# Wales on the
# Western Front

# Wales on the Western Front

*Edited by*
## John Richards

UNIVERSITY OF WALES PRESS
CARDIFF

First published by the University of Wales Press in 1994

www.uwp.co.uk

British Library Cataloguing-in-Publication Data
A catalogue record for this book is available from the British Library.

ISBN    978-1-78316-063-1

Printed by CPI Antony Rowe, Chippenham, Wiltshire

*In Memoriam (Easter 1915)*

The flowers left thick at nightfall in the wood
This Eastertide call into mind the men,
Now far from home, who, with their sweethearts should
Have gathered them and will do never again.

Edward Thomas
(Killed in action on Easter Monday, 1917)

# CONTENTS

# Contents

# ACKNOWLEDGEMENTS

The editor wishes to thank the following for their help in producing this book: Tom Dawkes, Louise Daly and Ann Thomas (all of the Senghennydd Library, University of Wales College of Cardiff); Peter Keelan (Salisbury Librarian); Norman Holme (Archivist, Royal Welch Fusiliers' Museum); Major Bob Smith (Curator, South Wales Borderers' Museum); Lieutenant Bryn Owen RN (Retd.) (Curator, Welch Regiment Museum); Christine Beresford (Curator, Regiments of Gloucestershire Museum); Diana Taylor for her word-processing skills; Ned Thomas (Director, University of Wales Press) for allowing me to see the proofs of Saunders Lewis's letters before publication.

The editor and the publishers express their grateful acknowledgements for permission to reproduce the following extracts:

Charles Clayton: from *The Hungry One* (Gomer, 1978). Reprinted by permission of Gwasg Gomer.

James Dunn: from *The War the Infantry Knew* (Sphere, 1989 edn.). Reprinted by permission of The Royal Welch Fusiliers.

Robert Graves: from *Goodbye to All That* (Cassell, 1957 edn.) and *Poems About War* (Cassell, 1988). Reprinted by permission of A. P. Watt Ltd. on behalf of The Trustees of the Robert Graves Copyright Trust.

Llewellyn Wyn Griffith: from *Up to Mametz* (Faber and Faber, 1931, reprinted Gliddon Books, 1988). Reprinted by permission of Hugh Wyn Griffith.

Ivor Gurney: from *Collected Poems of Ivor Gurney*, ed. P.J. Kavanagh (Oxford University Press, 1982). Reprinted by permission of Oxford University Press © Robin Haines, Sole Trustee of the Gurney Estate 1982.

*Acknowledgements*

Arthur Humphreys-Owen: from the manuscript diary of Captain Arthur Humphreys-Owen in the National Library of Wales. Reproduced by permission of Miss Elizabeth Humphreys-Owen.

David Jones: from *In Parenthesis* (Faber and Faber, 1963 edn.) Reprinted by permission of Faber and Faber Ltd.

Saunders Lewis: extracts from *Saunders Lewis: Letters to Margaret Gilcriest*, ed. M.S. Jones, N. Thomas and H.P. Jones (University of Wales Press, 1993). Reprinted by permission of Mair Saunders Jones.

Monmouthshire Territorials: from *With Rifle and Pick*, ed. Janet Dixon and John Dixon (Cwm Press, 1991). Reprinted by permission of John Dixon.

Siegfried Sassoon: from *Memoirs of an Infantry Officer* (Faber and Faber, 1965 edn.) Reprinted by permission of Faber and Faber Ltd.

Edward Thomas: from *Edward Thomas: A Portrait*, by R. George Thomas (OUP, 1985), and *The Collected Poems of Edward Thomas*, edited by R. George Thomas (OUP, 1978). Reprinted by permission of Oxford University Press.

Aneurin Williams: from transcript in *Stand To! Journal of the Western Front Association*, No. 29 (Summer 1990). Reprinted by permission of the editor.

W.G. Sweet: from 'A Memoir of the Final Advance 1918 by Sergeant W.G. Sweet', edited by Barry Johnson, from *Stand To! Journal of the Western Front Association*, No. 3 (Winter 1990). Reprinted by permission of the editor.

Every effort has been made to trace the copyright holders of the extracts in this volume. In the case of any queries, please contact the publishers.

# INTRODUCTION

The purpose of this book is to commemorate the experience of Welshmen on the Western Front, and to go a little way towards answering the question posed by a soldier's civilian friend: 'What is this war like?'[1] The aim has been to collect together writing which, individually and collectively, provides an impression of what it meant to be a soldier in the Great War. The pieces have been chosen, not necessarily for their literary merit, but to reflect as wide a range as possible of experiences, of Welsh military units, of people. With this in mind, the basis for selection has been that the authors should either be Welshmen or be describing the activities of the Welsh. Although several of the writers were Welsh-speaking the material has been chosen only from works in English – the inclusion of Welsh-language material was of course considered, but it was felt that the difficulties of producing satisfactory translations (especially of the verse) ruled it out for this volume.

The order of presentation is alphabetical (by authors' surnames). Exceptions to this have been made for the beginning and end of the war, so that Frank Richards appears first, describing his retreat from Mons. The anthology is brought to a close by W. G. Sweet and Vivian de Sola Pinto, who were both involved in the 'Advance to Victory'. Four appendices have been included for those who would like to know something about the military context: Appendix A provides some notes about the Army of 1914, particularly its Welsh units; Appendix B deals with the volunteer armies – Kitchener's men – whilst Appendix C lists the Welsh infantry units which served on the Western Front, and the dates on which they arrived. An

---

[1]Bernard Adams, *Nothing of Importance* (London: Methuen, 1917), p. xxvii.

outline chronology of battles is given in Appendix D.

The work is concerned only with the Western Front, but fighting went on in areas as diverse as eastern Europe, Egypt, Palestine, Arabia, the Balkans, Mesopotamia, Africa, and Italy – at sea and in the air, as well as on land. In one way or another, over 50 countries were drawn in. By the end, in 1918, more than eight million people were dead and many millions more had been wounded. Nearly two million Germans were killed in battle, and a similar number of Russians. Over a million Frenchmen died, whilst the British war dead amounted to almost 900,000 (two and a half times more than were to lose their lives in the Second World War).[2]

On the eve of the war the Welsh population numbered two and a half million of whom about 400,000 were men of military age, that is between the ages of twenty and forty. (Over half of them lived in Glamorgan, and 20 per cent in Monmouthshire.[3]) During the war the number of men who enlisted from Wales was 273,000, which means that about 70 per cent of this age group was recruited into the armed forces.[4] How did it come about that so many of these young Welshmen found themselves in France and Belgium, bearing arms against young Germans?

The years before the war had been a period of economic, political and military competition between the major powers of Europe. One manifestation of this was the attempt by Germany to erode Britain's naval superiority, a strategy which Britain saw as a threat to her vital interests, given the importance of protecting the sea-routes of her empire. By 1914 the rivalry had produced two camps: a 'Triple Entente' (Britain, France and Russia) and the 'Central Powers' (Germany and the Austro-Hungarian Empire).

The German government had for some years been concerned about the threat of 'encirclement' – an enhancement of the Triple Entente into proper military treaties. An alliance with a strong Austria-Hungary was thus crucial for the Germans,

---

[2]P. J. Haythornthwaite, *The World War One Source Book* (London: Cassell, 1992), p. 54.

[3]Derived from: Welsh National Executive Committee *Report* (Cardiff: Western Mail, 1921), p. 10. The population of Wales today (1991 census) is 2,798,500.

[4]War Office, *Statistics of the Military Effort of the British Empire during the Great War* (London: HMSO, 1922), p. 363.

since they did not wish to oppose the Triple Alliance unaided. The Austro-Hungarian Empire, however, was under constant threat from Slav nationalist movements, particularly those which worked to extend Serbia to include all Serbs in Bosnia, Herzogovina, Macedonia and Montenegro. There were many in both the Austro-Hungarian and German governments (the Kaiser and his Chief of Staff, General von Moltke, among them) who favoured an early 'preventive' war, with the aim of preserving the Empire by crushing the Serbs, even though this would probably involve a war with Serbia's traditional ally, Russia. Von Moltke's view was that action should be taken against Serbia as soon as possible, so that the Russian army could be fought before its current re-equipment programme was too far advanced.

On 28 June 1914 the Archduke Franz Ferdinand (heir to the Imperial throne) and his wife were murdered in Sarajevo by Gavrilo Princip, a Bosnian Serb. This was seized upon as the pretext for the preventive war, although the Austro-Hungarian government needed to be sure of Germany's support in the event of Russian intervention. The necessary assurances were given and so, on 23 July, a deliberately provocative and humiliating ultimatum was sent to the Serbian government. Two days later a conciliatory reply was received from Belgrade but, on 28 July, Austria-Hungary declared war on Serbia.

Two days later the Russians, in support of Serbia, began to mobilize their forces, which led the Germans to set in train their own mobilization. Germany had known for many years that a war with Russia would also involve a war against France, and so their plans for the conduct of such a conflict had been laid long before. The aim was to knock France out of the war quickly before transferring their attention, and troops, to the eastern front to deal with Russia. This scheme – known as the 'Schlieffen Plan' – allowed forty days for the defeat of France, and envisaged a vast enveloping advance through neutral Belgium, wheeling round to the west of Paris and then demolishing the French armies against the German frontier. The principal French response, based on their Plan XVII, would be an offensive in Alsace-Lorraine with any German strike through Belgium being held by a French army aided, they hoped, by an expeditionary force from Britain.

A crisis meeting of the British Cabinet, attended by Lloyd George, was held on 26 July, and the Royal Navy was ordered not to disperse from the exercises being held around the British Isles. Five days later Germany declared war on Russia, at the same time appropriating the Luxembourg railways to prepare for an attack through Belgium. On 2 August the German government demanded that their troops be allowed to pass unopposed through Belgium, stating that they knew that the French were about to enter that country – this was untrue. The Belgian government refused the outrageous request, and Germany declared war on France at 6.45 p.m. on 3 August 'making alleged violation of her frontier by patrols and her territory by aviators a pretext'.[5]

On the morning of 4 August four German armies crashed over the Belgian frontier on their way to France. At 4.00 p.m. the British government ordered the mobilization of the Expeditionary and Territorial Forces. Just after midnight the Foreign Office issued a statement:

> Owing to the summary rejection by the German Government of the request made by His Majesty's Government for assurances that the neutrality of Belgium will be respected ... His Majesty's Government have declared to the German Government that a state of war exists between Great Britain and Germany as from 11.00 p.m. on 4th August.[6]

Five days later the first British soldiers landed at Boulogne.

---

[5]*Official History of the War*, Vol. 1, p. 28. It continues: 'These allegations have since been admitted to be false.'
[6]Ibid., p. 29.

# FRANK RICHARDS

A Monmouthshire man, Frank Richards served with the pre-war Regular Army for eight years, mostly in India and Burma. By the summer of 1914 he had been a civilian for over five years and was working as a timberman's assistant in a colliery. On 5 August he rejoined his regiment at Wrexham and served, as a private, with the 2nd Royal Welch Fusiliers throughout the war. As part of the British Expeditionary Force they sailed from Southampton at 2 a.m. on 10 August 1914, arriving in Rouen that afternoon. The battalion was part of the 19th Brigade (along with the 1st Middlesex, 1st Cameronians and the 2nd Argyll and Sutherland Highlanders) which, on 24 August, arrived at a little village called Vicq.

~

## Le Cateau: the retirement[1]

It was at Vicq that we first realized that there was a war in progress. We advanced out of the village across open country. High shrapnel was exploding in the air some miles in front of us, and an officer and twelve of us were sent out about half a mile in front of the company and took up an outpost position at some crossroads. About midnight orders came for us to rejoin our company which was now lined up on a railway. Rations for the next day were issued out. The bread ration was a two-pound loaf between four men. It was the last bread ration we were to get for many a day, for our service had now begun in earnest. We marched all that night and the greater part of the

---

[1]Extract reproduced from F. Richards, *Old Soldiers Never Die* (London: Faber and Faber, 1933).

1

next day and dug trenches on the evening of the 24th August, outside a little village, the name of which I never heard, or else I have forgotten it. Old men and women from the village gave a hand in the digging. Whilst visiting outposts that evening Major Walwyn was shot through the foot with a spent bullet – the Battalion's first casualty in the War.

We were only in those trenches a few hours before we were on the march again; we didn't know where to, or why. We were issued out with an extra fifty rounds of ammunition, making in all two hundred rounds to carry. We marched all night again and all next day, halting a few times to fire at German scouting aeroplanes but not hitting one. At one halt of about twenty minutes we realized that the Germans were still not far away, some field-artillery shells bursting a few yards from my platoon, but nobody was damaged. We reservists fetched straight out of civil life were suffering the worst of this non-stop march, which would have been exhausting enough if we had not been carrying fifty pounds weight or so of stuff on our backs. And yet these two days and nights were only the start of our troubles.

We arrived in Le Cateau about midnight, dead-beat to the world. I don't believe any one of us at this time realized that we were retiring, though it was clear that we were not going in the direction of Germany. Of course the officers knew, but they were telling us that we were drawing the enemy into a trap. Le Cateau that night presented a strange sight. Everyone was in a panic, packing up their stuff on carts and barrows to get away south in time. The Royal Welch camped on the square in the centre of the town. We were told to get as much rest as we could. The majority sank down where they were and fell straight asleep. Although dead-beat, Billy, Stevens and I went on the scrounge for food and drink. We entered a café, where there were a lot of officers of other battalions, besides a couple of staff-officers, mixed up with ordinary troops, all buying food and drink. For three days officers and men had been on short rations. This was the only time during the whole of the War that I saw officers and men buying food and drink in the same café. I slept the sleep of the just that night, for about three hours. I could have done with forty-three, but we were roused up at 4 a.m. and ordered to leave our packs and greatcoats on the square.

Everyone was glad when that order was issued; the only things we had to carry now, besides rifle and ammunition,

were an extra pair of socks and our iron rations which consisted of four army biscuits, a pound tin of bully beef, and a
small quantity of tea and sugar. Iron rations were carried in case
of emergency but were never supposed to be used unless orders
came from our superior officers. Haversacks were now strapped
on our shoulders and each man was issued with another fifty
rounds of ammunition, which made two hundred and fifty
rounds to carry. At dawn we marched out of Le Cateau with
fixed bayonets. Duffy said: 'We'll have a bang at the bastards
to-day.' We all hoped the same. We were all fed up with the
marching and would have welcomed a scrap to relieve the
monotony. But we were more fed up before the day was
over. The Second Argylls who went to the assistance of the
East Yorks lost half of their battalion during the day, but we
simply marched and countermarched during the whole time
that this was going on.

We kept on meeting people who had left their homes and
were making their way south with the few belongings they could
carry. One little lad about twelve years of age was wheeling
his old grandmother in a wheel-barrow. They all seemed to
be terror-stricken. In every village we marched through the
church had been converted into a field-hospital and was generally full of our wounded. At about twilight we lined up in
a sunken road. I was the extreme left-hand man of the Battalion, Billy and Stevens being on my right. Our Colonel was
speaking to our Company Commander just behind us when up
the road came a man wheeling a pram with a baby in it and two
women walking alongside. They stopped close by me and the
man, speaking in English, told me that the two women were
his wife and mother-in-law, and that his only child was in the
pram. He was an Englishman, the manager of some works in
a small town nearby, but his wife was French. They had been
travelling all day. If they had delayed their departure another
hour they would have been in the enemy's hands.

Just at this moment a staff-officer came along and informed
our Colonel that all our cavalry patrols were in and that any
cavalry or troops who now appeared on our front would be
the enemy. He had hardly finished speaking when over a ridge
in front of us appeared a body of horsemen galloping towards
us. We immediately got out of the sunken road, and standing
up opened out with rapid fire at six hundred yards. I had only
fired two rounds when a bugle blew the cease-fire. This, I may

say, was the only time during the whole of the War with the exception of the German bugle at Bois Grenier, that I heard a bugle in action. The light was very bad, and the majority of the bullets had been falling short because we couldn't clearly see the sights of our rifles, but several horses fell. The horsemen stopped and waved their arms. We had been firing on our own cavalry who, I was told later, belonged to the 19th Hussars: I never heard whether any of them had been killed.

When we got back down in the sunken road the women were crying and the child was bawling, but the man seemed to have vanished. Stevens said, 'Where has he got to?' I asked the women but couldn't get a word out of them, only crying, when out from under the cover of the pram crawled the man. He commenced to storm and rave and wanted to know what we meant by all that firing which had terrified his wife and child. (He didn't say a word about his mother-in-law.) He said that he would report us. Billy got hold of him and said: 'Call yourself an Englishman! What the hell do you reckon you were going to do under that pram? For two pins I'd bayonet you, you bloody swine!'

'Fall in!' came the order, and we were on the march again. It was now dusk and I expect that family fell into the hands of the enemy during the night.

We retired all night with fixed bayonets, many sleeping as they were marching along. If any angels were seen on the Retirement, as the newspaper accounts said they were, they were seen that night. March, march, for hour after hour, without no halt: we were now breaking into the fifth day of continuous marching with practically no sleep in between. We were carrying our rifles all shapes and it was only by luck that many a man didn't receive a severe bayonet wound during the night. Stevens said: 'There's a fine castle there, see?', pointing to one side of the road. But there was nothing there. Very nearly everyone were seeing things, we were all so dead-beat.

At last we were halted and told that we would rest for a couple of hours. Outposts and sentries were posted and we sank down just off the road and were soon fast asleep. Fifteen minutes later we were woke up, and on the march again. We had great difficulty in waking some of the men. About ten yards from the side of the road was a straw rick, and about half a dozen men had got down the other side of it. I slipped over and woke them up. One man we had a job with but we got him going at last. By this time the Company had moved off, so we were stragglers. We came to some crossroads and didn't know which way to go. Somehow we decided to take the road to the right.

Dawn was now breaking. Along the road we took were broken-down motor lorries, motor cycles, dead horses and broken wagons. In a field were dumped a lot of rations. We had a feed, crammed some biscuits into our haversacks and moved along again. After a few minutes, by picking up more stragglers, we were twenty strong, men of several different battalions. I inquired if anyone had seen the 2nd Royal Welch Fusiliers, but nobody had. By the time that it was full daylight there were thirty-five of us marching along, including two sergeants. We got into a small village – I had long since lost interest in the names of the places we came to, so I don't know where it was – where we met a staff-officer who took charge of us. He marched us out of the village and up a hill and told us to extend ourselves in skirmishing order at two paces interval and lie down and be prepared to stop an attack at any moment. About five hundred yards in front of us was a wood, and the attack would come from that direction. The enemy commenced shelling our position, but the shells were falling about fifteen yards short. The man on my left was sleeping: he was so dead-beat that the shelling didn't worry him in the least and the majority of us were not much better. We lay there for about half an hour but saw no signs of the enemy. The staff-officer then lined us up and told us to attach ourselves to the first battalion we came across. I had to shake and thump the man on my left before I could wake him up. We marched off again and came across lots of people who had left their homes. Four ladies in an open carriage insisted on getting out to let some of our crippled and dead-beat men have a ride. We packed as many as we could into the carriage and moved along, the ladies marching with us. Late in the afternoon we took leave of the ladies. The men who had been riding had a good day's rest and sleep. If the ladies had all our wishes they would be riding in a Rolls-Royce for the rest of their lives.

During the evening when passing through a village I got news that the Battalion had passed through it an hour before. I and a man named Rhodes decided to leave the band and try and catch them up. During the next few days we attached ourselves to three different battalions, but immediately left them when we got news of our own. We wandered on for days, living on anything we could scrounge. It seemed to us that trying to find the Battalion was like trying to chase a will-o'-the wisp. But we were going the right way. All roads seemed to lead to Paris. One day, when we were on our own, not attached to any unit, Rhodes and I came across a band of gypsies in a wood and made them understand that we were very hungry. They invited us to the meal they were about to have, and I think we surprised them by our eating abilities. We thanked them heartily, and with bellies like poisoned pups staggered along again. It was the first square meal we had had since we left Amiens. The following day we came to a railhead. A train was in and an officer inquired if we had lost our unit. We said that we had, so he ordered us to get into the train which was full of troops who were in the same fix as ourselves.

No one knew where we were going to, but we all believed that we were going to Paris. One battalion that we had been with had been told by their officers that they were going to Paris for a rest. Everybody seemed to have Paris on the brain. We had a long train journey and I slept the greater part of the way. We detrained at a place called Le Mans. The only thing I can remember about this place was a large French barracks where we stayed and a street named after one of the Wright brothers of aeroplane fame. I expect I was too dulled with marching to notice anything more. We were there about a week and then got sent up country again. We picked the Battalion up just after they had passed through Coulommiers. I could not find Billy or Stevens; when I asked what had become of them I was told that Stevens had been missing after the Battalion left St Quentin. Then a man named Slavin said that Billy and himself had left the Battalion about fifteen miles from Paris. Billy had a touch of fever. They had got a lift in a motor lorry into Paris where Billy was admitted into hospital. Slavin said that he had stayed in Paris for four days and the last day he was there he saw Billy riding in a grand motor car with two French ladies; the way Billy waved his hand to him, anyone would have thought he was a bloody lord. Billy was lucky enough to be sent home, and I never saw him again.

# BERNARD ADAMS

John Bernard Pye Adams – known as 'Bill' – was born at Beckenham in Kent. Educated at Malvern and St John's College Cambridge, he gained a first-class degree in Classics before becoming warden of a hostel for Indian students in South Kensington, a post which he regarded as a prelude to missionary work in India. Adams was commissioned into the Royal Welch Fusiliers and joined the 1st Battalion on the Western Front. *Nothing of Importance*, first published in September 1917 (six months after its author had died of wounds at the age of twenty-seven), is described as 'a record of eight months at the front with a Welsh battalion: October 1915 to June 1916'. Captain Adams stressed: 'The events recorded are real and true in every detail. I have nowhere exaggerated; for in this war there is nothing more terrible than the truth.'

~

## The Working Party[1]

I think the 'working party' is realised less than anything else in this war by those who have not been at the front. It does not appeal to the imagination. Yet it is essential to realise, if one wants to know what this war is like, the amount of sheer dogged labour performed by the infantry in digging, draining, and improving trenches.

The 'working party' usually consists of seventy to a hundred men from a company, with either one or two officers. The Brigadier going round the trenches finds a communication trench

---

[1]Extracts reproduced from B. Adams, *Nothing of Importance: A Record of Eight Months at the Front with a Welsh Battalion, October 1915 to June 1916* (London: Methuen, 1917).

7

falling in, and about a foot of mud at the bottom. 'Get a working-party on to this at once,' he says to his Staff Captain. The Staff Captain consults one of the RE officers, and a note is sent to the Adjutant of one of the two battalions in billets: 'Your battalion will provide a working party of . . . officers . . . full ranks (sergeants and corporals) and . . . other ranks tomorrow. Report to Lt. . . ., RE, at . . . at 5.0 p.m. tomorrow for work on . . . Trench. Tools will be provided.' The Staff Captain then dismisses the matter from his head. The Adjutant then sends the same note to one or more of the four company commanders, detailing the number of men to be sent by the companies specified by him. (He is scrupulously careful to divide work equally between the companies, by the way.) The company commander on receiving the note curses volubly, declares it a 'd–d shame the hardest worked battalion in the brigade can't be allowed a moment's rest, feels sure the men will mutiny one of these days,' etc., summons the orderly, who is frowsting in the next room with the officers' servants, and says: 'Take this to the sergeant-major,' after scribbling on the note 'Parade outside Company HQ 3.30 p.m.,' and adding, as the orderly departs, 'Might tell the quartermaster-sergeant I want to see him.' Meanwhile the three subalterns are extraordinarily engrossed in their various occupations, until the company commander boldly states that it is 'rotten luck, but he supposes as So-and-so took the last, it is So-and so's turn, isn't it?' and details the officers; if they are new officers he tells them the sergeants will know exactly what to do, and if they are old hands he tells them nothing whatever. The 'quarter' (company quartermaster-sergeant) then arrives, and is told the party will not be back, probably, till 10.0 p.m., and will he make sure, please, that hot soup is ready for the men on return, and also dry socks if it turns out wet; he is then given a drink, and the company commander's work is finished.

Meanwhile the company sergeant-major has received the orders from the orderly, and summons unto him the orderly-sergeant, and from his 'roster', or roll, ticks off the men and NCOs to be warned for the working party. This the orderly-sergeant does by going round to the various barns and personally reading out each man's name, and on getting the answer, saying, 'You're for working party, 3.15 today.' The exact nature of the remarks when he is gone are beyond my province. Only, as an officer taking the party, one knows that at 3.25 p.m. the senior sergeant calls the two lines of waiting 'other ranks' to attention, and with a slap on his rifle, announces 'Working-party present, Sir,' as you stroll up. Working-parties are dressed in 'musketry order' usually – that is to say, with equipment, but no packs; rifles and ammunition, of course, and waterproof sheets rolled and fastened to the webbing belt. The officer then tells the sergeant to 'stand them easy', while he asks one or two questions, and looks once more at 'orders' which the senior sergeant has probably brought on parade, and at 3.30, with a 'Company-Shern! Slo-o-ope hip! Right-in-fours: form-fŏrs! Right! By the right, Quick *march*!' leads off his party, giving, 'March at *ease*, march-easy!' almost in one breath as soon as he rounds the corner. Then there is a hitching of rifles to the favourite position, and a buzz of remarks and whistles and song behind, while the sergeant edges up to the officer or the officer edges back to the sergeant, according to their degree of intimacy, and the working-party is on its way.

One working-party I remember very well. We were in billets at – – –, and really tired out. It was Nov. 6th, and on looking up my letters I find our movements for the last week had been as follows:

Oct.29th 9.0 a.m. Moved off from billets.
        12.0 midday. Lunch.
        3.0 p.m. Arrived in front trenches.
Oct.30th Front trenches.
Oct.31st Front trenches.
Nov.1st Relieved at 3.0 p.m. (The Devons were very late relieving us, owing to bad rain and mud.)
        5.30 p.m. Reached billets.
Nov.2nd Rain all day. Morning spent by men in trying to clean up. Afternoon, baths.
Nov.3rd 9.0 a.m. Started off for trenches again. It had rained incessantly. Mud terrible.
        1.0 p.m. Arrived in front trenches.
Nov.4th Front trenches. Rained all day.
Nov.5th 2.30 p.m. Relieved late again. Mud colossal. Billets 5.0 p.m.
Nov.6th. Morning. Cleaning up. Inspection by CO.
        Afternoon. SUDDEN AND UNEXPECTED WORKING-PARTY, 3.0p.m.–11.0 p.m.!!

Yet I thoroughly enjoyed those eight hours, I remember. There were, I suppose, about eighty NCOs and men from 'B'

Company. I was in charge, with one other officer. We halted at a place whither the 'cooker' had been previously despatched, and where the men had their tea. Luckily it was fine. The men sat about on lumps of trenchboards and coils of barbed wire, for the place was an 'RE Dump', where a large accumulation of RE stores of all description was to be found. I apologised to the RE officer for keeping him a few minutes while the men finished their tea; he, however, a second-lieutenant, was in no hurry whatever, it seemed, and waited about a quarter of an hour for us. Then I fell the men in, and they 'drew tools', so many men a pick, so many a shovel (the usual proportion is one pick, two shovels), and we splodged along through whitish clay of the stickiest calibre in the gathering twilight. An RE corporal and two RE privates had joined us mysteriously by now, as well as the second-lieutenant, and crossing H – – – Street we plunged down into a communication trench, and started the long mazy grope. The RE corporal was guide. The trench was all paved with trench-mats, but these were not 'laid', only 'shoved down' anyhow; consequently they wobbled, and one's boot slipped off the side into squelch, rubbing the ankle. Continually came up the message from behind, 'Lost touch, Sir!' This involved a wait – one, two minutes – until the 'All-up' or 'All-in' came up. (One hears it coming in a hoarse whisper, and starts before it actually arrives. Infinite patience is necessary. RE officers are sometimes eager to go ahead; but once lose the last ten men at night in an unknown trench, and it may take three hours to find them.) The other officer was bringing up the rear.

At last we reached our destination, and the RE officer and myself told off the men to work along the trench. This particular work was clearing what is known as a 'berm', that is, the flat strip of ground between the edge of the trench and the thrown-up earth, each side of a CT (communication trench).

When a trench is first dug, the earth is thrown up each side; the recent rains were, however, causing the trenches to crumble in everywhere, and the weight of the thrown-up earth was especially the cause of this. Consequently, if the earth were cleared away a yard on each side of the trench, and thrown further back, the trench would probably be saved from falling in to any serious extent, and the light labour of shovelling dry earth a yard or so back would be substituted for the heart-breaking toil of throwing sloppy mud or sticky clay out of a trench higher than yourself.

The work to be done had been explained to the sergeants before we left our starting-point. As we went along, the RE officer told off men at ten or five yards' interval, according to the amount of earth to be moved. Each man stopped when told off, and the rest of the company passed him. Sergeants and corporals stopped with their section or platoon, and got the men started as soon as the last man of the company had passed. At last up came the last man, sergeant, and the other officer, and together we went back all along. The men were on top (that is why the working-party was a night one); sometimes they had not understood their orders and were doing something wrong (a slack sergeant would then probably have to be routed out and told off). The men working like fun, of course, it being known, to every one's joy, that this was a piece-job, and that we went home as soon as it was finished. There was absolute silence, except the sound of falling earth, and an occasional chink of iron against stone; or a swish, and muttered cursings, as a bit of trench fell in with a slide, dragging a man with it; for it is not always easy to clear a yard-wide 'berm' without crumbling the trench-edge in. One would not think these men were 'worn out', to see them working as no other men in the world can work; for nearly every man was a miner. The novice will do only half the work a trained miner will do, with the same effort.

Sometimes I was appealed to as to the 'yard'. Was this wide enough? One man had had an unlucky bit given him with a lot of extra earth from a dug-out thrown on to the original lot. So I re-divided the task. It is amazing the way the time passes while going along a line of workers, noticing, talking, correcting, praising. By the time I got to the first men of the company, they were half-way through the task.

At last the job was finished. As many men as space allowed were put on to help one section that somehow was behind; whether it was bad luck in distribution or slack work no one knew or cared. The work must be finished. The men wanted to smoke, but I would not let them; it was too near the front trenches. And then I did a foolish thing, which might have been disastrous! The RE corporal had remained, though the officer had left long ago. The corporal was to act as guide back, and this he was quite ready to do if I was not quite sure of the way. I, however, felt sure of it, and as the corporal would be saved a long tramp if he could go off to his dug-out direct without coming with us, I foolishly said I had no need of him, and let him go. I

11

then lost my way completely. We had never been in that section before, and none of the sergeants knew it. We had come from the 'RE Dump', and thither we must return, leaving our tools on the way. But I had been told to take the men to the Divisional Soup Kitchen first, which was about four hundred yards north of X, the spot where we entered the CT and which I was trying to find. For all I knew I was going miles in the wrong direction. My only guide was the flares behind, which assured me I was not walking to the Germans but away from them. The unknown trenches began to excite among the sergeants the suspicion that all was not well. But I took the most colossal risk of stating that I knew perfectly well what I was doing, and strode on ahead.

There was silence behind after that, save for splashings and splodgings. My heart misgave me that I was coming to undrained trenches of the worst description, or to water-logged impasses! Still I strode on, or waited interminable waits for the 'All up' signal. At last we reached houses, grim and black, new and awfully unknown. I nearly tumbled down a cellar as a sentry challenged. I was preparing for humble questions as to where we were, the nearest way to X, and a possible joke to the sergeant (this joke had not materialised, and seemed unlikely to be of the easiest), when I recovered myself from the cellar, mounted some steps, and found myself on a road beside a group of Tommies emerging from the Soup Kitchen! My star (the only one visible, I believe, that inky night) had led me there direct!

## In Support

'Six days in billets: three days in support. Not particularly hard, that sounds,' I can hear someone say. I tried to disillusion people in an earlier chapter about the easiness of the 'rest' in billets, owing to the incessant working-parties. These were even more incessant during these four months. Let me say a few words then, also, about life in support trenches. I admit that for officers it was not always an over-strenuous time; but look at Tommy's ordinary programme:-

This would be a typical day, say, in April.

| | |
|---|---|
| 4 a.m. | Stand to, until it got light enough to clean your rifle; then clean it. |
| About 5 a.m. | Get your rifle inspected, and turn in again. |

| | |
|---|---|
| 6.30 a.m. | Turn out to carry breakfast up to company in front line. (Old Kent Road very muddy after rain. A heavy dixie to be carried from top of Weymouth Avenue, up via Trafalgar Square, and 76 Street to the platoon holding the trench at the Loop.) |
| 7.45 a.m. | Get your own breakfast. |
| 9 a.m. | Turn out for working-party; spend morning filling sandbags for building traverses in Maple Redoubt. |
| 11.30 a.m. | Carry dinner up to front company. Same as 6.30 a.m. |
| 1 p.m. | Get your own dinner. |
| 1 to 4 p.m. | (With luck) rest. |
| 4 p.m. | Carry tea up to front company. |
| 5 p.m. | Get your own tea. |
| 5.15 to 7.15 p.m. | (With luck) rest. |
| 7.15 p.m. | Clean rifle. |
| 7.30 p.m. | Stand to. Rifle inspected. Jones put his ugly boot out suddenly, just after you have finished cleaning rifle, and upsets it. Result — mud all over barrel and nose-cap. |
| 8.30 p.m. | Stand down. Have to clean rifle again and show platoon sergeant. |
| 9 p.m. | Turn out for working-party till 12 midnight in front line. |
| 12 midnight. | Hot soup. |
| 12.15 a.m. | Dug-out at last till |
| 4 a.m. | Stand to. |

And so on for three days and nights. This is really quite a moderate programme: it is one that you would aim at for your men. But there are disturbing elements that sometimes compel you to dock a man's afternoon rest, for instance. A couple of canisters block Watling Street; you *must* send a party of ten men and an NCO to clear it at once: or you suddenly have to supply a party to carry 'footballs' up to Rue Albert for the trench-mortar man. The Adjutant is sorry; he could not let you know before; but they have just come up to the Citadel, and must be unloaded at once. So you have to find the men for this on the spur of the moment. And so it goes on night and day. Oh, it's not all rum and sleep, is life in Maple Redoubt.

Three days and nights in support, and then comes the three days in the front line.

## *The Sniper*

Private Ellis had hard blue eyes that looked at you, and looked, and went on looking. They always reminded me of the colour of the sea when a north wind is blowing and the blue is hard and bright. I have seen two other pairs of eyes like them. One belonged to Captain Jefferies, the big game shooter, who lectured on Sniping at the Third Army School. The other pair were the property of a sergeant I met this week for the first time. 'Are you a marksman?' I asked him. 'Yes, sir! Always a marksman, sir.'

There is no mistaking those eyes. They are the eyes of a man who has used them all his life, and found them grow steadier and surer every year. They are essentially the eyes of a man who can watch, watch, watch all day, and not get tired of watching; and they were the eyes of my best sniper.

For Private Ellis had all the instincts of a cunning hunter. I had no need to tell him to keep his telescope well inside the loophole, lest the sun should catch on the glass; no need to remind him to stuff a bit of sand-bag in the loophole when he left the post unoccupied. He never forgot to let the sandbag curtain drop behind him as he entered the box, to prevent light coming into it and showing white through a loophole set in dark earth. There was no need either to make sure that he understood the telescopic sights on his rifle; and there was no need to tell him that the Boches were clever people. He never under-estimated his foe.

It was a warm day in early March. Private Ellis was in No. 5 Box, opposite Aeroplane Trench. This post was very cunningly concealed. Our front trench ran along a road, immediately behind which was a steep chalk bank, the road having originally been cut out of a rather steep slope. Just about five yards behind this bank was cut a deep narrow trench, and in this trench were built several snipers' posts, with loopholes looking out of the chalk bank. These loopholes were almost impossible to see, as they were very nearly indistinguishable from the shadows in the bank. Anyone who has hunted for oyster-catchers' eggs on a pebbly beach knows that black and white is the most protective colour scheme existing. And so these little black loopholes were almost invisible in the black and white of the chalk bank.

14

All the morning Private Ellis had been watching out of the corner of his eye a little bit of glass shining in Aeroplane Trench. Now Aeroplane Trench was a sap running out from the German front trench into a sunken road. From the centre sap two little branch saps ran up and down the road, and then slightly forward; the whole plan of it rather resembled an aeroplane and gave it its name. In it today was a Boche with a periscopic rifle; and it was this little bit of glass at the top of the periscope, and the nose of the rifle-barrel that Private Ellis was watching. Every now and again the glass and nose-cap would give a little jump, and 'plop' a bullet would bury itself in our front parapet. One of our sentries had had his periscope smashed during the morning, I was informed by a company commander with rather the air of 'What's the use of you and your snipers, if you can't stop them sniping us?' I told Ellis about the periscope, to which he replied: 'It won't break us, I guess, sir – two penn'orth of new glass for a periscope. It's heads that count.' In which remark was no little wisdom.

'Crack – plop', and after a long interval another 'Crack-zin-n-n-g', as a bullet ricocheted off a stone, and went away over the ridge and fell with a little sigh somewhere in the ground right away beyond Redoubt A. So it went on all the afternoon, while the sun was warming everyone up and one dreamed of the summer, and warm days, dry trenches, and short nights. Ellis had gone off rather reluctantly at midday, and the other relief was there. There was a slumbrous sensation about that brought on the feeling that there was no one really in the enemy trenches at all. Yet there was the little glass eye looking at us: it reminded one of a snake in the grass. It glittered, unblinking.

At about six o'clock I again visited the post. Ellis was back there, and watching as keenly as ever.

'No luck?' I remarked. 'I'm afraid your friend is too wily for you; he's not going to put his head over, when he can see through a periscope as well.'

Still Private Ellis said little, but his eye was as clear and keen as ever; and still the periscope remained.

'We must shell him out tomorrow,' I said, and went off.

At half-past seven we had 'stood down', and I was messing with 'B' Company, when I heard a voice at the top of the dug-out, and the servant who was waiting – Lewis, I think it was – said a sniper wanted to see me.

'Tell him to come down.'

15

Private Ellis appeared at the door. Not a muscle in his body or face moved, but his eyes were glowing and glittering. 'Got him, sir,' was all he said.

'What?' I cried. 'Got that Boche in Aeroplane Trench? By Jove, tell us all about it.'

And so to the accompaniment of a whiskey and Perrier he told us exactly what happened. It was not till well after 'stand-to', it appeared, that any change had occurred in Aeroplane Trench. Then the periscope had wobbled and disappeared below ground. Then there had been another long wait, and the outline of the sunken road had begun to get faint. Then slowly, very slowly, a pink forehead had appeared over the top, and as slowly disappeared. I wish I had been there to watch Ellis then. I can imagine him coolly, methodically sighting his rifle on the trench-edge, and waiting. 'I had to wait another minute, sir; then it appeared again, the whole head this time. He thought it was too dark to be seen ... Oh, he won't worry us any more, sir! I saw one of his arms go up, and I thought I could see him fall against the back of the trench. But it was getting so dark, I couldn't have seen him five minutes later at all.'

And if Ellis couldn't, who could?

Next day, and for many days, there was no sniping from Aeroplane Trench.

16

# WILFRED BOWDEN

Wilfred George Bowden was born at Gwendoline Terrace, Abercynon. Leaving school at thirteen, his first job was delivering milk for the Co-op., before becoming a 'telephone lad' – officially a Junior Clerk – at Abercynon railway station. His war service began on 15 February 1915 when, aged 16½, he enlisted at the Drill Hall in Pontypridd. Arriving at Haverfordwest, he joined the Second Line unit of his local Territorials, the 5th Battalion of the Welch Regiment. After about a year he was sent to the 4th (Denbighshire) Battalion of the Royal Welch Fusiliers which was attached to the 1st Division in France, (in September 1915 it became the Pioneer battalion of the 47th (London) Division).

—

## First Days in France[1]

*On his way to join his new battalion Wilfred Bowden, aged 17½, spent his first days in France at No.5 Infantry Base Depot, Rouen.*

On the second night of our arrival at No. 5 Infantry Base Depot, Rouen we were awakened some time before Reveille by a sergeant loudly enquiring whether there were any NCOs there. We were two Lance-Corporals, myself and one other, and it was the 'other' who announced his presence. The Sergeant ordered 'Yourself and five men parade in fifteen minutes, light marching order (i.e. no valise)'. When Reveille sounded and the rest of us got up, we wondered where they had gone. Our first parade was 'physical jerks'. When we returned, the mystery was solved.

---

[1]Extracts reproduced from W. G. Bowden, *Abercynon to Flanders and Back* (Risca: Starling Press, 1984).

Our colleagues, the early risers, were there, all six sitting most disconsolately about the tent and they met our enquiries in a very subdued manner. They had been taken to a rifle range, marched to the firing point where lay six rifles which they were warned not to touch until commanded. At the targets end, twenty-five yards away, sitting on a bench and bound, were three men, their backs towards them and a white circle indicating their hearts. They were told that the rifles contained cartridges, three were blank. On the command, 'Present', they were to aim! On the command 'Fire', to do so! On no account were they to operate the bolt. They did as ordered and were very upset, as I most certainly would have been. Just another incident indicative of the cruelty and futility of war.

## 'To Encourage the Others'[2]

*Wilfred Bowden was made a medical orderly, and marched south with his battalion, eventually arriving at the advanced divisional dressing station near Mametz Wood 'where only two weeks previously the Cardiff City Battalion had been halved'. Subsequently, he was at High Wood, Fricourt, Ypres, Arras and Bourlon Wood. The following incident took place just before the massive German onslaught of spring 1918.*

About the end of January 1918, we mustered for a battalion parade which was very unusual and we all wondered as to the purpose. The colonel handed over to the adjutant who came to the front equipped with a sheaf of papers which he read aloud. The burden of his speech was as follows:

'Private ... of the so-and-so regiment on the ... date is accused of cowardice in the face of the enemy. Was tried by General Court Martial on ... date and sentenced to death. Sentence duly carried out on the ... date.'

This was repeated for a considerable time, perhaps fifty or sixty cases, all with the same end, until the assembled battalion, very restive, emitted loud groans and noises of great disapproval which the authorities were unable to subdue. It reached a crescendo almost and whether the end of the list was reached or

---

[2]Voltaire: 'Dans ce pays-ci il est bon de tuer de temps en temps un amiral pour encourager les autres.' ('In this country [Britain] it is thought well to kill an admiral from time to time to encourage the others.' *Candide* (1759), Ch. 23.)

that the obvious resentment of the troops caused them to desist, I do not know. In retrospect and in the happening that followed it would appear that the High Command knew of an impending attack from the Germans, hence the reminder of the consequences inherent in the way that war, the acme of man's foolishness, has to be conducted. I had still a disturbing memory of the incident at Rouen rifle range two days after my arrival on French soil.[3]

## Prisoner of war

*The German offensive began on 21 March 1918. The 4th Royal Welch Fusiliers lost 117 men[4] and Wilfred Bowden was shot during hand-to-hand fighting in a trench.*

How long I remained in that place and condition I do not know, but I regained consciousness. What had happened to me? Where was I? My last impression was that I was dying. Open my eyes? But I am afraid! I am reaching normality quickly. I must open my eyes! I felt something about my chest so I looked up into the face of a brown-whiskered German searching my pockets; in fact, he has withdrawn my wallet! He was startled, jumped to his feet, and pointed a revolver at me. It didn't interest me one bit!!

No sign of fight in me so he stowed away his gun. He shouted and gesticulated to two unwounded British soldiers to come and look after their 'comrade' – the only word of sense to me. He indicated them to bandage me up with my field dressing. Until then I did not know exactly where I had been wounded. My gas mask haversack had caught much blood and was saturated. They pulled it off and threw it away. I recall spitting out bits of teeth and found difficulty in speaking.

As they hauled me to my feet and took me by the arm they told me that I had been shot through my neck, the bullet had apparently grazed my tongue, broke off most of my bottom teeth and emerged in the right corner of my mouth. On the road I

---

[3]During the Great War 312 men on the British side were shot for military offences. Fourteen were executed in Welsh units – eight for desertion and six for murder (J. Putkowski and J. Sykes, *Shot at Dawn* (Barnsley: Wharncliffe, 1989)).
[4]M. Glover, *That Astonishing Infantry: Three Hundred Years of the History of the Royal Welch Fusiliers (23rd Regiment of Foot) 1689–1989* (London: Leo Cooper, 1989), p. 187.

experienced difficulty in walking – loss of blood, I thought – although the two Tommies did their best.

And then came an act that I have always treasured. Walking towards us, alone, was the figure of a small, bearded German soldier with a pack on his back, high above his head. I must have looked pretty deplorable because he stopped, pushed me gently against the road bank (there were very few hedges in France). With a deal of trouble he took out his water bottle, removed the cork and emptied lovely, cold beer down my parched throat, patted me on the shoulder and moved on. I found it painful walking as my left leg appeared to stiffen, but my brain and reactions seemed normal. I noticed the stream of German transport moving westward and it seemed to me peculiar that most of it was horse-drawn. The vehicles themselves looked more like farm waggons than the more sophisticated variety I would have seen on our side.

Eventually we reached a roadside dressing station. My two companions left me to a one-man outfit whose rank I did not know. He changed my neck dressing, wiped my mouth and gave me an injection, whether for tetanus or a painkiller I did not know, so I sat down supported at my back by a hedge bank. I had no real idea of the time, I hadn't a watch, but I imagined it to be about 4.30 p.m. I was alone with this medical orderly for about half-an-hour when along trundled another of these horse-drawn 'gambo-like' vehicles on which there were three barrels, whether going to fetch water or returning from so doing I couldn't tell. My caretaker halted it and conversed with the three men who accompanied it. The upshot of the conference was that I was hauled up, to sit or to lie on top of those barrels, and we proceeded, destination unknown. Excruciating pain made me aware of my injuries, because my bottom teeth, practically shot away, with exposed nerves, made a fount of shooting stabs of pain, right to my head as each bump over the rough road provoked my discomforture and to the apparent amusement of my captors.

I should think we travelled thus for about half an hour when we entered Cambrai which appeared but little damaged. We stopped at a red brick building adjacent to the pavement where I was hauled down and taken towards its entrance. But we were held up by a diminutive figure of a young French housewife, apparently out shopping, who blocked our way. She appeared to me to be really crying and saying, 'Mon petit corporal' as she placed me against the wall of the building and unscrewed the stopper of a bottle, then poured quite a liberal quantity of wine into my mouth which was, to me, most refreshing. My captors then rescued me and propelled me into the building which appeared to be a small hospital. I was taken upstairs where an orderly assisted me to undress. He brought me a bowl of water to wash my face and hands and put me into a nice, clean bed. As soon as I was settled in, I looked around and noted that there were only six patients in a twenty-bed ward.

I was amongst the first casualties from this day's action. I noticed after having settled down that in the bed next to me was another British prisoner. There was little apparent movement. By the high boots at the bedside, he was a RFA man. Whilst I was taking in my surroundings and in particular, the man in the next bed, the door opened and a German soldier, in a most furtive and suspicious manner, moved over to the next bed, grabbed the high boots and very quickly and furtively slipped out. I remembered that my boots, ankle height were at my own bedside so I struggled out of bed, picked up my boots and tucked them into bed with me.

An orderly appeared with a trolley on which was a jug of coffee (ersatz) and a pile of black bread (not really black, but a dark brown). I was very glad of the drink, even though it was just coffee with neither sugar nor milk. I gesticulated that I couldn't eat; I pointed to my mouth and swollen tongue. He apparently got the message and with that continental shrug of the shoulders indicated that that was my misfortune, and so it was!

## Taken to Another Place

I remained there overnight and sometime around the next evening the orderly came to me and, by sign language, instructed me to get dressed. So far the only people I had seen there in charge were the orderlies who appeared occasionally and brought the same diet, which I continued to refuse, although I was getting very hungry and I felt very weak. He took me outside. At the corner of the street which appeared to adjoin the main road, was a street car, incidentally steam driven. He proceeded to propel me up the step on to the end platform. Inside were four beds – one above the other on either side of a gangway. A nurse hovered around, although no one took any notice of me! It was getting quite dark but we continued to trundle along. Eventually when we halted, a number of orderlies carried away the inmates of the car, amongst them I thought a few British soldiers. When

21

all had detrained the woman nurse, for the first time, noticed me. She shouted (a German habit) for me to get up and walk. By then cold, hungry – and very weak, I couldn't do this so I made no attempt to try. This 'lady' grabbed my coat collar and dragged me to the doorway. She jumped down and then again took hold of my collar. She dragged me out, and dropped me onto the cobbled roadside, about three feet below. I thought I should die! I was shocked with this impact, right to my brain, whilst she continued to yell at me, which attracted the attention of someone, obviously of some authority. He reprimanded her and insisted she took one side of me and together, they hauled me inside and upstairs to the top of what appeared to be some sort of Ecclesiastical place. Into a room I was deposited with about sixty unfortunates as myself.

I understand the place is Valenciennes.

There were no chairs or beds so everyone sat on the floor. It was very hot there due to the number present, and the fact that it was at the top of the building. The atmosphere was further fouled by the presence, in the centre of the room, of a large metal vessel which received the urinary contributions of the inmates; all reeked to high heaven! I slept very fitfully until daylight. We were all awakened by the arrival of a couple of Algerian-French prisoners, one of whom spoke good English. They brought mugs of hot ersatz coffee also the familiar lump of 'black' bread, which I could do nothing with, but the drink was lovely. Soon afterwards two German orderlies appeared and took hold of me. Sixty people – why me? Because I was nearest the door as they entered. They supported me under each armpit and took me down to the basement which had all the ablution facilities. They told me to take off my clothes – I think they assisted me – and indicated that I should climb onto a table constructed on top of struts or slats and lie down. I nearly jumped to the ceiling when a shower of ice-cold water descended on me. I was expected to so perform, because they almost rolled with laughter! I cannot recall being wiped dry but I dressed with assistance. They escorted me up a couple of floors to a big Ward and to an empty bed. We were all British wounded there, with all types of injury. The fellow next to me lay very still and did not speak, whilst I at this time could not form words, neither could I eat any of the bread they brought me, my tongue being swollen and sore.

Next morning when I awoke I noticed my next bed companion was as inert as before. His chest was exposed showing a round hole near his breast bone. I presume, as he endeavoured to breathe, he pumped away his life's blood, much of it saturating my side of the bed, which had been moved together in twos to make more room. He now lay dead, eyes wide open. I was very upset!

Again the two Algerians arrived with the same diet, coffee and bread, which of course I could do nothing with. I made this known to the one who spoke English. He told me that sometime in the morning a Catholic Priest would come around and I ought to enlist his help. I identified the priest as he went around the Ward, not speaking to anyone. I later found he was a monoglot German. However I started gesticulating, showing him uneaten bread, pointing to my poor mouth and gums; he smiled at me and left, re-appearing with a big blonde German doctor, dressed in operating white overalls, liberally spattered with blood. He examined my wound thoroughly. The priest, with the help of the Algerian, told me I was to be put on a milk diet. I am convinced this saved my life because I had surely been five days without a morsel to eat. Each time a food distribution was made, I, much envied by my neighbouring sufferers, had a bowl of some kind of pudding or gruel. The next night proved to be one of the most terrifying of my life.

Night had fallen and a minimum of light remained when an air raid alarm sounded. All was deathly still for minutes. Only hurried footsteps in corridors adjoining. Then that horrible drone of loaded aircraft – little consolation that they were British – and then the whine of falling bombs. At first in the vicinity, but not actually near us. With horrible nearness and very quickly, a terrific crash! Two windows blew in, shattered in fragments. The whole room littered with glass and debris as a stick of bombs dropped in the yard! All lights went out as absolute hysteria gripped this crowd of handicapped men, screaming and shouting. All guards and orderlies had gone to safer areas. I heard many of those most seriously maimed crying like children. I am sure I did not do that, but I buried my face in the pillow and blankets to escape that terrible, poignant noise. I prayed that I would emerge from this ordeal! I had no real idea of time or days. So much had happened! I felt I had spun around in a maelstrom. All the terrible happenings I had been watching on the perimeter. I felt my lacerated mouth, the row of broken-off teeth, the lump of congealed blood on my neck! I lay in a strange bed with strange faces, so many of them bearded, and heard foreign tongues. Common sense and appreciation of realities quietened my turbulent brain. I wondered why no one had examined me clinically. I was but one of the unfortunates!

How soon will I be amongst these nameless flotsams of war each morning I see being carried out to where, to what?

## On the Move Again – By Train

I had been in this place a week. Numbered and pointed out, by the help of the Algerian, we were told to dress and taken by ambulance to the railhead; into a train, eight to a compartment. We were all wounded in some way – feet, legs, arms, bodies, backs or heads – it was a painful business to sit in crowded conditions. In late afternoon we arrived in an area, flat and not apparently war-damaged – Brussels – and told to get out. There was no platform: which made it very difficult! We were directed to a field kitchen for coffee and bread which I couldn't eat, so it was back into the train, and on to 'somewhere'! Later when it was quite dark, we halted again. We were gradually getting to recognise the command 'Raus'.

At Cologne we were addressed by a civilian, very nicely really. He hoped our stay in Germany would not be too protracted and that we would return to our families soon. (His speech, though good, was not nearly as good as the bowl of soup they provided and certainly not as beneficial.) Back to the train we went again. (I should mention that it had no lights and that was the first night.) The bumping, boring, swaying and surging, accentuated our misery, punctuated by grouses, oaths and 'Thanks be to God', with occasional witticisms, which always abound.

It was known by my companions that I could not eat bread so it was frugally divided as an extra. Into the night! Clippity clop went wheels and rail joints! Destination unknown! I dozed! Grousings, cursings and loud imprecations of my fellows brought me back to reality.

I awoke in inky blackness and panic. We were hurtling through space – into Hell if its approaches were through noisy blackness – !

I had no idea what my reactions had been, but an arm was around my shoulders and a voice from the darkness said, 'Steady up Taff, we are alright. We are descending a slope.' And we proceeded on into the Fatherland.

This journey continued in this manner for three nights and four days. One of my compartment colleagues was a South

African, Billie Burton, from Pietermaritzburg in Natal; he was
of wonderful help to me. The times when I couldn't move fast
enough to collect my meagre food allowance, he got it for me;
in spite of each time having to persuade a suspicious German
that he was not trying to cheat an extra ration. He was, fortunately for me, able to make himself better understood because
he spoke Dutch (Boer), similar to German. We arrived in Berlin
and stood perhaps an hour in what appeared to be the main
railway station. A big bearded civilian appeared with a basket
of food. Before sharing it out, he demonstrated his knowledge
of English. He was handing a hunk of bread and a sausage to
the first man in the compartment and said to him, 'You find
it very difficult to fight against Germany? Ja.' The Englishman,
a Geordie (intent only on the bread and sausage, which was
being withdrawn) replied, 'What are you bothering about, you
square-headed bastard?' The German promptly took himself and
basket out onto the platform – so we had none! We stayed there
some time. Crowds of Berliners walked past, examining us, their
war booty!

## Prisoner-of-War Camp at Crossen

It was early morning when we reached a very pretty area,
Crossen, on Oder. We were crowded into lorries and driven
through a very nice little county town on its Eastern edges.
We passed a large redbricked building on our right, with
sentries at the entrance; a barrack for an Infantry Battalion.
On our left, on the rising ground, was our home for the
immediate future, the Prisoner-of-War Camp, officially designated 'Kriegsgefangenerlager' where we entered a large white-
washed building and waited. Later we were ordered to take off
all clothing and make a pile of garments in the centre of the
room. We were 'de-loused'.

We were again separated, those who had wounds went to the
camp hospital (Lazerette) for examination, where I stayed for two
nights (long enough to be frightened with the inadequacies of
treatment). In the next bed to me was Arthur Green, a Londoner,
who had a gaping gunshot wound which looked horrible to me,
above the knee a saturated bandaged bloody mass! Anyway I
was sent to the compounds, regarded as fit, and so lost contact
with Arthur Green on a daily basis.

The camp was an area of about thirty acres on a hillside. In
its centre was an open space, in the centre of which was a tall

wooden tower. Near the top a look-out area where two sentries patrolled always. At the bottom were four small field guns, each directed at every compound which led off from the centre, segregated by barbed wire. Around the perimeter of each compound were long single story white-washed barrack rooms, furnished with a two-tier platform on which the inmates slept, supplied with two thin covers (hardly worthy of the name – blanket). In the centre of each barrack was a flat topped brick fire-place, which enabled pots to be boiled. I was amazed at the quantity and variety of flotsam that men, who daily left the camp for work in and around, would bring back in their pockets, and indeed down their trouser fronts, either to burn or as scraps of food and vegetables to boil on this stove.

We were awakened each morning at 6 a.m. with a loud bugle-call, simultaneous with the entry into the barrack of an armed sentry, who stamped and raved around shouting 'Raus Englander Schweinhund!' A Roll was called and I was amused to hear of myself identified as Unter Offizier Vilfred Bofden, to which I soon became accustomed. We received one slice of black bread, about three inches diameter and three-quarters of an inch thick, no jam, no margarine, no butter or anything additional. We accepted a small enamel handbasin of gruel-type barley meal, until mid-day when the same handbowl received a ladle of boiled vegetables; no meat at all; no addition of condiment, which might have made it a little palatable. About 4 p.m. we received the same ration exactly of our morning issue, bread and barley meal. This was a starvation diet. We knew that if that was all we could ever expect, then for us – eventual death! Like others, I became afraid to venture across the expanse of the compound. I hugged the buildings around the edges. Hunger produced weakness and giddiness. I cannot even attempt to relate every day spent there; repetitive, horrible, hungry, boredom! The future appeared near hopeless.

*Wilfred Bowden was repatriated in December 1918, travelling in a Danish hospital ship from Danzig to Leith. After four days at Ripon Camp in Yorkshire he returned, at last, to Abercynon. His discharge papers were dated 15 February 1919 – four years, to the day, after his enlistment.*

# CHARLES CLAYTON

Charles Pritchard Clayton came from Garthmyl in Montgomeryshire. He was to become a university lecturer at Aberystwyth and then a member of the Welsh Schools' Inspectorate. In 1914 he was commissioned into the Special Reserve and by the following March was on his way to join the 1st Battalion of the Welch Regiment in the trenches. After being wounded at Ypres and recuperating in Britain he returned (in September 1915) to the Western Front – this time to the 2nd Battalion of his regiment, at Loos. By December 1916 he was Acting Lieutenant-Colonel commanding his battalion, after serving at Bazentin Wood, Fricourt and High Wood. Later in the war he attended a Senior Officers' School at Aldershot and was employed on staff duties in France.

~

## The Ypres Salient[1]

*In April 1915 the Germans made the first use of poison gas to aid their attack.*

The sun rises clearly, but at nine o'clock there seems to be a slight ground mist. As it gradually clears we frequently turn our eyes northward for there is a heavy bombardment going on. As a clear view opens out we can see enormous 'coalboxes'[2] exploding in and about the front and support lines a couple of miles away. Looking through my field glasses I can see men running about among the heavy black bursts and I can see parties bearing

---

[1] Extract reproduced from C. P. Clayton, *The Hungry One* (Llandysul: Gomer Press, 1978).
[2] Shell-bursts from heavy guns, with clouds of black smoke.

27

stretchers frequently making their way towards the rear. It is an anxious time, for if the line breaks there, our flank may be turned – at any rate we shall be in full view of the enemy.

A little later there is a lull in the bombardment and hoping to see something more hopeful I get out my glasses again. But there is something threatening in the sudden silence. I half expect to hear the heavy rifle fire and bombing of a hostile infantry attack; but what I see is even more disturbing. From the top of the slope where the 'coalboxes' have been making havoc there seems to be rising a line of small yellow clouds. Yet not rising but stealing along the ground. Gradually they spread and join together. As the cloud comes silently down the slight slope it seems to take the shape of a long roll of yellowish cotton wool, it is now so dense. From this distance its movement seems to be very slow. The sight of it brings a conviction that it is something ominous and threatening. The feeling is strengthened beyond any doubt when I discern small parties of men running madly in front of the dense cloud-roll. Sometimes some of them turn round and plunge into the cloud, but none seem to get out of it again. The sight, far away and indistinct as it is, is full of terrible significance. There seems no doubt but that the yellow roll is gas of some kind, a weapon not hitherto used in warfare and therefore of unknown power.

I cannot take my glasses away. The yellow fog gradually advances, throwing tentacles along trenches and hedges. There appears to be rifle fire from the German line but if there is a battle it is uncannily quiet. Now and then a retreating man falls, and in some places, where the cloud leaves a patch of ground clear, there appear to be bodies scattered about, but whether killed by the cloud or by rifles or earlier shelling it is impossible to tell. Some of those who fall on this side of the advancing cloud rise again and attempt time after time to stagger away from it. There is some fighting over in that direction in the afternoon but we fail to see what is happening. We can detect no movement in the stricken area.

Some tea has just been produced when Monty comes along and says that he has a job for me after tea. Stretcher bearers coming back from the front battalions on our left have reported that they have seen Germans behind our lines on that flank and some of the runners say they have been sniped at. I am to go out just before dusk with my platoon and hunt out every bit of cover I can find for about a mile to the left – the railway cutting, farms, buildings, copses and hedges. I am warned that there may be Germans anywhere from the railway embankment to the north. So after tea we set out. We thread our way in single file through the fields. We cross the railway and search the embankment, then form two parties and work up to each copse and farm from two points simultaneously.

Hunting the farms and farm buildings is quite interesting. In entering the lofts and attics – the most likely place for snipers – someone has to take the first chance. I find a revolver better than the men find rifles and usually get a look in as the doors are flung open. But we find no enemy. It soon gets too dark to see indoors and we have to use our torches. In one farmhouse, however, bursting suddenly into the kitchen, we find a fellow sitting at the table eating ravenously. The food appears to be stale scraps, left probably by the troops who last occupied the place. As we burst in, the lonely eater, hatless but in a British uniform, looks up but without excitement.

'Well', I demand, 'what are you doing here?'

'Getting some grub, I reckon', he replies casually, in a strong North American accent.

'What do you belong to?'

'Princess Pat's',[3] from a full mouth.

'Where's your regiment?'

'Guess there's not much left of it except me.'

'What are you going to do?'

'As soon as I've finished this I'm going back to have another dekko at those infernal devils who put that bloody gas over.'

We have some trouble to get him to come along with us but we have to insist for doubtless many Germans could speak like Canadians and certainly any sniper would not hesitate to get on a British uniform. He is the only prisoner we take, and after spending the night at our headquarters he is allowed to go back

---

[3]Princess Patricia's Canadian Light Infantry. 'The "Princess Pat's" had a strange beginning. A Captain of Militia, Andrew Hamilton Gault, was sufficiently wealthy to pay, in 1914, for the raising of a new regiment for service in the European War. He took the name of the daughter of the Duke of Connaught, Queen Victoria's third and favourite son and at that time Governor General of Canada. Recruitment came mainly from former soldiers of the British Army who had emigrated to Canada after the Boer War. At one stage, every regiment of the British Army (bar one) was represented in the Princess Patricia's Canadian Light Infantry's ranks.' (Roger Perkins, *Regiments of the Empire* (1989)).

by way of the reserve line to have a dekko at his enemy in the north. My impression is that he is a very sturdy fellow.

During the night 'A' Company receives a call, and Macaulay has to take out a platoon of the company to dig in on our left flank, north of the village and just behind the district that we have been searching. It is now known that the enemy has broken through the Zouaves and that the Canadians have been doubled up from their flanks – all as a result of that yellow cloud we watched so anxiously. The heavy gunfire has recommenced to the north of us and we now have two fronts, one facing east and the other north. We hear that every unit in the Division has been brought up and that the whole of the front line is being milked to find troops to throw into the gap. At Monty's order I go to get a bit of sleep while I may. In the afternoon Monty tells me that the Colonel of the N.F.s[4] has sent for two platoons and that I am to take command of them. I go to the Northumberland Headquarters on the edge of the village and report to the Colonel.

I find him down in the cellar, and he seems worried.

'How many men have you brought?'

'Sixty, sir.'

'Is that all you have in two platoons?'

'That's all now, sir.'

He mutters something and produces a rough plan of the village. Pointing to the last house on the road leading north he says that one of his captains is there.

'Your party will get 16 extra boxes of ammunition from the dump in the yard here and report as quickly as you can to Captain Dash. Then you will take your orders from him.'

I hurry back to my men and get them loaded up with the ammunition boxes. A few shells fall here and there about the village as we thread our way through the orchards but most of the firing is still to the northward. The boxes are heavy and our progress is slow. As we struggle along a runner comes to me with an order to hurry. Leaving Sergeant Laws to get the men along with the ammunition as quickly as he can I push ahead with the runner. Before we get to the house I can see the officer waving excitedly.

As I dash up he cries:

---

[4]Northumberland Fusiliers.

'For God's sake hurry your men along.'

'Well, what's the job?'

'There's no time to waste. Go straight along there in that direction', waving his hand to the northward, 'and try to get in touch with the next unit on the left.'

Our start lies along the broad paved road that leads out of the village. We are now standing in the shelter of the last house on the right. This road runs along the forward slope of some slightly raised ground, fully exposed from here northward to the enemy's fire from the east.

'Can you tell me where the enemy's positions are?' I ask.

'Somewhere out there.' He replied, vaguely swinging his arm north-east. 'You'll get under fire when you've gone about a hundred yards along the road. Get on.'

Assuring myself that all my party is ready in file behind me, I tell Sergeant Laws to send them after me at two yards' intervals and start walking up the road. As we start the shrapnel is bursting fairly thickly over the area in front of us. There is a certain amount of rifle fire, and now and then a machine-gun chatters noisily.

I soon have reason to damn that officer and his excitement. No sooner have I walked clear of the house thinking that I am fairly safe for the 'hundred yards' when a hostile machine gun suddenly blazes out from some point on my right and the bullets begin whistling round me and plopping into the bank on the left of the road. Trailing my rifle I put my head down, shouting to those behind: 'Come on.' I run for it. It seems that other hostile machine guns take up the chorus, and as I run the bullets throw up flashes from the paving under my feet, and seem to riddle the air all round. I keep it up for about two or three hundred yards and then, fearing that the men behind me are out of puff, I throw myself down on the left side of the road. There is practically no ditch, but the camber of the road will afford some little protection – better than nothing.

As soon as I have recovered breath I raise my head, to see how things fare behind. My next man is some yards behind and wriggling along the gutter towards me. The firing at us has slackened since we went down but quite a few bullets still strike the road and the slope above us. In front the slight gutter in which we lie peters out to nothing and there are no signs of troops in that direction as far as I can see. We can depend upon the machine guns opening again as soon as we get up.

Suddenly from just behind me comes the discharge of a rifle, followed by others. My men are retaliating. They are firing at some scraps of trench down in the hollow to the right of the road. I soon realise that those small trenches are our own. Parties sent out last night – possibly Macaulay's – have dug themselves in. I pass the word to cease fire, for our trouble comes from positions on the opposite slope, behind those bits of trench, and we cannot fire at our enemy without the risk of hitting our own people in the back. To myself I curse that captain fellow for failing to tell me that our own men were down there, and I curse him too, for telling me that we were safe for a hundred yards along the road, especially when my nearest man shouts: 'A lot of men are hit, sir.'

'Pass the word to get ready to advance.' I shout, realising that we can do no good here. Then having given time for the order to pass along I rise and run for it again with some, at any rate, of the men following. As the enemy sight our move their whole orchestra opens afresh, and again the sparks fly up from the stones. During the time which has elapsed since we first broke cover from the village the hostile observers have been chanting to the gunners, for now there is a heavy downpour of shrapnel round us. Luckily for us they don't seem to have realised that the ground rises here. Their time fuses are mostly too long and for every shell that bursts over our heads half a dozen explode comparatively harmlessly after they strike the earth.

After running about two hundred yards I seem to have left behind the heaviest machine gun fire and only a mild hail of bullets from riflemen continues. The machine guns, I'm afraid, are concentrating on the rear of my line. I am ready for a rest but there is not a scrap of cover anywhere to be seen. But to the left, some thirty yards up the slope, there is a high thorn hedge running parallel to the road. In itself it provides no cover against bullets and shell, but most hedges have ditches of some kind. I must chance it, and shouting 'come on', I climb the bank of the road and make up the slope. But I find no ditch at all. Not a vestige. But dropping to a walk behind the hedge I find that there seem to be few bullets, now that I am lost to view. So I pass on for a few yards looking vainly for any cover where we might dig in. Finding none I sit down to get my breath and wait for the men. But I must not wait for many here. To get us crowded behind this hedge and then to open intense machine gun and artillery fire upon it is just what the enemy would enjoy – and we should not.

Higher up the slope there seems to be a narrow ditch – it appears to lead a little higher up and further northward. We must not wait here, so I lead the way towards it. The shells are bursting very quickly now and I lose no time in getting the men down into it as soon as they arrive. It is only about nine inches deep and the same in width, and as it runs at an angle to the firing line it is enfiladed, but it gives a little cover from shrapnel splinters. To my surprise the fourth to arrive is Sergeant Laws. He says that there are no more men to come. The rest, he says, have either been hit or called back by the N.F. Captain when he realised what things were like on the road. Laws is certain that nearly all of the missing men have been hit. Prospects are not good, but it is of no use going back. We may yet be able to find the troops on our left. I notice a barbed wire entanglement further on, near the rest of the rise. There may be a trench there. Again I lead on, and as we move the bullets once more become plentiful. As I clamber through the wire entanglement I feel a sudden burning sensation in my left arm and wonder whether I have been hit but, seeing a trench before me, I do not stop to find out. The trench is filled with troops, grouped much too closely together. We lose no time in getting down among them for the fire we have drawn is still unpleasant.

They say they belong to the Northumberland Brigade, just fresh from England. They have no idea where the enemy is and are surprised when we tell them that they are practically the front line. They direct me to the officers' dugout and we pass along. I find the officers in a shallow timbered dugout which has about eighteen inches of soil over it. It seems a portion of the trench which has been broadened, deepened and covered leaving an entrance at either end. Bending down and peering into one of the entrances I ask for the Commanding Officer and tell him who I am and what I know of the position in front. He can give me no information about the position of any other troops. He refuses my offer of help in showing him positions in front and scouting to the left front. Then as I am about to speak again one of the thickly falling shells crashes through the roof within a foot or two of my head and explodes with a stunning roar inside the dugout. So sharply does the soil sting my face that I think for a moment that I am badly hurt. But as I draw my hand I find no blood.

Inside there is a clamour. I look in through the stifling smoke and can make out forms scrambling out through the opposite entrance. But somewhere in the reek there is a pitiful groaning, and groping forward I get hold of the hand of an officer who is trying to get to the door. I get him out and his men help me to lay him down in the trench. His head is all wet with blood, but I can find no large wound so we get bandages and bind it up. Leaving instructions with the Sergeant-Major about what to do with him I waste no time in hunting for the other officers but get back to where I left my men, rather anxious as to whether they are safe. I find them safe enough, and they have now been joined by three more who have got through behind us.

Seeing that we are still so few, and that some of the others appear to have been called back by the N.F. Officer, I decide to get back and report to the N.F. Colonel. We avoid the way by which we came. We should have little hope of getting back that way. We work back a little and enter the western end of the village. It is dusk when we get in. Down in the cellar I make my report. There is, of course, no welcome for us. The Colonel is anything but cordial. Of course our excursion has been a failure. I can tell him where the supports are, but I cannot tell him where the nearest front line post is. I can only say that from the farthest point to which we pushed along the road I could see no sign of any troops or trenches in front of the supports to which we had ultimately made our way. Finally he gruffly tells me to report to my Captain, which I am glad enough to do.

As we walk in among the dugouts in the twilight Monty meets us and he looks at me as if he sees a ghost. He seems to pull himself together with an effort and says quietly: 'Well I'm damned glad to see you again. A few of your men came in an hour ago and they told me you had been killed.'

'How many have come in?'

'Oh, only ten or a dozen altogether', he replies.

I sit down feeling rather sick. This means that only 17 or 18 are left out of the sixty. And they have been good fellows ... and they have all been through the fighting of these last weeks. Enough to show their quality. Monty's voice rouses me: 'You'd better go and get a bit of rest, you need it. I'm damned glad you're back, anyway.'

Somehow I cannot sleep although I am tired enough. So I take the ration party once more to the dump beyond the village. We carry for the N.F.s as well as for ourselves so I halt my party opposite their Headquarters which is still in the house on the south side of the road. While I go inside through a gap in the wall of the yard I leave the men with orders to lie close in the shallow ditch on the north side, for there are bullets frequently coming in from the north and smacking viciously against the wall. After I come out with my detailed orders I am just about to order the men to get up and come along when there is a duller impact and a yell. A young lad has failed to keep down in cover and we find he has been hit through the body low down. He is quickly carried through the wall to the dressing station and we move away down the village.

As we near the dump at the level crossing beyond the village a shrieking flight of shells plunges down, exploding at intervals along the left side of the road. Two or three men go down, but all except one gets up again. This one has a bit of shell in his leg, but he pluckily volunteers to find his way back to the nearest dressing station alone. One more of the original members of my platoon gone, another good fellow. But if his luck holds he will get to Blighty, and that's more than many of us are likely to do. The journey back with rather heavy loads, because of our small numbers, is accomplished without further loss, and this time I really am too tired to worry. But before I turn in I remember the feeling in my arm when I was under fire and now I find that there are two bullet holes in my sleeve one in front and one behind, but all that my arm shows is a dark red scar where the bullet has scorched the skin without actually cutting it.

The morning breaks fine and sunny, but we have little encouragement to think about the weather. Soon after daybreak we see fresh clouds of yellowish fumes drifting down from the northward and again the 'coalboxes' tear up the earth along the slopes towards which we adventured yesterday. We are gradually being surrounded as the line continues to break.

Yet I hear that we are holding out here in front of the village as strongly as ever. The remainder of our 'A' Company has been helping to clear the trench across the road where the big German trench mortar is still as active and devastating as ever. As they come back for a rest they tell us that three of the Royal Engineers who were helping them last night were killed by one of the big bombs.

I have just been gazing northward through my field glasses when Bryan of 'A' Company comes along the road, and I ask him what he thinks of it. He cannot be charged with false optimism, at any rate.

'We must all sell our lives as dearly as we can, according to the best approved traditions, I suppose', and he passes on.

In the afternoon there is a diversion. Hearing the German field guns open out vigorously, we see that their shells are bursting thickly about the slightly higher ground behind and to the north of the village. Then we see why they are shelling. Lines of British skirmishers are coming over the rise to support us and try to throw back the enemy from his advanced positions on our left. In long regular lines they come with two or three yards between each man, and a hundred or two hundred between each line. As they top the ridge and the shelling opens the bursts do them little harm. As they advance down the slope the shelling becomes more accurate; here and there we see men blown down, and some do not get up again, but still the skirmishers keep their lines and advance as if drilling on a parade ground. But now they are met by machine-gun fire from some point to the north of us and parts of their lines begin advancing on the run then lying down to fire while other sections rush forward.

And now comes real tragedy. The enemy seem to get their range, and down go several of the gallant skirmishers almost simultaneously in the middle of their rush. At the same time the guns seem both to quicken their fire and to become more effective. It is becoming a slaughter. It is terrible to watch and to be helpless to do anything. The lines are broken and there is a tendency to crowd to the left. The shrapnel is murderously effective now. It seems to sweep down whole sections of them. Some of them struggle helplessly after they fall. Nothing can help them now. Only one or two, out of all those lines manage to reach the shelter of the ruins of the village or get as far as our support trench.

We cannot help wondering why they were sent over that ridge in broad daylight. It seems almost as though some would-be-clever staff officer had some bright idea of flinging forward a line by map directions. No one who had been in this part of the Salient during the past 48 hours would have dreamed of trying to push lines of men down that slope in broad daylight and within easy machine gun range as well as full artillery observation. We do not want urgent and immediate help, and the posts to the north of us protecting our flank seem no worse off than they have been for the last day or two.

As dusk falls, more lines of skirmishers come over, these are not spotted and they get forward to the posts on our left without, as far as we can judge, the loss of a single man.

There follows another night of front line digging and ration carrying, and another day of watching the near bursts of the enormous trench mortar bomb and the more distant yet gradually approaching explosions of the 'coalboxes' to the north. We are nearly surrounded.

In the afternoon come secret orders which Monty imparts to me. Our front is to be vacated. We are to move back. The order of our going has been carefully detailed. The N.F.s whom we are now helping, have to pick out thirty of their men, thirty tough athletic fellows, and at nine o'clock tonight all except these thirty will move back. These thirty are to stay in the line, each with a sector to himself, and from 9 o'clock until midnight they are to move back and fore in their own sectors firing off rifles and star shells here and there in order to keep up the appearance of normal occupation of the line by our troops. At midnight they are to run for it, and try to get back to the new line some two or three miles to the west. If they have any wounded they must be left behind. Such are the orders for the thirty. Meanwhile the rest of us are to start back at nine.

Before we go we have to bury any ammunition that we cannot carry. Monty tells me to bury our reserve ammunition at the Company Headquarters, and I set my remaining men to work at once. In the garden behind the house we dig two graves – deep ones. In the bottom we stack the boxes. We fill in the soil, and on the top we place two wooden crosses with fictitious names on them. The enemy will not be able to tell them from genuine graves and will not trouble to disturb them.

We cannot help wondering during the evening whether the enemy will detect our purpose, but everything seems to continue normal except that the pressure on our immediate flank continues critical. A big new offensive may come at any moment.

Nine o'clock comes at last and we are soon threading our way through the ruins of the village for the last time. It is a relief to think that we shall not have any more journeys through this gloomy wreck of a place for rations with the feeling that the enemy is all the time closing round us.

But it is a weary march. It seems an age since we had a rest – even a wash – sometime in another life. There is just a hope that fresh troops will be holding the new line and that, if only for a day or two, we shall find some little sense of relief. But not far from Frezenberg, a small ruined hamlet which has been in the middle of the Salient, we are halted in the road. Monty is talking to a runner. The runner has been waiting for us. He brings orders and says he is our guide. Our slender hope of rest is gone and we are being led away to the north, back into battle.

Our hearts are heavy as we plod on over the rough ground in the darkness. Nobody speaks. We move very slowly. A few paces, and then a pause in order to make sure that those behind have closed up, for if once we lose touch we shall never find each other, and there is no visible trail. After struggling on for some time we cross an unfenced road. It comes from the northeast and goes on left towards Ypres. I am so tired that I am very nearly asleep on my feet.

But now I become conscious of noises along the road, mainly to the right. Subdued groaning, coughing, choking sounds. And as I cross the road I can see forms lying huddled about it. One of them gets up and staggers along a few yards towards Ypres, and then falls again in a fit of choking coughs. They are gassed men coming back from that fatal front where the terrible yellow cloud came down upon them. They are struggling step by step towards England – and dying in their tracks.

# EMLYN DAVIES

A farmer's son, Emlyn Davies lived near Oswestry and worked as a telegraphist for the Post Office. On his nineteenth birthday – 27 July 1915 – he volunteered at the local recruiting office and was posted to the 17th (Service) Battalion of the Royal Welch Fusiliers, which was in the 113th Brigade of the 38th (Welsh) Division. 'Reporting at Battalion Headquarters in Llandudno, I was assigned the regimental number 26413. Just ahead of me No. 26412 had been duly registered. He was a tall, good-looking, very nice boy. His name was Watcyn Emil Owain Griffith, son of the headmaster of Dolgellau Grammar School. We became bosom friends – for the remainder of his life.' (Watcyn was killed in action a year later.)[1] Emlyn Davies moved, with his battalion, to a tented camp at Flowerdown, near Winchester (twenty-four men to a bell tent) and later to a half-completed, muddy, hutted camp at Hazeley Down. After travelling across the Channel in *La Marguerite*,[2] the war took him to Laventie, Neuve Chapelle, Festubert, Givenchy and the battle of the Somme.

Transferred, because of his Post Office background, to the Brigade Signal Company, he served with 'F' Wireless Section (8th Army Corps) at Flamertinghe, near Ypres, and then at various listening posts in

---

[1]Watcyn Griffith died at Mametz Wood on 10 July 1916. Wyn Griffith's book *Up to Mametz* is dedicated 'to the memory of Private Watcyn Griffith'.
[2]*La Marguerite* was a paddle steamer which formerly operated around the north Wales coast. She was broken up in 1925.

the Ypres Salient.[3] In July 1917, a few days after his twenty-first birthday, he was with the 38th (Welsh) Division during the attack on Pilckem Ridge.

Invalided home with trench fever (February 1918) Emlyn Davies spent time in various medical and rehabilitation units in Britain. On 11 November 1918 he heard the bells pealing from Penrhos Church to celebrate the Armistice. Four months later he rejoined the Post Office. His chest troubles continued for many years.

~

## *Battalion Signaller*[4]

Much of my time in support areas was devoted to giving our group of signallers practice in the art of telegraphy. The rate of transmission expected of an Infantry signaller was eight words per minute. As a Post Office telegraphist, my rate exceeded thirty per minute. The boys used to gather around me either in the billet or outside, seated or prone, with whatever pieces of paper could be acquired. I would operate the key initially at ten words per minute for five minutes or so, then collect and examine the results, increasing the rate thereafter. There were some good boys in this section, some attaining twelve words per minute, and two or three, sixteen words per minute ...

After spending some weeks in the trenches, a call came to join a class in operating, and elementary electricity, at the Division School set up in La Gorgue. Two signallers from each of the twelve battalions assembled, under the instruction of NCO Williams, a Cardiff GPO telegraphist. The party was a happy one, kipping down in the lecture room. Here we were enlivened by the sparkling wit and humour of two Cockneys, members of the London

---

[3]A Memorandum by 1st Army, dated 27 October 1916 states: 'Listening sets have been in use by the French and Germans for nearly a year; by the British for 8–9 months, although no definite organisation was established until April.' The Memorandum gives examples of British transmissions which breached security, for example, 'Tell the officer one patrol is going out tonight'; 'Trench State: Officers 14, Other Ranks 845'; 'You have challenged the South Wales Borderers to a football match tomorrow, haven't you?' (Memorandum in J. Ferris (ed.), *The British Army and Signals Intelligence during the First World War* (Alan Sutton for Army Records Society, 1992).)
[4]Extracts reproduced from E. Davies, *Taffy Went to War* (Knutsford: Knutsford Secretarial Bureau, 1976).

Welsh. Their tales were expressed largely in unprintable English; sessions of uproarious merriment resulted. Captain Bowyer, RE, came to know of the circumstances in which a qualified telegraphist was in attendance at a class designed for elementary purposes. Rather than send me back to the battalion, he had me transferred to the Instrument Repair Workshop where I learned to execute minor repairs. Moreover, I was given an Operating Test with a view to transfer to a Signal company, and passed it. There was, however, no vacancy, therefore I returned to the Battalion on completion of the current course ...

Whilst signallers, by Army regulation, did no fatigues, presumably because they were always on call, we carried the same weight as any other ranks, indeed our weight exceeded that of any other. Not only full pack with rifle but signalling equipment also. This included rolls of spare wire, a case containing tools and earth pins in addition to the telephone-telegraph set. Up the line we were responsible for maintaining communications with HQ, each of the four companies, often to additional posts in support areas and, most essential, to artillery batteries covering our sector. We were at the beck and call of the Company Commander for whom we also acted as runners.

Our numerous lines ran alongside the trenches and were vulnerable to shellfire. Then our immediate task was to trace the breakage, taking with us spare lengths of wire in the event of a gap, or a series of gaps, so that connection could be effected quickly. More often than otherwise, the breakages occurred during a barrage when communications were vitally and urgently necessary. It was no pleasant task to trace the lines and repair them ...

At Zuytpeene, a village 20 miles away and some five miles from the hill town of Cassel (which housed the Headquarters of General Sir Hubert Plumer, GOC, Second Army), a Wireless Signalling School had been established. Packed off there for one month's course had its advantages; comfortable billets in a small Chateau standing in parkland; plentiful food; discipline correct but not bullish; no marching; no machine gun bullets; heaven, in short. And withal, a glorious spell of September sunshine. The classes were attended by representatives of each of the Divisions comprising the Second Army, Irish, Welsh, Scottish, English, Australians and New Zealanders, intermingled in happy and interesting concordance.

The instructors, mainly GPO Telegraphists, were reasonable and efficient, making the course profitable and interesting. It consisted of learning the elementary principles of Electricity and Magnetism, and in Wireless Telegraphy. Lectures, demonstrations and the practice of communication in this medium were included in the curriculum.

## The Wireless Section

On one of the Section's operators receiving wounds I was sent to replace him at Potiyzhe Wood.

In the Salient some eight stations were operating in teams of three. At Potiyzhe, because the set-up included a very sophisticated instrument in addition to the normal examples in use, there were six operators. It was so sensitive that the occupants had to tread the floor very gently indeed, also to speak in lowered voices. Every sound was re-echoed, drowning any other incoming signals. Potiyzhe was one of the eight such posts dotting the Salient front areas ... the dugout had been scratched out of a mound beyond which lay a sparse wood on rising ground. Three sides were fairly solid, the front curtained with groundsheets, the roof with a two foot depth of sandbags. Sides and roof dripped with water. The parlour/workshop/dining room/bedroom was roomy enough to house the six occupants and their gear. A three-tiered bank of timbered frames, the mattress consisted of wire netting having the softening aid of any clean sandbags which could be acquired ... The purposes of wireless posts were fourfold. When lines were cut by shellfire, messages were transmitted to appropriate Commanders in the rear; as listening posts to enemy installations; as 'policemen' to our own infantry transmissions. The rule of conduct forbade the use at all times of messages containing language in plain English; the prescribed code must be adhered to. Unauthorised messages had to be recorded and reported. Mainly we were kind to our friends, only infrequently reporting their naughty misdeeds. The fourth dimension was to record radio transmissions made by Observation Aircraft, engaged in noting the effect of our artillery's shelling of indicated enemy targets. A diagram of clock-face design with concentric lines at stated distances, each crossing of the lines leading to the numerals were either lettered or numbered. By this means the actual spot within yards upon which a shellburst was observed would be noted and transmitted to the Battery Commander. 'WW' indicated a washout or 'not observed'. 'OK' meant 'It's a Bull' whereon that ranged target continued to receive the violent attention of the gunners ...

Aerials were often cut and brought down by shell fire and immediate erection of a replacement was essential. The first requirement was a suitable object, usually at least one tree some fifty to a hundred feet high, preferably two trees fifty to a hundred yards apart. The method of erection was first to attach a guy wire to the aerial, secured to it and insulated from it. The length of the aerial was decided. The guy wire had to be of a length as would allow it to clear the tree and to land at a point where it could be secured to the trunk. To the stem of a rifle grenade, previously defused, the guy wire was secured. The stem was pushed into the rifle's bore. Firmly held with its butt resting lightly on the ground, the rifle leaned at about forty-five degrees, the grenade was fired. With good luck and much practice the contraption sailed over and beyond the tree and secured, the home end of the aerial was similarly treated. The firing of a rifle grenade produced a considerable kick, too violent for firing from the shoulder ...

At this juncture it may be appropriate to describe the instruments in use in a Trench Wireless Post. The sets were light and to a simple, even primitive design, crystal type and having a morse key. Later a one-valve set was introduced; again later to include two valves; a considerable improvement, but remaining far inferior to those used by the Germans. Signals received normally never exceeded R5; R7 volume was desirable. At R1, R2 and R3 our normal was difficult and sometimes impossible to read. Reception was further complicated by the vast number of transmissions heard simultaneously. The operator had to concentrate upon his allocated station, picking up its individual tune in competition with other stations of greater strength. To wear headphones for a four-hour session imposed considerable strain upon the aural functions. It was no fun ... It was our practice to take down the daily communiqué transmitted by the British, French and German authorities in triplicate; sending one copy to the Brigadier, one to the nearest infantry Commander, retaining the third. Reception was made more difficult by reason of loud and persistent German transmission from their station at Bruges. Consequently much jamming resulted, often rendering the communiqués devoid of sense. In these instances we inserted in the place of the missing words 'Jammed'. Often there were more jams than words, in which event copies would not be distributed.

*Emlyn Davies was sent on a week's course to Corps Headquarters in a chateau at Proven:*

Clad in every possible aid to keeping tolerable warmth, we carried out officer-directed experiments for the possible use of 'ground aerials', on the premise that aerials at the front suffered destruction. They also drew fire. The drill was to lay the insulated aerials along the ground to a depth of one foot. For this one needed the tools and the brawny arms of a village blacksmith. A foot of frosted earth to pierce. It was nigh impossible. Lighting upon an idea to use a small pond in which to drive the earth-pins proved effective. The experiments proved largely successful. Six months later at Armentires, with the addition of Power Buzzers fitted with two valves, and fixing on the two ends of the aerials, one on either side of the set, the earth-pins, effective signals could be transmitted over a distance of a thousand yards. The effectiveness of transmissions proved infinitely increased over the Crystal Set whose use was superseded by the Power Buzzer and the new aerials ...

I was recalled and sent for a stint of duty at Intelligence GHQ, some 25 miles to the rear. It was a well-equipped establishment. In the operating room were perhaps a dozen operators decorated with headphones, and two NCO cipher decoders. On the desk beside them lay a thick volume, containing, no doubt, the answers to every code under the sun. Every known signalling device was there; simple and complicated, wireless sets, sounders and what not. Outside the hut a directional aerial swivelled on its base. Every morning each operator was handed a note indicating the enemy station to which he was to listen. 'Concentrate on this one Station alone and get everything.' Enemy transmissions despite their multiplicity of origin were more easily received than our own ...

Our next port of call was to the extreme right of the Division's holding, based upon Fleurbaix. Normally each such cross was well marked by the German gunners. Fleurbaix was no exception. Shelling was in progress, therefore we cut blindly across rough country to Sailly au Bois, in front of which our post stood, in yet another British made 'shelter'. It was then a quiet area, both as regards the eternal gunnery and the work we had to perform.

It rested mainly on 'policing' the infantry signallers in their frequent unauthorised effusions. Poor lads; they were as cheesed off, or perhaps more so, than ourselves, and perhaps with more justification. We recorded their departures from faith. We did not report a tithe of them, sometimes taxing our imagination to offer garbled, and sometimes incomprehensible messages. The boys, nevertheless, could not forgive our true recordings. Perhaps they relented a little when we told them of our omissions and inventions. I had been an infantryman too.

Twelve inches of snow fell in quick time. Collecting on our aerials, sagging and breakage followed. 'Stick 'em up again, Taffy.'

# JAMES DUNN

*The War the Infantry Knew*, which Wyn Griffith thought to be 'one of the finest of war books', is a diary of the activities of the 2nd Battalion, Royal Welch Fusiliers. It is described on the title page as being 'founded on personal records, recollections and reflections, assembled, edited and partly written by One of their Medical Officers' – in fact Captain J. C. Dunn, a temporary officer in the Royal Army Medical Corps. Of Scottish parentage, James Dunn was born in New Zealand, but raised and educated in Scotland. Although medically qualified, he volunteered to fight in the South African War, serving as a trooper in the Montgomeryshire Yeomanry. In 1914, at the age of forty-three, he volunteered again and became doctor to the 2nd Royal Welch.

~

## The Battle of Loos, 1915[1]

*This was to see the first use by the British of chlorine gas (the Germans had used it at Ypres in April). In the attack, against the German 6th Army, the 2nd Royal Welch Fusiliers were to advance on the left flank.*

### September 4th
The Battalion, in reserve and now in Béthune, had to find large working-parties daily. No one got much rest during September. There were fatigues for everyone, whether in or out of the trenches. A new front line was dug in Nomansland in the Cambrin sector. Everywhere assembly trenches were dug behind

---

[1]Extracts reproduced from J. C. Dunn, *The War the Infantry Knew, 1914–1919* (London: Sphere Books, 1989 edn.).

the support line, and gun-emplacements were dug in it. Stores for bridging trenches, ladders for getting out of them, had to be carried. Large and heavy metal cylinders, slung from a pole, that weighed on the shoulders of two men, were carried from Annequin cross-roads to be dug into the front line. The official name for the content of these cylinders was 'accessory'. It was a crime to call it 'gas'. No printable vocabulary could repeat what the men called it as they struggled and sweated up the narrow angular trenches, which were festooned with loose telephone wires that gripped sometimes the throat, sometimes the feet. – New batteries rolled in behind us, flung up emplacements in the chalky soil, and registered: all with the barest pretence of secrecy. Troop, train, and wagon movements were unconcealed. There was so much to be seen and sought for by both sides that observers excitedly poked their telescopes through the slits of the most cunningly contrived observation posts, 'O-pips', so that they flashed in the sun like heliographs. And air activity increased greatly on both sides . . .

*September 24th*
The morning sky grey. There was more rain; after breakfast it became only a drizzle. Later in the day there was a beautiful and complete rainbow against a louring sky behind the Germans. There has been more din all day, and the enemy has been retaliating. The wind, what there is of it, is unfavourable to us; very disquieting. The evening was still dry but, after dark, black and ragged clouds from the south drifted low across the waxing moon. The Argylls' MO was eloquent with exuberant optimism, the Middlesex MO just quietly hopeful, when we met at night to discuss arrangements. According to the official forecast and programme the gas is to lay out all the Germans, the leading battalions have just to walk over, the supports do any needed mopping-up: there will likely be some resistance at Les Briques farm and walled orchard, 1,000 yards distant: then the advance will continue through Auchy to Haisnes, nearly two miles off. Both these villages are trenched, wired, and loopholed. Where will my dressing station be? 'Where it is tonight', I said, 'unless the wind change, and I see no promise of a change.' Then we had words, but parted on an understanding. The happy-go-lucky tone of our infantry programme jarred on me in the circumstances.

Brigade Orders gave the Battalion its assembly position and

required it to support the Middlesex, but gave no time for its advance or other detail. In Battalion Orders it was calculated that our leading Companies would be forming in the front line as the last of the Middlesex went over. The morning had been spent fitting and preparing: Orders were issued and explained. After the final inspection of the awful gas-masks of that period the men were dismissed until evening. There was a Battalion dinner with the GOC and Staff of the 24th Division, who were taking over the billet, as unexpected guests. It was a cheery affair at the start, but there was a shadow on it, and the diners were too pre-occupied to keep up the cheeriness to the end. At 10.45 we left Béthune and marched the 9 kilometres to Cambrin, where RE stores were collected. The night was very dark, it poured with rain all the way. The march was a depressing affair, which 'C' company tried to enliven by a constant repetition of 'China, China, Chinatown', but without great success.

*September 25th*
'B' Company reached its assembly trench, some 200 yards behind the front line, about 1 o'clock, and lay down to await zero. The assembly trenches were deep and cramped. Everyone was inconvenienced by his kit and equipment. Besides rifle, bayonet, 200 rounds of ammunition, and extra ration, every man had to carry a pick or shovel or other tool, and several new and unwieldy bombs known as 'cricket balls'. The matchstriker on which the bomb fuse had to be lighted had become so wet as to be useless until it might dry. All had to wear a rolled PH helmet[2] on the head, ready to be pulled down at a moment's notice; a cap was balanced on top of it, and the whole was tied on with a piece of string passed under the chin. Things might have been worse, for although the night was cold the pouring rain had become lighter showers. A rum issue was to be served out an hour before the attack. Freeman countermanded his Company's issue, to the dismay of his men and more than dismay of those who saw it poured over the ground. 'A' Company lost theirs.

Heavy gun-fire awakened me in No. 1 Harley Street. No notice of zero hour had reached me, so I ran upstairs to a paneless attic window that was out of bounds. A grey watery sky: shells bursting on the German front line, and

---

[2]The Phenol Helmet was an early form of gas mask.

a line of smoke forming on our front: the air was raw, it was nearly windless; there was some crackling of small arms, a bit like sticks kindling. I ran down and called the men, pulled on some clothes, and rushed round to Wimpole Street, a shallow communication trench in which we had made a dressing-station of a sort by digging into the side and sandbagging a rafter roof. We were overwhelmed at once by a score or two of slightly wounded, who said, 'All's going well', and breathless men who said they were 'gassed', though few looked like it.

Zero, 5.45, had found the Battalion ready to move up to support the 1st Middlesex, 'C' and 'B' Companies leading. The whir-r-r of shell splinters mingled with the zipp and whiplash crack of rifle and machine-gun bullets over its assembly trenches. What followed can be understood only in the light of what happened in front. Our artillery treated the German front line with rapid fire; the shooting was good – but the garrison had been withdrawn to the support line. At the same time the Special Gas Company opened the cocks of the cylinders. The unfavourable wind had been reported early to the Brigadier, and he applied to have the gas countermanded – without avail. What wind there was caused it to drift along the line from right to left and to fall back into the trench. Men in the front line got mouthfuls of it, and some became panicky. Gas helmets were adjusted. While the wearers were being stifled in them, the German artillery opened on the crowded trench with well-aimed fire which caused casualties. The first rearward stream of walking wounded began, and the scared, including many of the gas merchants, went with them. Some disorder had been caused, but the Old Line steadied itself. Scaling-ladders were put in position, and other final preparations were made.

The infantry assault was not to start until 6.30 – 'to let the gas act'. During the time of waiting to go over German shells were bursting on the front line and communication trenches. A portion of the Middlesex climbed out of their trench ahead of the time-table to escape the gas, and began a forward movement. The Argylls climbed out on time from both front and support trenches; the cover given by craters let some of the first wave get to the German wire; the second wave dashed forward and was checked by their own front line and wire. 'Forty officers and 800 men shot down in five minutes' summarises the Brigade's attack.[3]

The main items of this scene were reproduced on the rest of the front of the 2nd Division. The 6th Brigade at Cuinchy was more affected by the gas, which put most of its machine-guns out of action. Elements of only one 2nd Division unit got a footing in the German position: one machine-gun prevented the replenishment of its ammunition, and it was bombed out. On the right of the Division, gas, and the direction of the wind relative to the trenches, was a great factor in a considerable and promising initial success.

The CO had left the soil-covered shelter dug into the side of a trench, in which HQ was temporarily housed, to meet his Companies in the front line. When he arrived there it was not yet clear of the Middlesex, apart from casualties. What he saw of the attack was 'forlorn little groups' that assembled in front of the wire and dissolved in trying to go forward, and the Germans standing shoulder to shoulder on their fire-steps, visible from the breast upwards, firing deliberately. The attack was failing, it had already failed, and his Companies were not yet in the trench: 'I[4] thought we were eternally disgraced.' He climbed on the parapet to try to see them, but a Middlesex officer pulled him down. After ordering everyone still in the trench to advance he went in search of his own men. While he and Owen were in the communication trench near the front a shell burst overhead, wounding him in the forehead and arm.

When 'C' and 'B', the leading companies, began to move forward at 6.30 the support line and communication trenches were being fairly heavily shelled. They could see nothing; and they knew nothing of the state of affairs in front. 'With[5] Freeman were Pattison – the Company Sergeant-Major – a few bombers, and me. We had gone only a short distance

---

[3]The Argylls' casualties that day were 330, early estimates were 500. The Middlesex lost over 450.
[4]Brigadier O. de L. Williams.
[5]Captain P. Moody.

when the trenches were found blocked with debris, walking wounded, runners and stretcherbearers, so progress was terribly slow. When we arrived at what was expected to be the front line, but proved to be the support line, Freeman found that only 20 of his men had got through the jam and kept up with him. As his Company was due in the front line in twenty minutes, he sent Pattison and me over the top to find and bring in the others. During the search, in which we failed, Pattison – hearing a shell coming – dropped on his face. When the dust and smoke had cleared he was in the fresh shell-hole of a 5.9 in a sitting posture. Collecting himself, he remarked, 'That one nearly had me', and carried on. Just as we two returned to Freeman to report our failure Colonel Williams ran forward with a wound over an eye, from which the blood ran down his face. He was very concerned; he had seen that the Middlesex attack was failing, so he ordered the troops in the vicinity to advance at once over the top to support it. At that moment Freeman collapsed – it was proved afterwards that he had died of acute heart failure. I led the small party forward. Six had become casualties by the time the front line was reached. Most of the party thought, in the excitement and confusion, that it was the German trench. ('The sight of the trench was horrible, it was literally packed with wounded, dying, and dead men; one had the greatest difficulty in avoiding treading on them.') And the scene beyond was the same. The ground was strewn with dead and wounded in numbers diminishing with the distance; many of the wounded were crawling back through the grass. Gas was still rising from cylinders in our trench; and, drifting up from the right, it came back over our line and fell into the trench for lack of a breeze to disperse it: thus many of the helpless wounded were gassed. Again I made search for the main body of my Company and, having found it, reported to HQ for orders. Owen, who was commanding now, because the CO had gone to hospital, told me in characteristically picturesque language to advance. I thought of the tactical situation as it had appeared to me, but went and got the Company into line. 'C' Company were in position; they too had been held up by wounded Middlesex working their way down, though their move had been through a less busy traffic route.

The[6] Battalion attack was a forlorn hope. About 8 o'clock the officers blew their whistles and over we went, 'B' Company on our left. I saw no shells bursting over the German trenches, so, the morning being bright and sunny, the German riflemen and machine-gunners took their toll of us undisturbed. 'C' Company may have gone 40 yards and then the line just fell down. Samson was very badly hit, and died later in the day; Goldsmith and I were badly wounded; the casualties among the men were heavy.

Half of 'B' Company fell in 30 yards. Since there was no prospect of the remaining 200 yards being covered by more than a handful, I ordered the remainder of the Company to halt and scratch themselves in. This was done with remarkable rapidity. The pre-arranged plan of advancing by rushes of alternate platoons never had a chance to function. At 9 o'clock a runner was given a message to HQ. As there was no reply by 10.30 another message was sent. Then we were ordered to stand fast, ready to take part in another attack that was to be made at 11 o'clock, the appearance above the parapet of the bayonets of the fresh wave would inform us when to move.

'A' and 'D' Companies had assembled in Maison Rouge Alley, in front of Cambrin Church; their progress to the support and front lines was somewhat similar to that of 'C' and 'B'. Their further advance was countermanded by Owen, who had watched the useless sacrifice of 'C' and 'B'. They waited expecting anything, but the impossibility of infantry action on this front was represented by Owen and the other Officers commanding. At noon they relieved the Middlesex, and the Cameronians relieved the Argylls. They helped to tidy up and to fan the gas out of the trenches. Stanway was given command of 'C' Company. The breakthrough by the divisions on the right had become known, infantry movements could be seen; the artillery behind us had switched to the right. By 4 o'clock Moody, 'tired of looking for these bayonets, returned for orders – no earthworm ever crawled closer. At HQ I was greeted by the Acting CO with the exclamation "Hullo! I thought you were dead", and told to go and bring the men back. Having had no food for about twenty-two hours, I was grateful for a square inch of chocolate from Rugg, the Intelligence Officer, who appeared to have nothing in particular to do. The companies were withdrawn with difficulty.

---

[6]Captain H. Blair.

Men were sent back singly through the long autumn grass of Nomansland to leap quickly into the trench on reaching the parapet, where ready hands helped them in.'

During these hours the wounded were being helped, and helping each other, and more wounds were being incurred in the helping. Blair 'was out of the picture with a fractured pelvis. A less wounded man near me wanted to carry me in, but I told him we would both be shot; however, he started to get up and was wounded again immediately. I crawled back slowly and was laid in the bottom of the trench, where I was nearly suffocated with gas before the doctor came and had me moved to a narrow communication trench; I lay there for five hours. No stretcher could be used even if one had been available. Eventually I was carried down slung on my puttees between two rifles. It was an exceedingly painful journey. Once clear of the trenches the medical arrangements were very good.'

As soon as it was dark parties went out and did excellent work bringing in the wounded and the dead. Work in the Dressing-station went on into the night, for twenty-one hours in all without food or pause. One of our batteries, about 200 yards in rear, had sprayed the ground beside us with shrapnel from muzzle-bursts now and then; twice one of us was well peppered with ricochets, but the bullets had no penetration. Of some scores of men of the Brigade and flank Brigades who came complaining of gas, few were affected to any appreciable extent; lots of men who had nausea and intense headache remained at duty. There was a period of watery sunshine in the morning, the rest of the day was overcast and there were hours of drizzle or more.

The night was dry. There was quiet on the Brigade front except . . .

*September 26th*

. . . for occasional shells, some of them tear-gas. During the morning, while Thomas, OC 'A' Company, was watching the action still going on in front of Vermelles, he was shot by a sniper. A man also was killed and eight were wounded. The day, otherwise, was uneventful for us, since the expected diversion on the Brigade front was not called for. Two dead Middlesex officers having been found in Nomansland during the night stripped of their uniform, a warning was issued, so everyone in the uniform became suspect. Empty gas cylinders were removed and replaced by full ones, whereat Owen excelled himself in speaking his mind to the Gas Officer. Our dead were buried in Cambrin Cemetery. The action had cost the Battalion seven officers and 113 other ranks killed and wounded, nearly all in two Companies.

# M. St H. EVANS

The war diary and letters (mostly to his mother) of Lieutenant M. St Helier Evans were published in 1952.[1] Their author was commissioned on 29 October 1914 (at the age of eighteen) into the 9th Battalion of the Welch Regiment, which had just been formed at Cardiff. It landed in France in July 1915 as part of the 58th Brigade[2] of the 19th (Western) Division, known as the 'Butterfly' Division because of its badge.[3] After recovering from wounds he returned to France in April 1916, just before his twentieth birthday and was soon employed in conducting a draft of reinforcements from Etaples to the 9th Royal Welch Fusiliers whose 'Colonel is Sir David Davies, a multi-millionaire by the way (lucky man); he has been recalled to attend parliament ...'[4] By the end of May he was 'not sorry to be back with THE Regiment'.[5] The 9th Welch were on the Somme engaged in preparations for the forthcoming offensive and were involved in 'this bloody fighting'[6] for the village of La Boiselle; his company lost sixty men. Lieutenant Evans was to take part in the advance to the Hindenburg Line and the Flanders offensive of 1917.

---

## The Battle of Messines: 7–14 June 1917

3 June 1917
Domestic news at a low ebb; kit is down to 35lb; we cannot be expected to dress the rate these pettifogging orders arrive; we

---

[1]*Going Across, or With the 9th Welch in the Butterfly Division: Being Extracts from the War Letters and Diary of Lieutenant M. St Helier Evans*, edited by Frank Delamain (Newport, Mon.: R. H. Johns, 1952).
[2]The brigade consisted of 9th Cheshire, 9th Royal Welch Fusiliers, 5th South Wales Borderers, and 9th Welch.
[3]It was part of Kitchener's 2nd New Army.
[4]See M. St Helier Evans, *Going Across*, p. 20.
[5]Ibid., p. 28.
[6]Ibid., p. 44.

are left helpless. I am trying to outwit the Transport Officer by getting a lighter bag with a padlock. I took the NCOs to see a model of the landscape we propose soon to project Jerry from; it is real artistry, ruins are shown with bricks, trenches by concrete, roads of wood, woods by twigs; most ingenious, contours are indicated, more than that, they are clearly defined. There should be no mistake. I talked to my platoon about it. We are on tip-toe, I could not rise to the heights of Henry 5th's eloquence but we came a good second. The setting for my *en avant, mes enfants* harangue was in keeping with the increased tempo, the tapestried background, the ceaseless rumble of traffic, the mutter and roar of guns working to a frenzy, in a crescendo of open diapason. Then followed a lecture on machine guns and one more working party under Royal Engineers' guidance for carrying stores from Poppy Lane Dump to our new Assembly Line . . . They are making us cry at last. Fritz has found the way to accomplish this by a low down dirty trick. This new Tear Shell, it is more annoying than lethal, it renders one ineffective if blinded with watering eyes, a sickly poison nevertheless, the batteries are swamped with it, we have walked across several emplacements evacuated as a result. A limber was caught by shells the other night just before we came along, the driver, two horses and mules were lying dead on the road. One of our boys, F. Baker, was killed. This salvo came down in answer to an SOS.

On our return from the working party a shattering explosion was heard and felt, it was a dump of ours going up, a dense billowing cloud was all that was left of this valuable cargo. In a trice, we were flat in a handy ditch. To round off this roseate night a balloon of ours in flames lit up the countryside incarnadined . . . I am keeping two blankets as nights strike chill after the day's heat; do not imagine for an instant that I am suffering from Cold Feet. If we could last out the Somme, we can thumb our noses at the future which rushes at us big with fate. And we are ready.

The Band is improving under the guidance of QMS McCavitt who was in the Empire Band, Cardiff, he also qualified for the Guards. The YM[7] has become generous, refused payment for some purchases. Fattening us for the slaughter. May only be in the line twenty-four hours, keeping our heads well under.

---

[7]YMCA canteen.

A tri-plane squadron is over us, they look clumsy but powerful, I count them each time and it is a relief to see they are all present and correct.

I take off my hat to our Div. Field Guns, everywhere we go, they follow like ministering angels; when called upon to cut the Hun wire or to put down a barrage or answer an SOS they rain down a hail of iron, spreading a curtain over our heads. The guns are sleek, business like and kept spotless, green wheels and shining brass hubs, the crew as usual have a totally inadequate protection. No praise can be too high for these gunners. Somehow, except for occasionally meeting the Forward Observation Officers, we do not get the chance to make their acquaintance.

I finish this on the 6th, it is the eve of a great day, perhaps the most momentous in our lives; from hints you will have gathered where we are. It has been a strenuous time getting all in order. One night the routes up had to be reconnoitred for an overland track, nothing is left to chance. Harris has gone down with gassing, they put some over when we were working; I was in another part and on going out only got a slight whiff of it, it reduced us to streaming eyes. Everything is ready, flares for plane contact, rifle grenades, wire-cutters, bombs, fans for plane signals and I shall carry a VL[8] Pistol. Bazentin licked us into shape to face this. Must confess it gives that feeling waiting for the pistol to unleash us for the Half Mile.

## 9 June 1917
Somewhere the other side of the old Hun Line. One hardly knows where or how to begin, the last few days we have been in a nightmare daze ... Yes, we were bang in the middle of this stunt and haven't yet been relieved properly though drawn back to near the original front line. When we go out there will be a chance to write a fuller account of our impressions. I am extremely busy being the only officer left in the company ... I can say now it was Wytschaete we took, Messines is away on our right flank ... We went over the top at 3.30. Three large mines on our immediate front – there were others – were blown. In one a whole company of Huns went up. Cheers. We were to have taken the 3rd and 4th lines, but it was all too simple, we just walked into them, thanks to the guns blasting every inch.

---

[8]Very Light – a signal pistol.

This most intense barrage cleared the way and what Huns were left ran up to us with their hands up.

They are too demoralized to make a big counter attack – just yet – the first twenty-four hours is the critical time. Hope they will not attempt it. May be moving further up this evening. Most of the Hun guns are drawn back and what they have left are firing at extreme range.

This is just to reassure you as to my safety, thank God, but at what a cost. I must try to tell you later. The officers in reserve have kindly sent us oranges, tinned fruit, meat and salmon.

## 13 June 1917

Hope the Field Cards have reached you. The hoped-for relief did not come so here we are still in the line. B is in front (as generally). We occupy a concrete pill box. The Hun was one up on us with these shelters which will stand up to most shells, a really heavy direct will squash them like egg shells; they have given us a lot of trouble; they have slits for machine guns and a determined crew could hold up a Brigade with enfilade fire. This Bosche strong point is in a wood named Bug Wood. Not very refined. So you see we have a safe place to run to. They say the Hun has very few batteries, which is a comfort. That remains to be seen.

Hope to get relieved in a few days, it is too bad to keep us in so long. A week ago tonight we marched up in the stilly night waiting for what the morrow's dawn would bring forth. I wondered who would live to tell the tale. I cannot exaggerate the tension, discomforts and the heat. Must dilate on that later. But I am thankful to have been spared, we can all do with a rest and a wash. Not carrying any washing kit, my thin pair of socks are worn to a thread and I had to wear a light pair of boots as the heavy ones were crippling; the blister is better. After all my lectures on feet too. The biter bit. I hope all this is not boring you. My shirt is in threads. Every night we are all on duty, carrying up rations, material, etc.

A wonderful sight to see our planes. Now and again the air is thick with them. One came down in flames last night, hit by machine gun from the ground. Watkins, our runner, has returned from leave. Hughes, our waiter, has not turned up, we fear he has been nabbed for another regiment, we should be sorry to lose him as he had got into our ways.

Have not troubled this time to collect many souvenirs. Any

papers collected have gone to the Adge[9] for onward transmission. Intelligence will scrutinise. Last night, with Stanton
and a party of Scouts and Snipers, we went outside for what
proved an interesting night walk; we were on fresh ground
thanks to our late advance; information was urgently required.
It was not known where the enemy were, how far had he gone
back, had he dug in and what lay between us and him, what
was the nature of the ground? All this was for us to determine.
This was indeed virgin ground though inaptly adjectived; it is too
chaste a term for anywhere so polluted by its late owners. We set
out in fine style, eight of us; we crawled over the parapet from our
line in Rose Wood, all was quiet, there seemed little need to continue creeping; victory had gone to our heads, let us be bold and
walk. We did so and went on our hind legs in a kind of Gaby
Glide fashion. There were many uninjured trees on the route
and these hold secrets; we are not enamoured with woods –
not under these conditions – so we moved circumspectly. That
night in the Salient at Zouave Wood made me wary. I try by con-
centration to pick up messages from the minds of the opposite
people, this may sound odd and it is difficult to explain, it may
be some form of latent instinct inherited from distant ancestors
or telepathy. It was worth trying anyhow. This was the longest
patrol for distance any of us have yet accomplished, we estimated it at 600 yards, thus considerably more than is the average
width of No Man's Land. It is almost impossible to judge exactly
as this time we had no map and no aerial photographs to help us;
in daylight the ground shrinks, periscopes and field glasses dis-
orientate; when we get there, all is changed and elusive. It was
the first patrol I have ever properly enjoyed unless we recall that
cold night at that tree stump down at Hébuterne. We were vastly
amused finding a Hun dummy battery, simple but effective, three
tree trunks on cart wheels; from the air this might well fox us, but
as there were but few shell holes in the vicinity we deducted
our gunners with range and locating instruments had not been
fooled. In my official report a lot was made of this, it is just
what 'they' love to hear about. In the dark these deceived us,
we thought we had captured some real guns without a blow.
We swallowed our chagrin and resisted dawdling among those
trees. On and on with many a pause, peering and listening, no

---

[9]The Adjutant of his battalion.

sounds escape us and we seem to have developed cats' eyes. Then ahead a ridge of earth confronted us, it was not a crater at that long way from the lines, it looked like recent digging, was this a parados or parapet, in other words had we lost direction and come upon a trench from the rear? By this time we were lying flat as pancakes. It was obviously a trench of sorts, we were bound to come to one sooner or later, there had been no rumours of a general withdrawal to the Rhine. So there was no alternative, it had to be explored.

With our ears to the ground there were no sounds. We could not spend all night in that position, something must be done, furthermore, our moon tables warned us that time was not on our side. I do not pretend to be foolhardy enough to risk my men's lives (or my own) by sauntering around in moonlight. Already the darkness was less opaque. It was up to me to do something about it so I crept to each man to impart a simple plan of campaign, 'give me a moment to get over, follow quickly and spread right and left'. And I knew they would. At this point all instincts failed me; we little knew what we were going into. We slid over and down the incline head first. Ho, within! No answer, it was all empty. We groped around. But what is this? A find at last, signs of recent habitation, we see what look like letters, documents, papers. Knowing how Intelligence delight in such finds, they gobble them up, digest the contents and assess the crumbling morale and cheer our troops with Comic Cuts,[10] we started to collect these prizes gleaming in what light there was and to me it seemed getting too light. Then one of my men whispered to me, 'Please sir, we are in a latrine.'

Too true we were, and didn't we know it. We floundered on and made our way down this short trench obviously an isolated post and there lying anyhow were three bags full. Bombs of a type we had not seen, one knows the egg bomb and potato masher all too well. This is where our Sherlock Holmes' stuff comes in useful. Why is this post empty, left invitingly open for us to walk into? Normally a forward post is manned by night and may be vacated by day. No good soldier would ever leave an overcoat behind, even on the hottest night there comes the chill of dawn. We would crime any man leaving his coat, how much stricter then would a Prussianized army be. Why leave

---

[10]The regular summaries of activity produced by the Intelligence Officers.

valuable bombs? The answer must be, our victory had weakened their morale, they may have seen us and in the dim light had multiplied our numbers, their hearts failed them and discretion was the better part of valour. It has often been mine, hence the understanding.

Possibly too the unorthodox approach to and capture of their *sanctum sanctorum* had upset all the rules and regulations as laid down in their manual of warfare, this ruthless and entirely unexpected development determined their flight.

Apart from the material we had inadvertently collected, when we got into the post proper, there was an indefinable sense of recent presence, a kind of echo of those who had left.

On the other hand, the enemy is no fool. Never despise your enemy is one of the first maxims. Was this a trap, were we the flies in the web? It all looked too good to be true. Then ensued a debate. What about taking the bags of bombs and overcoat as lawful loot? Having lately placed a booby trap ourselves and heard of the tricks played on us in captured dugouts, I disliked the idea of moving these articles. They were left as found. We climbed out of this curious place and went on with greater care, found a road and beyond it Green Wood. We thought we were seeing things when without warning there appeared to float up a large red disc looming through the trees; it gave us a start, in our tautened state we were so intent on finding earthly bodies we had forgotten the heavenly. It reminded us of Bairnsfather's cartoon where the wife at home gazes in rapture and Old Bill out here curses the moon in no measured terms. We decided that Green Wood is at the moment nobody's business. No lights, no sounds. Just watchfulness and a brooding silence all pervading. After the war, if God is so minded, some one will avoid woods o'nights like the plague and leave them to poets and lovers wrapped up in themselves. We got home safely.

*19 June 1917*

A fortnight since our great attack. It seems longer than that; after weeks of intensive preparation it has all died down quickly. The credit must go to the Artillery. It was colossal. Twelve per cent more guns than in any war in history. Miles back there were guns of all calibres, dumps large and small hidden in ditches and behind hedges and trees and all was camouflaged. Railways had been run forward, wide and narrow gauge. Haig was watching from one of the hills, not Kemmel, but perhaps the Scherpenberg or Schomberg. We left Murrum Bidgee Camp on the Wednesday evening, at 10.15 to be exact. No smoking or talking was allowed while going up to the Assembly lines. As some NCOs and I had previously reconnoitred the route, Z track, I took the lead. The night was calm, so were we in this atmosphere of suppressed excitement and expectancy. There was a slight heat haze. The guns were keeping up a desultory fire, nothing out of the ordinary and no shells came back at us. A plane flew over us a few times as though searching, we imagined it must be an enemy, suspicious. Later we learnt that they were not certain when the attack would commence. From their vantage points they must have known something was afoot. Colonel Godfrey rode along with us and tried to make conversation. I must have seemed unresponsive, there was so much to think about and so little time left.

We got to the jumping off trench at midnight, saw all the men settled into their allotted places with scaling ladders for the jump to come. Saunders, Morris and I rested in a shelter, the time went quickly. At 2.15 I gave rum to half the company. Nearly every man was asleep which was most sensible, if there had been time we could have all so slept. At 3 a.m. we arose to be going. This was indeed the lull before the storm.

Our watches on wrist had been synchronised, there was nothing we had forgotten. In my hand I carried a card showing the exact minute at which we should reach certain coloured lines, the time and place where the barrage would lift and fall, we were to keep close to it. I carried too, a Very Light pistol with coloured flares in case needed.

At 3.10 the mines went up and every gun belched and machine gun overhead fire joined in. The noise defied description. There had never been anything like it – ever. We were literally rocked from side to side, the whole earth gulped, heaved, shuddered and vomited a vast spume from its bowels. The debris shot up, towered up hundreds of feet and hurtled down. By then the first wave was over and racing ahead. Nag's Nose simply vanished in one vast cloud of smoke and flame. For me this was symbolical for this day would blot out more than that. At this stage a few shells came over, for which and for once I salute the German gunners for their bravery in being able to stand up to the pulverizing avalanche falling around their batteries. They must have been swamped; we had located every battery. Two regiments in our Brigade went first, took their objectives and we were to follow and go right on to the final objective on the top of the ridge. Just at the time of your thunderstorm, 3.30, at first faint gleam of dawn, we took the great plunge towards the unknown. The smoke from the mines and fog created an artificial darkness into which we leapt. In the vast crater that had been Nag's Nose, a blue flame was flickering; we had to traverse this and had to tread lightly over the damp, spongy subsoil. 'A' Company seemed to lose direction somewhat owing to the smoke laden air and appeared to be charging ahead straight for Wytschaete. They would therefore swing too much to the right. What had been the village was planned to be their right flank. By the way, a few days before this we watched our guns erase Wytschaete entirely. It disappeared like a conjuring trick, just smoke and dust. When we got there after waiting three years, it was simply rubble and brick-red powder.

During the battle we were able to reorganise. Our Company had the tendency to align with 'A', with the result that some casualties were caused. The Grand Bois proved no obstacle, thanks to the guns; there was to be no second Mametz Wood this time; our guns had cut all the wire and a new invention, Thermite, which burns anything or anybody and gets hotter on exposure to air had cleared the way. Coming through the wood, five enemy ran towards us with their hands up. I had to prevent our men killing them. One has to stifle personal feelings. When a man throws up the sponge, he loses something more than his liberty. The rules of war are that men who have found themselves forced to give in, shall be given the right to live. So that, more desirous to see them dead, duty urged me to protect them. Rather ironical as I have so much to revenge.

Our first objective, the Blue Line, existed only in name, no trench was left, everything except a few pill-boxes was beaten out of recognition. At this stage Saunders and I pulled out our maps and had a lucky escape, we were within an ace of being blown up by one of our own shells falling short, it fell at our feet; it was a miracle – no other word for it – how we survived the day. That was not the only near shave. But, I say this without bragging, nothing seemed to matter, one could have walked into hell, as indeed we were, without a tremor. I cannot understand it myself. I can assure you I had not had an overdose of rum either. I cannot remember if any.

Soon after this, Saunders got hit in the lung and was taken back. This left me alone as Morris was wounded in two places by our shells. Two hours to wait at the Blue Line and then on. Again a shell fell short, it hit one of our lads, a mercifully quick going out for him, he fell limp and his journey was over.

I sent a runner with urgent request to the Adjutant to get on to the battery at fault. We dragged Morris into a shelter and waited for that exasperating gun to stop. M. was hit by shrapnel in the leg and arm, it passed the latter penetrating the breast near the heart. The doctor said it was a lucky escape. It was some hours before he could be carried back. During the advance up to the Green Line, a rabbit, scared out of its wits, ran out of its burrow.

We reached our final objective, the Green Line bordering the road from Wytschaete to St Eloi. Here we started to dig in. Most of our men hale from the Rhondda Valley and they dug then as though back in their mines; we soon had a semblance of a trench. It was then that the Colonel sent Fitz Simmonds to help, it was a help too; he would make me take a sip of his whisky, the first time I had ever tasted it, it must be an acquired taste. Then the men called for me. At such times they must turn to someone. I went along and looked down. On the floor of the new trench poor little Waggett of my platoon was dying from loss of blood, an enemy shell had hit him and there was nothing we could do. His white face and slender body was piteous, he looked sacrificial. So young, so innocent, so at rest after the storm. I must have seen hundreds killed, but this memory will never be effaced. One noticed as so often, how kindly death comes, it draws aside the mask we wear leaving a poise, a serenity, clean and decent as God would have us be, maybe after His own image.

They must have thought me heartless when I turned away. I had no words. They buried the poor fragile body in a shell hole near by and we carried on. Having the Company on my hands I was not near Sergeant Owen when he was struck, no one will give me any details and there is no good done by wanting to know. It is grief beyond words. His mother is heart broken, so am I. He lived at Resolven, Neath, and had the Platoon No. 6 since the Battalion was formed early in the war. He took the greatest pride in having the best turned out Platoon, we could rely on him to cope with any situation, he was invariably calm, considerate and courteous. I first got to know him well that terrible night at Mametz, when we had to get a carrying party through. It is at such times a man's true worth shines out and the absurd barrier that divides our ranks is brushed aside. It is especially hard luck when the countless perils we have passed unscathed are recalled.

Only a few days before we went into the line, near one of those villages, we were having our last conversation and were joking about recommending one another for medals. He was hopeful of getting through.[11]

There is nothing more to say. These grand fellows have shown the way and surely will be ready to help us over when the great adventure ends. Then we have lost Corporal Manning, D.J. Evans and others.[12] It only remains to carry on unquestioning the unfathomable, inscrutable decrees.

The battle moved on. Another Division leapfrogged on to Oostaverne and later we moved forward for two hours into the wood of that name. A cooling rain fell. Lieutenant Salmon was attached to us. It was about now that I saw a new model tank snaking along. If only we had had hundreds we might have broken right through. As Bridges would say, we were on top of the roof that day. Two of our balloons down in flames.

---

[11]Sergeant Thomas Owen was killed on 7 June. Born at Resolven, he had enlisted at Neath.
[12]Sergeant David John Evans, from Tredegar, joined the Monmouthshire Regiment at Abergavenny. He was killed, serving with the 9th Welch, on 7 June.

# ROBERT GRAVES

Robert Graves arrived on the Western Front in May 1915. He had close connections with Wales: his father had been made a Bard at the 1902 National Eisteddfod in Bangor and owned a house in Harlech (an area to which Robert was very attached). It was the secretary of the Harlech golf club who made the first contact with the Royal Welch Fusiliers, which Graves joined at Wrexham on 12 August 1914. He was nineteen. When he went to France (in May 1915) he found, to his disgust, that he was to be posted to the 2nd Battalion of the Welch Regiment which, in the tradition of regimental rivalry, he looked upon as being inferior to his own. In *Goodbye to All That*, one of the most famous of books about the war, he writes about his new battalion, and his introduction to the front line in a coal-mining area of northern France. The 2nd Welch were, at this time, trying to recover from their severe losses at Aubers Ridge on 9 May.

~

## *The Welch Regiment, at Cambrin*[1]

I had heard little about the Welsh Regiment, except that it was tough and rough, and that the Second Battalion, to which we were going, had a peculiar regimental history as the old Sixty-ninth Foot. It had originally been formed as an emergency force from pensioners and boy-recruits, and sent overseas to do the work of a regular battalion – I forget in which eighteenth-century campaign. At one time, the Sixty-ninth had served as marines. They were nicknamed the 'Ups and Downs', partly because '69' makes the same sense whichever way up it is written. The 69

---

[1]Extract from Robert Graves, *Goodbye to All That* (London: Cassell, 1957 edn.).

was certainly upside-down when we joined. All the company officers, with the exception of two boys recently posted from Sandhurst, and one Special Reserve captain, came from other regiments. There were six Royal Welch Fusiliers, two South Wales Borderers, two East Surreys, two Wiltshires, one from the Border Regiment, one from the King's Own Yorkshire Light Infantry. Even the quartermaster was an alien from the Connaught Rangers. There were still perhaps four time-serving NCOs left in the battalion. Of the men, perhaps fifty or so had got more than a couple of months' training before being sent out; some had only three weeks' training; a great many had never fired a musketry course. All this, because the First Division had been in constant hard fighting since the previous August; in eight months the battalion had lost its full fighting strength five times over. The last occasion was at Richebourg on May 9th, one of the worst disasters hitherto. The Division's epitaph in the official communiqué read: 'Meeting with considerable opposition in the direction of the Rue du Bois, our attacks were not pressed.'

The battalion's ranks were made up first with reservists of the later categories, then with re-enlisted men, then with Special Reservists of pre-war enlistment, then with 1914 recruits of three or four months' training; but each class in turn had been expended. Now, nothing remained to send, except recruits of the spring 1915 class, with various sweepings and scourings. The First Battalion had, meanwhile, suffered the same heavy losses. In Cardiff the Welsh Regiment advertised: 'Enlist at the depôt and get to France quick.' The recruits were mostly men either over-age or under-age – a repetition of regimental history – or with some slight physical disability which prevented them from enlisting in regiments more particular than the Welsh.

I still have the roll of my first platoon of forty men. The figures given for their ages are misleading. On enlistment, all over-age men had put themselves in the late thirties, and all under-age men had called themselves eighteen. But once in France, the over-age men did not mind adding on a few genuine years. No less than fourteen in the roll give their age as forty or over, and these were not all. Fred Prosser, a painter in civil life, who admitted to forty-eight, was really fifty-six. David Davies, collier, who admitted to forty-two, and Thomas Clark, another collier who admitted to forty-five, were only one or two years junior to Prosser. James Burford, collier and fitter, was the oldest soldier of all. When

I first spoke to him in the trenches, he said: 'Excuse me, sir, will you explain what this here arrangement is on the side of my rifle?' 'That's the safety-catch. Didn't you do a musketry-course at the depot?' 'No, sir, I was a re-enlisted man, and I spent only a fortnight there. The old Lee-Metford didn't have no safety catch.' I asked him when he had last fired a rifle. 'In Egypt, in 1882,' he said. 'Weren't you in the South African War?' 'I tried to re-enlist, but they told me I was too old, sir. I had been an old soldier in Egypt. My real age is sixty-three.' He spent all his summers as a tramp, and in the bad months of the year worked as a collier, choosing a new pit every season. I heard him and David Davies one night discussing the different seams of coal in Wales, and tracing them from county to county and pit to pit with technical comments.

The other half of the platoon contained the under-age section. I had five of these boys; William Bumford, collier, for instance, who gave his age as eighteen, was really only fifteen. He used to get into trouble for falling asleep on sentry duty, an offence punishable with death, but could not help it. I had seen him suddenly go to sleep, on his feet, while holding a sandbag open for another fellow to fill. So we got him a job as orderly to a chaplain for a while, and a few months later all men over fifty and all boys under eighteen got combed out. Bumford and Burford were both sent to the base; but neither escaped the war. Bumford grew old enough by 1917 to be sent back to the battalion, and was killed that summer; Burford died in a bombing accident at the base-camp. Or so I was told – the fate of hundreds of my comrades in France came to me merely as hearsay.

The troop-train consisted of forty-seven coaches, and took twenty-four hours to arrive at Béthune, the railhead, via St Omer. We detrained at about 9 p.m., hungry, cold and dirty. Expecting a short journey, we had allowed our baggage to be locked in a van; and then played nap throughout the journey to keep our minds off the discomfort. I lost sixty francs, which was over two pounds at the existing rate of exchange. On the platform at Béthune, a little man in filthy khaki, wearing the Welsh cap-badge, came up with a friendly touch of the cap most unlike a salute. He had orders to guide us to the battalion, at present in the Cambrin trenches, about ten kilometres away. Collecting the draft of forty men we had with us, we followed him through the unlit suburbs of the town – all intensely excited by the noise and flashes of the guns in the distance. None of the draft had been out before, except the sergeant in charge. They began singing. Instead of the usual music-hall songs they sang Welsh hymns, each man taking a part. The Welsh always sang when pretending not to be scared; it kept them steady. And they never sang out of tune.

We marched towards the flashes, and could soon see the flare-lights curving across the distant trenches. The noise of the guns grew louder and louder. Presently we were among the batteries. From about two hundred yards behind us, on the left of the road, a salvo of four shells whizzed suddenly over our heads. This broke up *Aberystwyth* in the middle of a verse, and sent us off our balance for a few seconds; the column of fours tangled up. The shells went hissing away eastward; we saw the red flash and heard the hollow bang where they landed in German territory. The men picked up their step again and began chaffing. A lance-corporal dictated a letter home: 'Dear auntie, this leaves me in the pink. We are at present wading in blood up to our necks. Send me fags and a life-belt. This war is a booger. Love and kisses.'

The roadside cottages were now showing more and more signs of dilapidation. A German shell came over and then whoo-oo-oooooooOOO-bump-CRASH! landed twenty yards short of us. We threw ourselves flat on our faces. Presently we heard a curious singing noise in the air, and then flop! flop! little pieces of shell-casing came buzzing down all around. 'They calls them the musical instruments,' said the sergeant. 'Damn them,' said my friend, Frank Jones-Bateman, cut across the hand by a jagged little piece, 'the devils have started on me early.' 'Aye, they'll have a lot of fun with you before they're done, sir,' grinned the sergeant. Another shell came over. Everyone threw himself down again, but it burst two hundred yards behind us. Only Sergeant Jones had remained on his feet. 'You're wasting your strength, lads,' he said to the draft. 'Listen by the noise they make where they're going to burst.'

At Cambrin village, about a mile from the front trenches, we were taken into a ruined chemist's shop with its coloured glass jars still in the window: the billet of the four Welsh company-quarter-master-sergeants. Here they gave us respirators and field-dressings. This, the first respirator issued in France, was a gauze-pad filled with chemically-treated cotton waste, for tying across the mouth and nose. Reputedly it could not keep out the German gas, which had been used at Ypres against the Canadian Division; but we never put it to the test. A week or two later came the 'smoke-helmet', a greasy grey-felt bag with a talc window to look through, and no mouthpiece, certainly ineffective against gas. The talc was always cracking, and visible leaks showed at the stitches joining it to the helmet.

Those were early days of trench warfare, the days of the jam-tin bomb and the gas-pipe trench-mortar; still innocent of Lewis or Stokes guns, steel helmets, telescopic rifle-sights, gas-shells, pill-boxes, tanks, well-organized trench-raids, or any of the later refinements of trench warfare.

After a meal of bread, bacon, rum, and bitter stewed tea sickly with sugar, we went through the broken trees to the east of the village and up a long trench to battalion headquarters. The wet and slippery trench ran through dull red clay. I had a torch with me, and saw that hundreds of field mice and frogs had fallen into the trench but found no way out. The light dazzled them, and because I could not help treading on them, I put the torch back in my pocket. We had no mental picture of what the trenches would be like, and were almost as ignorant as a young soldier who joined us a week or two later. He called out excitedly to old Burford, who was cooking up a bit of stew in a dixie, apart from the others: 'Hi, mate, where's the battle? I want to do my bit.'

The guide gave us hoarse directions all the time. 'Hole right.' 'Wire high.' 'Wire low.' 'Deep place here, sir.' 'Wire low.' The field-telephone wires had been fastened by staples to the side of the trench, and when it rained the staples were constantly falling out and the wire falling down and tripping people up. If it sagged too much, one stretched it across the trench to the other side to correct the sag, but then it would catch one's head. The holes were sump-pits used for draining the trenches.

We now came under rifle-fire, which I found more trying than shell-fire. The gunner, I knew, fired not at people but at map-references – crossroads, likely artillery positions, houses that suggested billets for troops, and so on. Even when an observation officer in an aeroplane or captive balloon or on a church spire directed the guns, it seemed random, somehow. But a rifle-bullet, even when fired badly, always seemed purposely aimed. And whereas we could usually hear a shell approaching, and take some sort of cover, the rifle-bullet gave no warning. So, though we learned not to duck a rifle-bullet because, once heard, it must have missed, it gave us a worse feeling of danger. Rifle-bullets in the open went hissing into the grass without much noise, but when we were in a trench, the bullets made a tremendous crack as they went over the hollow. Bullets often struck the barbed wire in front of the trenches, which sent them spinning with a head-over-heels motion – ping! rockety-ockety-ockety-ockety into the woods behind.

At battalion headquarters, a dug-out in the reserve line, about a quarter of a mile behind the front companies, the colonel, a twice-wounded regular, shook hands with us and offered us the whisky bottle. He hoped that we would soon grow to like the regiment as much as our own. This sector had not long before been taken over from a French territorial division of men in the forties, who had a local armistice with the Germans opposite – no firing, and apparently even civilian traffic allowed through the lines. So this dug-out happened to be unusually comfortable, with an ornamental lamp, a clean cloth, and polished silver on the table. The colonel, adjutant, doctor, second-in-command, and sig-nalling officer had just finished dinner: it was civilized cooking – fresh meat and vegetables. Pictures pasted on the papered walls; spring-mattressed beds, a gramophone, easy chairs: we found it hard to reconcile these with the accounts we had read of troops standing waist-deep in mud, and gnawing a biscuit while shells burst all around. The adjutant posted us to our companies. 'Captain Dunn of 'C' is your company commander,' he told me. 'The soundest officer in the battalion. By the way, remind him that I want him to send in that list of DCM recommenda-tions for the last show at once; but not more than two names, or else they won't give us any. Four is about the ration for any battalion in a dud show.'

Our guide took us up to the front line. We passed a group of men huddled over a brazier – small men, daubed with mud, talking quietly together in Welsh. They were wearing waterproof capes, for it had now started to rain, and cap-comforters, because the weather was cold for May. Although they could see we were officers, they did not jump to their feet and salute. I thought that this must be a convention of the trenches; and indeed it is laid down somewhere in the military text-books that the courtesy of the salute must be dispensed with in battle. But, no, it was just slackness. We overtook a fatigue-party struggling up the trench loaded with timber lengths and bundles of sandbags, cursing plaintively as they slipped into sump-holes or entangled their burdens in the telephone wire. Fatigue-parties were always encumbered by their rifles and equipment, which it was a crime

71

ever to have out of reach. After squeezing past this party, we had to stand aside to let a stretcher-case pass. 'Who's the poor bastard, Dai?' the guide asked the leading stretcher-bearer. 'Sergeant Gallagher,' Dai answered. 'He thought he saw a Fritz in No Man's Land near our wire, so the silly booger takes one of them new issue percussion bombs and shots it at 'im. Silly booger aims too low, it hits the top of the parapet and burst back. Deoul! man, it breaks his silly f—ing jaw and blows a great lump from his silly f—ing face, whatever. Poor silly booger! Not worth sweating to get him back! He's put paid to, whatever.' The wounded man had a sandbag over his face. He died before they got him to the dressing station.

I felt tired out by the time I reached company headquarters, sweating under a pack-valise like the men, and with all the usual furnishings hung at my belt – revolver, field-glasses, compass, whisky-flask, wire-cutters, periscope, and a lot more. A 'Christmas-tree' that was called. Those were the days in which officers had their swords sharpened by the armourer before sailing to France. I had been advised to leave mine back in the quartermaster-sergeants' billet, and never saw it again, or bothered about it. My hands were sticky with the clay from the side of the trench, and my legs soaked up to the calves. At 'C' Company headquarters, a two-roomed timber-built shelter in the side of a trench connecting the front and support lines, I found tablecloth and lamp again, whisky bottle and glasses, shelves with books and magazines, and bunks in the next room. I reported to the company commander.

I had expected a grizzled veteran with a breastful of medals; but Dunn was actually two months younger than myself – one of the fellowship of 'only survivors'. Captain Miller of the Black Watch in the same division was another. Miller had escaped from the Rue du Bois massacre by swimming down a flooded trench. Only survivors had great reputations. Miller used to be pointed at in the streets when the battalion was back in reserve billets. 'See that fellow? That's Jock Miller. Out from the start and hasn't got it yet.' Dunn did not let the war affect his morale at all. He greeted me very easily with: 'Well, what's the news from England? Oh, sorry first I must introduce you. This is Walker – clever chap from Cambridge, fancies himself as an athlete. This is Jenkins, one of those elder patriots who chucked up their jobs to come here. This is Price – joined us yesterday, but we liked him at once: he brought some damn good whisky with him. Well, how long is the war going to last, and who's winning? We don't know a thing out here. And what's all this talk about war-babies? Price pretends ignorance on the subject.' I told them about the war, and asked them about the trenches.

'About trenches,' said Dunn. 'Well, we don't know as much about trenches as the French do, and not near as much as Fritz does. We can't expect Fritz to help, but the French might do something. They are too greedy to let us have the benefit of their inventions. What wouldn't we give for their parachute-lights and aerial torpedoes! But there's never any connexion between the two armies, unless a battle is on, and then we generally let each other down.

'When I came out here first, all we did in trenches was to paddle about like ducks and use our rifles. We didn't think of them as places to live in, they were just temporary inconveniences. Now we work here all the time, not only for safety but for health. Night and day. First, at fire-steps, then at building traverses, improving the communication trenches, and so on; last comes our personal comfort – shelters and dug-outs. The territorial battalion that used to relieve us were hopeless. They used to sit down in the trench and say: "Oh, my God, this is the limit." Then they'd pull out pencil and paper and write home about it. Did no work on the traverses or on fire positions. Consequence – they lost half their men from frost-bite and rheumatism, and one day the Germans broke in and scuppered a lot more of them. They'd allowed the work we'd done in the trench to go to ruin, and left the whole place like a sewage farm for us to take over again. We got sick as muck, and reported them several times to brigade headquarters; but they never improved. Slack officers, of course. Well, they got smashed, as I say, and were sent away to be lines-of-communication troops. Now we work with the First South Wales Borderers. They're all right. Awful swine, those territorials. Usen't to trouble about latrines at all; left food about to encourage rats; never filled a sandbag. I only once saw a job of work that they did: a steel loop-hole for sniping. But they put it facing square to the front, and quite unmasked, so two men got killed at it – absolute death-trap. Our chaps are all right, but not as right as they ought to be. The survivors of the show ten days ago are feeling pretty low, and the big new draft doesn't know a thing yet.'

'Listen,' said Walker, 'there's too much firing going on. The men have got the wind up over something. If Fritz thinks we're jumpy, he'll give us an extra bad time. I'll go up and stop them.'

Dunn went on: 'These Welshmen are peculiar. They won't stand being shouted at. They'll do anything if you explain the reason for it – do and die, but they have to know their reason why. The best way to make them behave is not to give them too much time to think. Work them off their feet. They are good workmen, too. But officers must work with them, not only direct the work. Our time-table is: breakfast at eight o'clock in the morning, clean trenches and inspect rifles, work all morning; lunch at twelve, work again from one till about six, when the men feed again. "Stand-to" at dusk for about an hour, work all night, "stand-to" for an hour before dawn. That's the general programme. Then there's sentry-duty. The men do two-hour sentry spells, then work two hours, then sleep two hours. At night, sentries are doubled, so working parties are smaller. We officers are on duty all day, and divide up the night into three-hourly watches.' He looked at his wristwatch. 'By the way,' he said, 'that carrying-party must have brought up the RE stuff by now. Time we all got to work. Look here, Graves, you lie down and have a doss on that bunk. I want you to take the watch before "stand-to". I'll wake you up and show you around. Where the hell's my revolver? I don't like to go out without it. Hello, Walker, what was wrong?'

Walker laughed. 'A chap from the new draft. He had never fired his musketry course at Cardiff, and tonight he fired ball for the first time. It went to his head. He'd had a brother killed up at Ypres, and sworn to avenge him. So he blazed off all his own ammunition at nothing, and two bandoliers out of the ammunition-box besides. They call him the "Human Maxim" now. His foresight's misty with heat. Corporal Parry should have stopped him; but he just leant up against the traverse and shrieked with laughter. I gave them both a good cursing. Some other new chaps started blazing away too. Fritz retaliated with machine-guns and whizz-bangs. No casualties. I don't know why. It's all quiet now.'

# Sospan Fach[2]

## (The Little Saucepan)

Four collier lads from Ebbw Vale
Took shelter from a shower of hail,
And there beneath a spreading tree
Attuned their mouths to harmony.

With smiling joy on every face
Two warbled tenor, two sang bass,
And while the leaves above them hissed with
Rough hail, they started 'Aberystwyth'.

Old Parry's hymn, triumphant, rich,
They changed through with even pitch,
Til at the end of their grand noise
I called: 'Give us the "Sospan" boys!'.

Who knows a tune so soft, so strong,
So pitiful as that 'Saucepan' song
For exiled hope, despaired desire
Of lost souls for their cottage fire?

Then low at first with gathering sound
Rose their four voices, smooth and round,
Till back went Time: once more I stood
With Fusiliers in Mametz Wood.

Fierce burned the sun, yet cheeks were pale,
For ice hail they had leaden hail;
In that fine forest, green and big,
There stayed unbroken not one twig.

They sang, they swore, they plunged in haste,
Stumbling and shouting through the waste;
The little 'Saucepan' flamed on high,
Emblem of hope and ease gone by.

Rough pit-boys from the coaly South,
They sang, even in the cannon's mouth;
Like Sunday's chapel, Monday's inn,
The death-trap sounded with their din.

---

[2]This poem and the one which follows are taken from Robert Graves, *Poems About War* (London: Cassell, 1988).

\* \* \* \*

The storm blows over, Sun comes out,
The choir breaks up with jest and shout,
With what relief I watch them part –
Another note would break my heart!


## *Sergeant-Major Money*[3]

It wasn't our battalion, but we lay alongside it,
  So the story is as true as the telling is frank.
They hadn't one Line-officer left, after Arras,
  Except a batty major and the Colonel, who drank.

'B' Company Commander was fresh from the Depôt,
  An expert on gas drill, otherwise a dud;
So Sergeant-Major Money carried on, as instructed,
  And that's where the swaddies began to sweat blood.

His Old Army humour was so well-spiced and hearty
  That one poor sod shot himself, and one lost his wits;
But discipline's maintained, and back in rest-billets
  The Colonel congratulates 'B' company on their kits.

The Subalterns went easy, as was only natural
  With a terror like Money driving the machine,
Till finally two Welshmen, butties from the Rhondda,
  Bayoneted their bugbear in a field-canteen.

---

[3]This poem is based on an incident which occurred three months before Robert Graves joined the 2nd Welch. In *Goodbye to All That* (pp. 96–7) he describes the miscreants as 'young miners' who stated that they had shot the Sergeant-Major by mistake, meaning to have killed their platoon sergeant. The soldiers involved were Company Sergeant-Major Hugh Job Hayes from Kingston-upon-Thames (aged 32), Lance-Corporal William Price (aged 41) and Private Richard Morgan (aged 32). They were all regular soldiers – 'Hughie' Hayes had enlisted at the age of 14 and had fought in the Boer War. He was shot by Price and Morgan, who were drunk, and died on 21 January 1915. The two men were tried by a General Court Martial held at Lillers on 6 February, and shot by a firing squad on 15 February. The victim and his murderers are buried in Béthune Town Cemetery. (Sources: Putkowski and Sykes, *Shot at Dawn*, p. 33; *Soldiers Died in the Great War: Part 45*, p. 13.)

Well, we couldn't blame the officers, they relied on Money;
  We couldn't blame the pitboys, their courage was grand;
Or, least of all, blame Money, an old stiff surviving
In a New (bloody) Army he couldn't understand.

                                                    1917.

# LLEWELLYN WYN GRIFFITH

Born at Llandrillo-yn-Rhos, Llewellyn Wyn Griffith went to Blaenau Ffestiniog County School and Dolgellau Grammar School, where his father was headmaster. He became employed by the Inland Revenue, first in Liverpool and then in London where (still working for the Revenue) he read for the Bar at the Middle Temple.

On the outbreak of war, aged twenty-four, he enlisted as a private soldier in the 7th Battalion, Royal Welch Fusiliers. In January 1915 he was commissioned into the 15th (1st London Welsh) Battalion, which he joined in Llandudno where it was part of the new 38th (Welsh) Division. Wyn Griffith served with his battalion in France, before filling staff posts at Brigade, Divisional and Corps level. He was mentioned in dispatches for his conduct at Mametz Wood (where his brother, Private Watcyn Griffith, was killed) and was awarded the OBE (Military) and the Croix de Guerre.

After leaving the army he went back to the Inland Revenue, retiring with the grade of Assistant Secretary in 1952. Wyn Griffith became well known for his public activities, including broadcasting, literature and the Arts Council. He was chairman of the Honourable Society of Cymmrodorion, and received a CBE (in 1961) and an honorary D. Litt. from the University of Wales. He died in 1977.

*Up to Mametz* was published in 1931, and is dedicated to the memory of his brother.[1]

~

## Inspections

Every day, and sometimes more than once a day, the Colonel would inspect his battalion front. No one knew the hour of his

---

[1] Llewellyn Wyn Griffith, *Up to Mametz* (London: Faber and Faber, 1931).

coming. Nothing escaped that keen eye of his – bad duckboard here, there a weakening in the wall, fire-step to be repaired in one bay, two men had dirty rifles, one man did not know where company headquarters stood, three men did not know where to find the ammunition boxes, and one lance-corporal seemed doubtful where the gas alarm was situated. He would enter our dug-out, take out his note-book, and begin his chronicle of shortcomings. The law of average must hold, and there must have been occasions when he asked a man of normal intelligence where the bombs were stored, and heard the simple truth told without hesitation, but I was never made aware of such strokes of good fortune. I knew only too well that if the Colonel must ask a searching question, it would be hurled at the most stupid man in the company.

He was a good officer, and a kindly man, who concealed his feelings in spurts of sharp and sudden sentences.

'Get that parapet higher, d'ye see?'

'Yes, sir.'

'No good tinkering at the bay, see? Rebuild it.'

'Yes, sir.'

'Don't like that bomb-store, d'ye see?'

'Yes, Colonel.'

'Dam dirty rifle one fellow had: jump on his sergeant, see?'

'I will, sir.'

'Well, I must be going on ... No thanks, I won't have a drink ... Good morning.'

In the nature of things, there can be little cordiality between a Colonel and his junior officers in war time, but we respected him and liked him, and felt that his brusque ways were not the whole of the man. There was an underlying sympathy with a young man bearing a heavy burden of responsibility, though it was well concealed on a morning parade when we were out of the line. He was considerate in small things; once only did I know him to accept an offer of whisky and water in a company dug-out in the trenches, on a day of sweltering heat, and then he looked at the bottle to see how much we had before he accepted. He declined our hospitality on many occasions when he was obviously tired, from an unselfish disinclination to impoverish us. If on his visit he found the company commander asleep, he would not let him be disturbed: greater men than he were not so considerate.

The Brigadier was a daily plague.[2] He had won the Victoria Cross and the Distinguished Service Order in the South African War. He was slight, athletic in build, and good-looking: his mind was slow in working, but tenacious to the point of obstinacy. He spoke slowly, in a prim way – his fellow regular officers called him 'Jane'. It would be a misuse of words to call him brave, but he was certainly fearless. I have heard an uncharitable company commander, labouring under a grievance, say that he was too stupid to be frightened of anything but reason. He took a delight in exposing himself to fire, quite forgetting that the infantry officer who was his unwilling companion was being forced into a foolhardy challenge of the powers that troubled him day and night, when the Brigadier was far away from the line. He had little sense of humour, but I once saw him laugh at an incident that might have brought trouble upon my head.

It was a cold and wet night, and I was following him along my sector, listening to an interminable catalogue of minor faults. We came to a Lewis Gun post, and as we approached it the gunner fired a drum of ammunition. He did not recognize the General, who asked him:

'Was it you firing then?'

'Yes.'

'What were you firing at?'

'Don't know.'

'Then why did you fire?'

'Just to bloody well amuse myself', said the stubborn Welsh collier, in his close-clipped South Wales speech. The General turned away and laughed, to my great relief ...

The Brigadier wore a mackintosh jacket over his uniform, a pair of mackintosh trousers over his breeches, and a steel helmet that tended to slide over his left ear. There was no visible mark of rank at first, but later he fixed on his helmet the crossed sword and baton. His real badge of office was a wooden staff exactly

---

[2]Brigadier-General Llewellyn Alberic Emilius Price-Davies (born on 30 June 1878) had been commissioned into the King's Royal Rifle Corps in 1898 and served in the Boer War. He was promoted to major in September 1915 and to (temporary) brigadier in November 1915, when he took up the command of the 113th Brigade. His Victoria Cross had been awarded for an action at Blood River Poort in the Transvaal in September 1901. His brother-in-law was Sir Henry Wilson, at this time commanding IV Corps.

four feet six inches long, and with this he tested the height of the top layer of sandbags on the parapet over the fire-step. It was decreed that this height of four feet six inches must never be exceeded – there was little danger of any shortage, but a tall man standing on the fire-step felt acutely conscious of his upper eighteen inches. This mackintoshed figure, with boyish face and pouting expression, conscientiously measuring his staff against the trench wall, and finding a quiet satisfaction in the rare tallying of the two heights, commanded a force of three thousand men. In the stagnant condition of our war-making, it might be said that though he was the titular head of this body, to which he issued orders, he commanded no one. He elaborated for our benefit orders he had received from above, but he was no prime mover. He led no one, nor did he ever taste the thrill of throwing mass against mass. We were tenants of an estate of mud, and he was high bailiff, holding us to a careful tenancy, meticulous even in his overseeing of our domestic economy. He was zealous in his administration, sparing not himself, nor others, struggling manfully with a burden that appeared to us to be a little too large for his capacity, and concealing this by an untiring expenditure of physical energy.

On rare occasions we were 'at home' to more distinguished visitors. The Divisional Commander, Staff Officers of the Division and Corps would move quietly and quickly through our trench in the early morning. We knew them not, save by their red tabs and badges of rank, but they asked no awkward questions and were easily entertained. They did not seem to belong to our army. We noticed that they were circumspect in their choice of day and time for such a venture, and we envied them their short sojourn in our wilderness. The lines that follow were written on one such occasion, and I see now that they are but a reflection of the immemorial contempt of the infantry:

> There they go round the company front
> To see the poor devils that bear the brunt
> Of ev'ry strafe and trench mortar stunt,
> On a dull and misty morning.
>
> What if the Hun should see them come?
> They'd vanish as soon as my tot of rum,
> But well do they know that the guns are dumb
> On a dull and misty morning.

# The Concert

On our last evening in Riez Bailleul, the Sergeant-Major came to the Company Headquarters to say that the men were anxious to give a concert. A piano had been found, and for a small fee the owner was willing to allow us to take it to the orchard for the evening, provided we kept a tarpaulin over it to 'keep out the damp.' Would the officers come, and would I persuade the Adjutant to play the piano?

A man of undoubted administrative ability, with a knowledge of one half of the world of the day that made backwoodsmen of us all, added to a large acquaintance with its more prominent citizens, he had sauntered through many occupations before attaining a large measure of success as a journalist. Through all his varying moods there ran one thread that gave a continuity to his changeful personality, and that was his love of music. He was an attractive pianist, not of the highest order of technique, but endowed with a capacity to make others share in his own delight in playing. Yes, he would play, and he would accompany the songs.

We assembled in the orchard in the dusk, a hundred and fifty men lying about on the trodden grass, talking and smoking. A thin haze of tobacco smoke hung as a pale blue shadow against the darkening sky, and two candles in the piano sconces gave a round blur of yellow light. The air was still, and in the distance a rumble of far-off shell fire served as an echo to the thunder of a limbered wagon passing along the road. We sang a chorus or two to unstiffen the minds of all, to weld us into a unity of mood.

Some forms had been lashed together to make a precarious platform, and on this the Sergeant-Major, by virtue of his office, president and prime mover of such an enterprise, stood to announce that Corporal Jackson 'would oblige', following the time-honoured formula, by singing a song.

Corporal Jackson was greeted enthusiastically by all as he stepped up. At some time or another he had been on the stage, according to the best informed of the company – 'made a lot of money in 'is day, 'e 'as, an' 'e carn't 'arf dance'. He walked across to the piano.

'Music?' said the Adjutant, with a smile.

'No sir, got no music.'

'What are you going to sing?'

'"Don't Stop Me", sir.'

'I don't know it – what's the tune?'

Jackson bent down and hummed into the Adjutant's ear.

'Right you are, Corporal ... Carry on.'

'Will you play a few bars of introduction first, sir, and then play the tune for the dance after each chorus?'

Corporal Jackson walked to the centre of the stage and gave an expert shuffle with his feet to test its stability. 'Mind them boots, Corporal, the Quarter's looking', shouted some irrepressible member of the company.

It was a third-rate song, sung by a fourth-rate singer, followed by a second-rate clog dance, but in the remoteness of that green orchard in Flanders, far from any standard of comparison, it claimed and held approval for its own sake. The words of the chorus still remain, wedded to a jerky tune, both trailing an air of days long passed away:

> Don't stop me, don't stop me,
> I've got a little job to go to,
> 'Twas advertised in ninety-eight,
> If I'm not there I'll be too late ...

Another corporal, fat and tenorish, sang 'Thora', hanging precariously on its sentimental slopes, curving his mouth into a wonderful vowel fantasy over the

> *Noightin-gales in the brenches,*
> *Stawrs in the mej-jic skoy.*

A good hard-working Corporal, though his belt was a perpetual worry to him in his convexity.

But the evening grew to its grand climax when the stern-faced Sergeant-Major stood grimly on the stage, thin-lipped and hawk-eyed, to sing a ballad of Northern Lands. Every line in his face, and every contour in his spare body, gave the lie to his opening words:

> *Oh, Oh, Oh, I'm an Eskimo,*
> *And I live in the Land of Snow ...*

The rest of the song has faded, but that sense of contradiction is still vivid. He had to sing it twice because he could remember no other.

Private Walton hunched his shoulders and adjusted the weight of his body carefully from one leg to another until he found a position of stable equilibrium, mental as well as physical. From his pocket he pulled out a mouth-organ, wiped it carefully on

83

the under-side of his sleeve, shook it and tapped it gently against his palm, presumably to remove any crumbs of tobacco or biscuit, and suddenly burst into a wild harmonic frenzy. From the welter of common chord and seventh there rose a recognizable tune, emphasized by the tapping of his foot, and he stimulated the whole company to song. When the audience had gathered sufficient momentum, he stopped to wipe his mouth-organ.

The next performer was Signaller Downs, who roused the community to a long-drawn-out sequence of 'Nev-vah Mind' in Gertie Gitana's undying song, a song that declined in speed as it grew in sentiment. The moon rose in the blue-grey sky, mellowing the darkness and deepening the shadows under the trees, turning the orchard into a fine setting for a nobler stirring of the spirit. Over the subdued chatter of many voices and the noise of an occasional lighting of a match came the silvery spray of notes from the piano. The Adjutant was playing quietly to himself, meditating in music. The talking ceased, and men turned away from their comrades to listen, until there was dead silence under the trees to make a background for the ripple of the piano.

The silence broke in upon the player and he removed his hands from the keyboard for an instant. The world seemed to plunge into a deep pool of silence before the applause began, enough of a gap to show that his listeners had been travelling with him into another land. He played it again, and as he turned away from the piano he whispered to me, 'I told you that they could appreciate good music if they got the chance.' A summer night in an orchard, with a moon low in the sky, and in the heart of each man a longing – if music could not speak in such a setting it were not music.

## Mametz Wood

The General was cursing last night at his orders.[3] He said that only a madman could have issued them. He called the Divisional Staff a lot of plumbers, herring-gutted at that. He argued

---

[3]Brigadier-General Horatio James Evans was born at Penralley, Rhayader, on 7 June 1859, and had fought in the Afghan and Boer Wars. 'He thought the plan of attack was stupid and he said so.' (Colin Hughes, *Mametz: Lloyd George's Army at the Battle of the Somme* (London: Gliddon Books, 1990), p. 18.)

at the time, and asked for some control over the artillery that is going to cover us, but he got nothing out of them. 'We are not allowed to attack at dawn; we must wait for the show at Contalmaison, well away on our left.'

'We'll get a good view of that show from Pommiers Redoubt.'

'I dare say, but don't you think that it is a funny thing to keep us waiting in the lobby? We are going to attack Mametz Wood from one side, and Contalmaison is on the other side of the Wood – why shouldn't both attacks be made at the same time? It would spread out the German fire.'

'I suppose it would spread out ours too', said Taylor, 'but if you are going to start asking "Why" about orders you'll soon be off the Staff or off your head. You might as well say, "Why attack the Wood at all?"'

'But I do say that, Taylor. Look at it now – it's a forest. What damage can our guns do to that place? If you had a good dug-out near the edge of that wood, and a machine-gun, how many men would you allow to cross that slope leading up to the Wood? You'd mow them down as soon as they stood up.'

We had reached the high ground at Pommiers Redoubt, and, standing in a trench, scanning the Wood with our glasses, it seemed as thick as a virgin forest. There was no sign of life in it, no one could say whether it concealed ten thousand men or ten machine guns. Its edges were clean cut, as far as the eye could see, and the ground between us and the Wood was bare of any cover. Our men were assembled in trenches above a dip in the ground, and from these they were to advance, descend into the hollow, and cross the bare slope in the teeth of the machine-gunners in the Wood. On their right, as they advanced across the bullet-swept zone, they would be exposed to enfilade fire, for the direction of their advance was nearly parallel to the German trenches towards Bazentin, and it would be folly to suppose that the German machine-guns were not sited to sweep that slope leading to the Wood.

'I'm not surprised that the General cursed when he got his orders', said Taylor. 'The truth about the Brigadier is that he's got too much sense. He was soldiering when some of the fellows above him were still playing marbles. I'm going to see my signallers ... I'll see you later.'

A little further along the trench a group of officers were engaged in a discussion over a map spread out on a box.

85

I went up to speak to them, and found that this was the head-quarters of a group of Heavy Artillery concerned in the bombardment of Contalmaison, and about to wipe it off the map, as I gathered.

Taylor came up out of a dug-out. 'We're through to the old Brigade Headquarters, the Division, and to the battalions. How long we'll be through to the battalions is another story', he said.

The General arrived with the Brigade Major and the Staff Captain, looked around him quickly, and turned to me.

'Have you found a good place for us?'

'Yes, sir, there's room in the signallers' dug-out, but this is a good place for seeing.'

'It's close on seven o'clock. Are we through to everybody, and have the battalions reported that they are in position?' he asked.

'Yes, sir.'

'Then send out the report that Brigade Headquarters has opened here. You stay with me, and be ready to take down any orders or messages when the time comes.'

With this he went to consult with the Brigade Major. I stood on a step in the side of the trench, studying the country to the East and identifying the various features from the map. Our guns were quiet, and, although everybody within sight was moving, there was a weird stillness in the air, a brooding menace. Why was I standing here when men I knew were lined up in readiness to expose their bodies to a driving sleet of lead? The thought of the days' torment, doomed, as I thought, from its beginning, to bring no recompense, weighed like a burden of iron. The sound of a heavy bombardment, some distance away to our left, broke in upon the silence and grew to a storm of noise and smoke. Contalmaison was the target, prominent upon a hill until the smoke obscured the hill-top, turning it into a dark cloud hung between a blue sky and brown-pitted earth. Out of this cloud, at intervals of some minutes, an orange sheet of flame made an effort to escape, only to be conquered and smudged out by the all-pervading smoke. It did not seem possible that there could be guns enough in France to create such a fury as this, and my mind went back to the artillery fire of 1915 and early 1916. Our trench bombardments were things of no importance when con-trasted with this, and I felt half ashamed to remember that they had frightened me.

At eight o'clock the artillery began its bombardment of the edge of Mametz Wood. A thousand yards away from where I stood, our two battalions were waiting. I read the orders again. The attack was to be carried out in three stages, beginning at half-past eight, reaching in succession three positions inside the Wood, under the protection of an artillery barrage. Smoke screens were to be formed here and there. Everything sounded so simple and easy.

A few minutes after eight, all our telephone wires to the battalions were cut by the enemy's reply to our fire. There was no smoke screen, for some reason never explained – perhaps someone forgot about it. This was the first departure from the simplicity of the printed word. Messages came through, a steady trickle of runners bringing evil news; our fire had not masked the German machine-guns in Mametz Wood, nor in the wood near Bazentin. The elaborate time-table suddenly became a thing of no meaning, as unrelated to our condition as one of Napoleon's orders; our artillery barrage was advancing in mockery of our failure, for we were two hundred yards away from the Wood.

A message arrived from the Division. In twenty minutes' time, the artillery would begin another bombardment of the edge of the Wood, and under cover of this we were to renew the attack – in twenty minutes. We were a thousand yards away from the battalions, with no telephone communication; there were maps at Divisional Headquarters, they knew where we were, they knew where the battalions were, and they knew that our lines were cut. A simple sum in arithmetic ... Our operation was isolated; no one was attacking on either flank of our Brigade, so that there was complete freedom of choice as to time. With all the hours of the clock to choose from, some master-mind must needs select the only hour to be avoided. He did not ask himself whether the order could reach its ultimate destination in time ... the answer to that sum in arithmetic.

Every attempt to move near the Wood was met by a burst of frontal and enfilade machine-gun fire. Shells were falling, taking a steady toll of lives. Later, another order came from Divisional Headquarters. We were to attack again, to make a third effort to penetrate this wall of lead. The General gave some orders to his Brigade-Major, called me to accompany him, and we set out for Caterpillar Wood and to reach the battalions. Although the day was fine, the heavy rains of the preceding days had turned the chalky soil into a stiff glue. The hurry in our minds accentuated the slowness of our progress, and I felt as if some physical force was dragging me back. Haste meant a fall into a shell hole, for we had abandoned the attempt to move along the trench. Shrapnel was bursting overhead, and a patter of machine-gun bullets spat through the air. We passed through Caterpillar Wood, and in a disused trench on our left I saw an Artillery officer. I turned off to ask him whether his telephone was working, and learned that he was in communication with a Heavy Artillery Group somewhere beyond Pommiers Redoubt. I ran down the trench to rejoin the General, and we dropped down the bank into the nullah between Caterpillar Wood and Mametz Wood, passing a stream of 'walking wounded' making their way out.

There was a dug-out in the bank, with scores of stretchers down on the ground in front, each stretcher occupied by a fellow creature, maimed and in pain. This was the Advance Dressing Station; twenty rounds of shrapnel would have made stretchers unnecessary. Along the bare ridge rising up to Mametz Wood our men were burrowing into the ground with their entrenching tools, seeking whatever cover they might make. A few shells were falling, surprisingly few. Wounded men were crawling back from the ridge, men were crawling forward with ammunition. No attack could succeed over such ground as this, swept from front and side by machine-guns at short range. Down in the nullah we were out of sight of the enemy, but fifteen minutes of shrapnel would have reduced the brigade to a battalion, and every minute that passed seemed to bring nearer the hour of our inevitable annihilation. We were caught in a trap, unable to advance, unable to withdraw without being observed. It must ever remain one of the many mysteries of the War why the enemy did not pound us with shell fire, for this was so obviously the only place of assembly.

The time was drawing near for the renewal of the attack, for another useless slaughter. Casualties in officers had been extremely heavy, and the battalions were somewhat disorganized.

'This is sheer lunacy,' said the General. 'I've tried all day to stop it. We could creep up to the edge of the Wood by night and rush it in the morning, but they won't listen to me ... It breaks my heart to see all this.'

'If I could get you through on the telephone, would you talk to them again?' I asked.

'Of course I would, but all the wires are cut, and there is no time to go back.'

'I know of a telephone to an Artillery Group, and they might get you through to the Division,' I answered.

'Find out at once whether I can get through,' he replied.

I hurried up to the trench where I had seen the Artillery officer and found that his wires were still uncut, and as I ran back to the General I prayed in my heart that they would hold; the lives of some hundreds of men depended upon it. It did not occur to me that words sent along that wire might fail in their object, that someone sitting far away would look at a map and say, 'No, you must reach that Wood at all costs.' Seen in its stark reality, our position was so hopeless that a dispassionate account of it must convince any one, even at a distance of six miles, that to remain where we were would be no less calamitous than to try to advance. The enemy had shown no desire to hold that exposed ridge with men, for his bullets were defence enough, and in a short space of time his artillery must realize that there was a magnificent target in that hollow between the ridge and the bank.

When I came back to the hollow, I could not find the General. I ran from one group of men to another, working my way up the ridge, until I found him organizing the defence of the position against any possible counter-attack. Shells did not seem to matter; my whole existence, up to that very minute, had been of no importance to the world, but my original conversation with that Artillery officer, so obviously prompted by what men call Destiny, could lead to the saving of hundreds of lives, and must not fail to do so. I knew that I had been 'chosen' for this. Ten minutes later I sat in the trench while the General spoke on the telephone, tersely describing the utter folly of any course of action other than a gradual withdrawal under cover of outposts, and quoting figures of our casualties. He was arguing with determination. There was opposition, but he won. As I jumped up to start on our way back to the ridge, he stopped me.

'Wait a minute. They are shelling this bank, and this message must get through. Give me a sheet of paper,' said he. He wrote down his order for the withdrawal and gave it to me. 'You go one way, and I'll go another way. Join me in the hollow. Go as fast as you can.' With this he went down the trench, and I ran and stumbled down the bank, still feeling perfectly safe in the hands of Destiny.

Two hours later the General and I were dragging our way from the nullah and back towards Pommiers Redoubt. We sat down in a trench to let a file of men pass by, and I suddenly noticed that his face was grey and drawn.

'Have you eaten anything since this morning?' I asked him.

'No ... have you?' he replied. 'I feel whacked.'

'Will you wait here a few minutes – I'll be back soon,' I said.

I had seen a dug-out, and I went inside it. Some signallers were lighting a fire to boil a mess-tin full of water; they lent me an enamel cup, and in it I put a tablet of compressed tea. The brew was strong and the water was not boiling, but it was a warm drink, and I took it back to the General. It revived him, and we munched our biscuits as we walked along.

Back again to Pommiers Redoubt, but with a difference, in the flat greyness of approaching dusk. The noise of the guns had died down to a sullen scale-practice, with an occasional, and almost accidental chord, so different from the crashes of the day. Stretcher-bearers, bowed forward under their straps, were carrying their burdens of suffering across the ploughed and pitted slopes.

'How did you come to find that telephone?' asked the General.

'I happened to notice the Artillery officer on my way down, and I went to ask him if his line back was working. Don't you remember my leaving you?'

'No, I don't remember ... Well, it saved the lives of some hundreds of men, but it has put an end to me.'

'Why do you say that?'

'I spoke my mind about the whole business ... you heard me. They wanted us to press on at all costs, talked about determination, and suggested that I didn't realize the importance of the operation. As good as told me that I was tired and didn't want to tackle the job. Difficult to judge on the spot, they said! As if the whole trouble hadn't arisen because someone found it so easy to judge when he was six miles away and had never seen the country, and couldn't read a map. You mark my words, they'll send me home for this: they want butchers, not brigadiers. They'll remember now that I told them, before we began, that the attack could not succeed unless the machine guns were masked. I shall be in England in a month.'

He had saved the Brigade from annihilation. That the rescue, in terms of men, was no more than a respite of days was no fault of his, for there is no saving of life in war until the eleventh hour of the last day is drawing to an end. It was nearly midnight when we heard that the last of our men had withdrawn from that ridge and valley, leaving the ground empty, save for the bodies of those who had to fall to prove to our command that machine guns can defend a bare slope. Six weeks later the General went home.

# IVOR GURNEY

Ivor Bertie Gurney was a Gloucester man, the son of a tailor, and was trained as a musician. From May 1916 he served on the Western Front as a private in the Gloucestershire Regiment. After the war he produced many poems and songs, whilst doing a variety of jobs. He suffered several 'breakdowns' and lived in psychiatric hospitals until his death on Boxing Day 1937.

In this poem Ivor Gurney recollects his experience of entering the trenches for the first time, and salutes with gratitude the unexpected humanity he found there, from a Welsh battalion. The 2/5th Glosters arrived in France on 25 May 1916, going into the trenches at Laventie six days later. They were 'under instruction' from the 15th (London Welsh) Battalion of the Royal Welch Fusiliers.

~

## First Time In

After the dread tales and red yarns of the Line
Anything might have come to us; but the divine
Afterglow brought us up to a Welsh colony
Hiding in sandbag ditches, whispering consolatory
Soft foreign things. Then we were taken in
To low huts candle-lit, shaded close by slitten
Oilsheets, and there the boys gave us kind welcome,
So that we looked out as from the edge of home.
Sang us Welsh things, and changed all former notions
To human hopeful things. And the next day's guns
Nor any line-pangs ever quite could blot out
That strangely beautiful entry to war's rout;

Candles they gave us, precious and shared over-rations –
Ulysses found little more in his wanderings without doubt.
'David of the White Rock', the 'Slumber Song' so soft, and
that
Beautiful tune to which roguish words by Welsh pit boys
Are sung – but never more beautiful than there under the
guns' noise.[1]

---

[1]From P. J. Kavanagh (ed.), *Collected Poems of Ivor Gurney* (Oxford: Oxford University Press, 1982).

# ARTHUR HUMPHREYS-OWEN

The National Library of Wales possesses the Army Correspondence Book and Journal kept by Captain A. E. O. Humphreys-Owen for the period 13 October to 9 November 1917, when he was Officer Commanding 'D' Company of the 10th (Service) Battalion, Royal Welch Fusiliers.[1]

Arthur Erskine Owen Humphreys-Owen was born on 16th June 1876 at Berriew in Montgomeryshire, the year in which his father, Arthur Charles Humphreys inherited the Glansevern mansion and estate, taking the arms and additional surname of Owen. The estate was of about 4,000 acres and included most of the eastern part of Berriew parish from the Severn to Castle Caereinion. A. C. Humphreys had been called to the Bar in 1864, was chairman of Montgomeryshire County Council from 1889, and Liberal MP for the shire from 1894 to 1905. He was the first chairman of the Central Welsh Board, which was responsible for the inspection of intermediate and secondary schools. Arthur Humphreys-Owen and his wife, Maria, produced a son and three daughters.

The son, Arthur Erskine Owen Humphreys-Owen was educated at Harrow, Trinity College, Cambridge, and in Germany. From 1898 to 1904 he was in the diplomatic service, but resigned on inheriting the Glansevern and Llanrug estates. In 1908 he became high sheriff of his county, a year after marrying Isabelle, the daughter of Sir Edward Sassoon, Bart. They had a son, born in 1908, and a daughter.[2]

The date of his original army commission has not been traced, but on 1 October 1909 (at the age of 33) he was promoted to captain in the 7th (Montgomeryshire) Battalion (Territorial Force) of the Royal Welch

---

[1]Army Correspondence Book: Glansevern VII (14600). Journal: Glansevern VII (14812).

[2]Information about Glansevern and Humphreys-Owen is from C. L. J. Humphreys, 'The Charles Humphreys of Montgomery and Berriew', *Montgomeryshire Collections*, Vol. 70 (1982), p. 54; E. H. C. Davies, 'Glansevern', *Montgomeryshire Collections*, Vol. 72 (1984), pp. 53–62.

Fusiliers. As he is recorded as having qualified as an interpreter (he was fluent in French and German) in 1905, it may be assumed that he had started his military service in the 7th Battalion's predecessor – the 5th (Volunteer) Battalion. A month after the outbreak of the Great War he was recommissioned (as a second lieutenant) in his territorial battalion, regaining his captain's rank on 28 September 1916, having spent a period on attachment to the 6th (Service) Battalion, the Dorset Regiment.[3]

In the autumn of 1917 he was serving with the 10th (Service) Battalion of the Royal Welch Fusiliers, which had been formed on 16 September 1914 as part of Kitchener's third New Army.[4] Since arriving in France it had seen some intense fighting including the attack on Delville Wood where, in July 1916, the South Africans were enduring so heroically and Corporal Davies and Private Hill won Victoria Crosses before the battalion was relieved, having lost 228 men. November of 1916 found the Battalion attacking the village of Serre, and discovering themselves to be isolated after taking three lines of trenches. After taking part in the Arras offensive in the spring of 1917, the 10th Battalion was again in action (at Zonnebeke near Polygon Wood) late in September, suffering 43 killed, 211 wounded and 38 missing.[5] The manuscripts held by the National Library of Wales were produced about a fortnight later.

The extracts which follow have been arranged in chronological order, with intercalated entries from the battalion war diary,[6] to provide a brief insight into an officer's day-to-day experience of the battle zone. At this time, Captain Humphreys-Owen was forty-one years old.

~

*Saturday 13 October 1917 (Journal)*
Fine day. Companies parade and inspection by CO in the morning. Pritchard has gone off to the CCS,[7] not cured of the wound in his head. I am taking over the company. The platoon commanders are Gutteridge, Arnold, Jones, the bombing officer and Hunter (away on leave). In the afternoon I go over to Ovillers and get a bath there, then have tea with 'C'

---

[3]The author is indebted to Mr Norman Holme, Archivist at the Royal Welch Fusiliers Museum, for information about Captain Humphreys-Owen.
[4]E. A. James, *British Regiments 1914–1918* (London: Samson Books, 1978), p. 67.
[5]M. Glover, *That Astonishing Infantry: Three Hundred Years of the History of the Royal Welch Fusiliers* (London: Leo Cooper, 1989), pp. 145–7, 153, 155–6, p. 161.
[6]F. N. Burton and A. P. Comyns, *The War Diary (1914–18) 10th (Service) Battalion Royal Welch Fusiliers* (Plymouth: William Brendon and Sons, 1926).
[7]Casualty Clearing Station.

Mess of Division details. Meet a decent fellow there, Redmond, who has constructed an old ruined house into a very cosy place, and is planning an officers' club; Canteen and Men's Club across the street. On to Belagnies and dine at the club there with the CO and other officers and play bridge. Lose 22 francs. Captain Adamson is going to take charge of 'D' company for the first tour of the trenches as he knows the system.

*Sunday 14 October (Journal)*
*Captain Humphreys-Owen went to the Casualty Clearing Station at Ovillers to have a tooth filled. Afterwards:*
Walk to Bapaume and have lunch at the Club. Write letters. Walk on to Belagnies and tea at the Corps Club there. Back to Mess. Play Bridge. Win 5 francs.

*Monday 15 October (Journal)*
Very cold night. Frost on the ground. A lot of shooting in the night. On court martials the whole day from 10.00 a.m. – 4.00 p.m. in the Suffolk camp close. Two officers, two NCOs have gone up the line from each company to look around. The Corps news is that six German submarines have surrendered at Dover. There is also a yarn that a separate Treaty of Peace with Austria was all but signed last June. Got a letter from Belle.

*Tuesday 16 October (Journal)*
I went up the line with Sergeant Powell. Passed through village of Ecouste – all in ruins, got into the communication Trench the other side and had to walk up it three-quarters of an hour before reaching the front line. Inspected the sector to be held by our company. A rather ragged front line Trench and the German line about 80 yards off. There are several points in our line from which the Bosch can observe our movements, but he didn't snipe me – didn't even send over any TMs.[8] The whole ground is full of old battle relics – corpses, equipment, arms, ammunition, etc. roll out wherever digging has to be done. Went to the Company Headquarters which is an old Bosch dug out – very deep. Our left is actually in the village of Bullecourt. On the way

---

[8]Trench mortars.

back from Ecouste I could see right over the German lines. A very fine day.

*Wednesday 17 October (Journal)*
Court Martial work all day at the 2nd Royal Scots. Lunch: Officers' Mess. Tea: Club. Went to preside at Battalion entertainment in the evening.

*Thursday 18 October (Journal)*
Perfectly fine day. Court Martial work all day at the Royal Scots. Tea at the Club. Got a letter (long one) from Belle. Heavy strafe going on in the line tonight.

*Friday 19 October*
*War Diary*: The battalion entrained at Mory Abbey, de-trained at Ecouste, and marched to the trenches, where it relieved the 8th Battalion The King's Own (Royal Lancaster Regiment) in the Bullecourt Sector.
*Journal*: We go up into the line tonight to relieve the King's Own. Went up by light railway arriving at Ecouste about 10. Marched up from there. Got to Batt. Hdqrs. about 11 and into the front line about 12. A few dud or gas shells fired at us on the way. We hold about 400 yds. of front line – with 'A' company on our left, our bit being Foxtrot Lane to 50 yards beyond March post and Company Hdqrs. is a deep dug out in London Reserve.

*Sunday 21 October (War Diary)*
Casualties – killed: one O.R.
A draft of 3 rank and file joined the battalion.

*Monday 22 October (Correspondence Book)*
*Report on Reconnaissance*
1.  Object. German Dug Out in No Man's Land, 30 yards outside parapet of February Post.
2.  Party consisting of two officers and four other ranks thoroughly searched this dug out at 8.00 p.m. October 22nd.
3.  Four entrances led down about 30 feet deep to a long gallery about 100 yards long. Eight compartments facing the staircases opened off gallery, and one on the other side.

4. This Dug Out appears to have been constructed to hold a complete unit of 200 infantry if necessary.
5. The whole dug-out was littered with corpses and appears to have been taken by surprise and gassed. No man had his equipment on.
6. The patrol thoroughly searched the corpses and rubbish which littered the whole place, but nothing of value in the way of documents could be found. Such newspapers etc. that were found are enclosed, also shoulder badges off greatcoats.

*Tuesday 23 October (Journal)*
Nothing very unusual during this tour. The first night while over in the open looking at our wire – one of our fellows nearly shot me. Hardly any of these men have been in the line before. Every evening we send out wiring parties and also work upon improving our trenches which are pretty muddy in parts and exposed.

*Friday 26 October (Correspondence Book)*
5.00 a.m. From: O.C. 'D' Company
    To: Adjt. Battn. Hdqrs.
    By runner.
    Indents: SAA[9] 5000
    Sandbags 250
    Intelligence: No shelling. No Trench Mortars.
    No aerial activity.
    Work Report: Instruction in wiring and improving LG[10] emplacements. Two wiring parties sent up to front line.
6.45 a.m. To: Batt. Adjt.
    By Fullerphone[11]
    Socks have been changed and feet rubbed; three hot meals provided during last 24 hours.
3.15 p.m. To: Batt. Adjt.
    By runner.

---

[9]Small arms ammunition.
[10]Lewis gun.
[11]An instrument invented by Captain A. C. Fuller to try to minimize interception of messages by the enemy.

Lt. Arnold reported to me this morning that Sgt. Baverstock, who was senior NCO with the wiring party, last night remained in the Trench and did not come out to the wiring party. Lt. Arnold states that as the party were running out into No Man's Land he ordered two men to remain behind and assist in handing out the material, and to follow when all material was out. Sergeant Baverstock heard this order, and remained behind himself with another private the whole time the party were working. He alleges he understood that was the meaning of Lt. Arnold's order.

I do not wish to bring a serious charge against this NCO as there is no evidence for this, but I consider him under the circumstances quite unfit to retain his rank.

*Journal*: We were relieved by 'C' Company this morning and marched down into Ecouste Lane in reserve. Here we are in dug-outs under the Bank in the sunken road. We just keep quiet all day and clean up. They got several pretty close to us however. Thursday night one dropped behind me – the next across the road – the third near Seel's dug-out – who jumped out and came to my dug out for shelter.

*Saturday 27 October (Correspondence Book)*
5.00 a.m. *To: Batt. Adjt.*
By runner.
Indents: SAA – Nil
Grenades – Nil
RE Material – Nil
Intelligence Summary: Half a dozen enemy shells fell north of Ecouste–Noreuil Road rear 'D' company-lines about 7.00 p.m.
Work Report: Cleaned up arms and equipment. Two working parties of 21 OR[12] and officer each to front line. One party to Tunnelling Company RE of 15 OR.
*War Diary*: The battalion was relieved in the trenches by the 8th Battalion the King's Own (Royal Lancaster Regiment) and marched to camp at Mory.

---

[12]Other ranks.

*Friday 2 November (Correspondence Book)*
Return of Officers: Lt. Hunter; Lt. Jones (Bombing); Lt. Arnold (Physical Drill); Lt. Gutteridge (Musketry); Lt. Seel (Lewis Gun).

*Sunday 4 November (War Diary)*
The battalion marched to the Bullecourt Sector and relieved the 8th Battalion The King's Own (Royal Lancaster Regiment) in the trenches.

*Monday 5 November (Correspondence Book)*
5.00 a.m. *To Batt. Adjt.*
Indents: Iron Sheets 50
Sandbags 500
Work Report: Relief of Sector taken from King's Own.
*To Mess President*
The Officers' Mess would like some eggs, cheese, tinned fruit-salad, sauce, mustard. No whisky is needed but more lime juice. Other Officers' Messes in the line get real tinned butter, which is excellent. Make a note of it. Also apples. Charcoal for fuel is needed, also candles.
4.00 p.m. *To Batt. Adjt.*
By runner.
Your No.6 of the 4th says Fullerphone only to be used for *very urgent messages.* How does this affect the 3.30 a.m., 2.00 p.m. and 4.00 p.m. reports referred to in your No.4 of the 4th?
6.15 p.m. *To Batt. Adjt.*
Great difficulty in preparing hot meals for the men, as there is no fuel supplied as before.
Intelligence Report: About 4.00 p.m. 5th inst. our guns apparently shelling target at U.22 d 6.6 were dropping short at U.22 d 5.3. Some in front and some in rear of January post. This was reported by wire immediately as the safety of the post was involved. Some hostile shelling by TMs between 4.45 and 5.30 p.m. 5th inst. Direction of wind at 3.00 a.m. 6th inst: South.
Work Report: All posts attended to by their garrisons. Trench between February and March improved and duck-boarded.

*War Diary*: Casualties – died of wounds (gas): Lieut. H. W. Rayner (attached to 76th Trench Mortar Battery) and Pte A. G. Jones;[13] wounded (gas): Pte A. Colley; Pte F. Calder; Pte W. H. Gilleard; Pte W. H. Hall; Pte R. P. Jones; Pte H. Anscombe.

*Wednesday 7 November*
*War Diary*: The battalion was relieved in the trenches by the 8th Battalion the King's Own (Royal Lancaster Regiment) and marched to camp at Mory.
*Correspondence Book*: Reference enclosed letters from Messrs. Cox,[14] has claim been made for my Field allowance, also for Ration allowance from Sept. 15 to October 6th inclusive at 1/9*d* per day, also for Maintenance allowance 3rd Oct. to 6th Oct. inclusive at 15/- a day, also cab fares at 2/6*d* a day Oct. 3rd to Oct. 6th.
Is the Messing allowance of 5½*d* a day paid to the individual officers, or to the Mess President in reduction of Mess Expenses?

*Friday 9 November*
*War Diary*: A draft of 84 rank and file joined the battalion.
*Correspondence Book*: 6.45 a.m. Trench state of company here is 102. 76 are going up line tomorrow.

*On Monday 19 November 1917, the 10th Royal Welch Fusiliers were relieved by the 12th (Service) Battalion of the Prince of Wales's Own (West Yorkshire Regiment). The Royal Welchmen marched off to camp at Forreuil, but a week later they returned to man the trenches at Bullecourt.*

*By 1918 Captain Humphreys-Owen had become second-in-command of the 14th (Service) Battalion of his regiment, until he was wounded in action on 23 August 1918 near La Boiselle. After the war he returned to Glansevern, giving his occupation (in Who's Who in Wales) as 'land-owner'. He was a barrister-at-law of Lincoln's Inn, cites his religion as 'Churchman' and lists his recreations as horticulture and reading. He was a member of the Athenaeum.[15] In 1929 he disappeared, in London,*

---

[13]Private Albert Jones, who died of wounds on 5 November, was born at Bridgnorth, enlisted at Ironbridge and had served in the Montgomeryshire Yeomanry.
[14]The agents responsible for army pay and allowances.
[15]A. Mee (ed.), *Who's Who in Wales* (Cardiff: *Western Mail*, 1920).

*and was never heard of again. His wife lived on in Hampshire, being a member of the county council and a magistrate, whilst his sisters stayed on at Glansevern until they moved to a nursing home (the last one died in 1955). The property was sold in 1951 and the family papers deposited in the National Library.*

# DAVID JONES

David Jones was a London Welshman, intensely conscious of his Welsh identity. His father, from Holywell in Flintshire, became a printer in London, later becoming business manager of *The Christian Herald*, the Nonconformist weekly. His son became an art student, continuing his studies after the war at the Westminster College of Art. In 1921 David Jones was received into the Roman Catholic church and went to live in Sussex in order to work with Eric Gill, who later migrated to Capel-y-ffin near Abergavenny. David Jones spent a good deal of time there, but became almost a recluse, living in hotels and boarding houses. Exhibitions of his paintings were held in Chicago, Venice, New York and London.

Private David Jones disembarked in France, with the 15th (1st London Welsh) Battalion Royal Welch Fusiliers in January 1915. Wounded at Mametz Wood in July 1916 (at the age of twenty-one), he returned to the front in October, serving at Ypres and around Bois Grenier until being invalided home with trench fever. He wrote nothing during the war but published the prose poem *In Parenthesis* in 1937. T. S. Eliot thought it 'a work of genius' and it has been described as 'one of the most original works of art to come out of the First World War ... an evocation of war more poignant in the very extensiveness of its references, the controlled range of its voice, than any of the stripped, personal lyrics of Sassoon or Owen'.[1] It has also been shown to be an accurate record of places and events. The following

---

[1] E. Ward, *David Jones: Mythmaker* (Manchester, 1983).

passage² begins with the soldiers waiting, anxiously, to attack. (The foot-notes, which begin here at no. 7, were provided by David Jones.) His battalion, initially in reserve, was sent into the attack almost immediately.

～

## Mametz Wood

Perhaps they'll cancel it.
O blow fall out the officers cantcher, like a wet afternoon
or the King's Birthday⁷.
   Or you read it again many times to see if it will come different:
you can't believe the Cup wont pass from
or they wont make a better show
in the Garden.⁸
Won't someone forbid the banns
or God himself will stay their hands.
It just can't happen in our family
even though a thousand
and ten thousand at thy right hand.

Talacryn doesn't take it like Wastebottom, he leaps up & says he's dead, a-slither down the pale face – his limbs a-girandole
at the bottom of the nullah,
but the mechanism slackens, unfed
and he is quite still
which leaves five paces between you and the next live one to the left.
   Sidle over a bit toward where '45 Williams, and use all your lungs:
   Get ready me china-plate⁹ – but he's got it before he can hear you, but it's a cushy one and he relaxes to the morning sun and smilingly, to wait for the bearers.

---

²Taken from David Jones, *In Parenthesis* (London: Faber and Faber, 1963 edn.).
⁷*O blow fall out the Officers*. To hear the bugle sound 'Fall out the Officers' was welcome to men on a wet day doing field exercises. It connoted the break off of operations.
  *King's Birthday*. A holiday for HM Forces – after the ceremonial parade.
⁸ *or you read it . . . in the Garden*. Cf. the Gospels (narrative of the Agony and of the Betrayal).
⁹*china-plate*. From 'china-plate', rhyming slang for 'mate'.

Some of yer was born wiv jam on it
clicked lucky and favoured
                    pluckt brand from burning
and my darling from unicorn horn with only a minute to go,
whose wet-nurse cocked a superstitious eye to see his happy
constellation through the panes.

But it isn't like that for the common run and you have no men-
suration gear to plot meandering fortune-graph nor know
whether she were the Dark or the Fair left to the grinding.

Last minute drums its taut millennium out
you can't swallow your spit
and Captain Marlowe yawns a lot
and seconds now our measuring-rods with no Duke Josue
nor conniving God
to stay the Divisional Synchronisation.

So in the fullness of time
    when pallid jurors bring the doomes
    mooring cables swipe slack-end on
barnacled piles,
and the world falls apart at the last to siren screech and
screaming vertical steam in conformity with the Company's
Sailings and up to scheduled time.

As bridal arranged-paraphernalia gets tumbled – eventually
and the night empties of these relatives
if you wait long time enough
and yesterday puts on to-day.
    At the end of the suspense
come the shod feet
hastily or laggard
or delayed –
but anyway, no fretting of watch on the wall nor their hysteria,
can hamper nor accelerate
exact kinetics of his advent
nor make less miserable his tale to tell
    and even Mrs Chandler's tom
will stiffen one Maye Mornynge
to the ninth death.

Tunicled functionaries signify and clear-voiced heralds cry
and leg it to a safe distance:
leave fairway for the Paladins, and Roland throws a kiss —
they've nabbed his batty for the moppers-up
      and Mr Jenkins takes them over
and don't bunch on the left
for Christ's sake.

      Riders on pale horses loosed
and vials irreparably broken
an' Wat price bleedin' Glory
Glory
Glory Hallelujah
and the Royal Welsh sing:
Jesu
      lover of me soul ... to *Aberystwyth*.
But that was on the right with
the genuine Taffies
      but we are rash levied
from Islington and Hackney
and the purlieus of Walworth
flashers from Surbiton
men of the stock of Abraham
from Bromley-by-Bow
Anglo-Welsh from Queens Ferry
rosary-wallahs from Pembrey Dock
lighterman with a Norway darling
from Greenland Stairs[10]
and two lovers from Ebury Bridge,
Bates and Coldpepper
that men called the Lily-white boys.
Fowler from Harrow and the House who'd lost his way into
this crush who was gotten in a parsonage on a maye.
Dynamite Dawes the old 'un
and Diamond Phelps his batty[11]
from Santiago del Estero
and Bulawayo respectively,

---

[10]*Greenland Stairs*. In Rotherhithe.
[11]*his batty*. Interchangeable with 'china' (see note 9) but more definitely used of a most intimate companion. Jonathan was certainly David's 'batty'.

both learned in ballistics
        and wasted on a line-mob.

Of young gentlemen wearing the Flash,
from reputable marcher houses
with mountain-squireen first-borns
prince-pedigreed
from Meirionedd and Cyfeiliog.
C. of E. on enlistment eyes grey with mark above left nipple
probably Goidelic from length of femur.
Heirs also of tin-plate lords
from the Gower peninsula,
detailed from the womb
        to captain Industry
if they dont cop a packet this day
nor grow more wise.
Whereas C. S. M. Tyler was transferred from the West Kents
whose mother sang for him
at Mary-Cray
if he would fret she sang for lullaby:
      *We'll go to the Baltic with Charlie Napier*
she had that of great uncle Tyler
Eb Tyler, who'd got away with the Inkerman bonus.[12]

Every one of these, stood, separate, upright, above ground,
blinkt to the broad light
risen dry mouthed from the chalk
vivified from the Nullah without commotion
and to distinctly said words,
moved in open order and keeping admirable formation
and at the high-port position[13]
walking in the morning on the flat roof of the world
and some walked delicately
sensible of their particular judgment.

---

[12]*Mary-Cray.* Kentish village on outskirts of London.
  *We'll go to the Baltic ... Inkerman Bonus.* Popular song from the period of
Napier's Russian expedition:
  We'll go to the Baltic with Charlie Napier
  And help him to govern the Great Russian Bear.
It is the first song I can remember my mother singing me.
[13]*the high-port position.* Regulation position at which to hold rifle, with bayonet
fixed, when moving toward the enemy. It was held high and slantingly across
the body.

Each one bearing in his body the whole apprehension of that innocent, on the day he saw his brother's votive smoke diffuse and hang to soot the fields of holocaust; neither approved nor ratified nor made acceptable but lighted to everlasting partition.
Who under the green tree
had awareness of his dismembering, and deep-bowelled damage; for whom the green tree bore scarlet memorial, and herb and arborage waste.

Skin gone astrictive
        for fear gone out to meet half-way –
bare breast for –
to welcome – who gives a bugger for
the Dolorous Stroke.[14]

But sweet sister death has gone debauched today and stalks on this high ground with strumpet confidence, makes no coy veiling of her appetite but leers from you to me with all her parts discovered.
   By one and one the line gaps, where her fancy will – howsoever they may howl for their virginity
she holds them – who impinge less on space
sink limply to a heap
nourish a lesser category of being
like those other who fructify the land
like Tristram
Lamorak de Galis
Alisand le Orphelin
Beaumains who was youngest
or all of them in shaft-shade
at strait Thermopylae
or the sweet brothers Balin and Balan
embraced beneath their single monument.
   Jonathan my lovely one
on Gelboe mountain
and the young man Absalom.
White Hart transfixed in his dark lodge.
Peredur of steel arms

---

[14]*Each one ... and arborage waste ... Dolorous Stroke.* Cf. Genesis iv; Malory, book xvii, ch. 5; Canon of the Mass, Prayer, 'Quam Oblationem', and Malory, book ii, ch. 15.

and he who with intention took grass of that field to be for
him the Species of Bread.
    Taillefer the maker,
and on the same day,
thirty thousand other ranks.
And in the country of Béarn – Oliver
and all the rest – so many without memento
beneath the tumuli on the high hills
and under the harvest places.[15]

But how intolerably bright the morning is where we who are
alive and remain, walk lifted up, carried forward by an
effective word.

But red horses now – blare every trump without economy,
burn boat and sever every tie every held thing goes west and
tethering snapt, bolts unshot and brass doors flung wide and
you go forward, foot goes another step further.

The immediate foreground sheers up, tilts toward,
like an high wall falling.
There she breaches black perpendiculars
where the counter-barrage warms to the seventh power where
the Three Children walk under the fair morning

---

[15]*shaft-shade.* Cf. Herodotus, book vii, *Polymnia*, Dieneces' speech.
*sweet brothers ... monument.* Cf. Malory, book ii, ch. 19.
*White Hart transfixed.* Cf. *Richard II*, Act v, Sc. vi.
*Peredur of steel arms.* Peredur. The *Percivale* of the romances called 'of
steel arms' in the Triads, and by the Gododdin poet: 'Peredur with arms
of steel ...' (he commemorates other warriors, and proceeds) ' ... though
men might have slain them, they too were slayers, none returned to their
homes.'
*with intention ... Species of Bread.* In some battle of the Welsh, all reference
to which escapes me, a whole army ate grass in token of the Body of the
Lord. Also somewhere in the Malory, a single knight feeling himself at the
point of death makes this same act.
*Taillefer ... other ranks.* Cf. Wace, *Roman de Rou*: 'Then Taillefer, who sang
right well, rode before the duke singing of Carlemaine and of Rollant, of
Oliver and the vassals who died at Renchevals.'
*country of Béarn ... harvest places.* Not that Roncesvalles is in the Béarn country,
but I associate it with Béarn because, once, looking from a window in Salies-
de-Béarn I could see a gap in the hills, which my hostess told me was indeed
the pass where Roland fell.

and the Twin Brother[16]
and the high grass soddens through your puttees
and dew asperges the freshly dead.

There doesn't seem a soul about yet surely we walk already
near his preserves; there goes old Dawes as large as life and
there is Lazarus Cohen like on field-days, he always would
have his entrenching-tool-blade-carrier hung low, jogging
on his fat arse.

They pass a quite ordinary message about keeping aligned
with No. 8.

You drop apprehensively – the sun gone out,
strange airs smite your body
and muck rains straight from heaven
and everlasting doors lift up for '02 Weavel.
You cant see anything but sheen on drafting particles and
you move forward in your private bright cloud like
one assumed
who is borne up by an exterior volition.

You stumble on a bunch of six with Sergeant Quilter getting
them out again to the proper interval, and when the chemical
thick air dispels you see briefly and with great clearness what
kind of a show this is.

The gentle slopes are green to remind you
of South English places, only far wider and flatter spread and
grooved and harrowed criss-cross whitely and the disturbed
subsoil heaped up albescent.

Across upon this undulated board of verdure chequered
bright
when you look to left and right
small, drab, bundled pawns severally make effort
moved in tenuous line
and if you looked behind – the next wave came slowly, as suc-
cessive surfs creep in to dissipate on flat shore;
and to your front, stretched long laterally,

---

[16]*seventh power ... Three Children ... Twin Brother.* Cf. Book of Daniel, ch.iii.
Here I identify 'The Great Twin Brethren' at the battle of Lake Regillus
with the Second Person of the Blessed Trinity – who walked with the Three
Children in the fiery furnace.

and receded deeply,
the dark wood.

And now the gradient runs more flatly toward the separate
scarred saplings, where they make fringe for the interior thicket
and you take notice.
   There between the thinning uprights
at the margin
straggle tangled oak and flayed sheeny beech-bole, and fragile
birch whose silver queenery is draggled and ungraced
and June shoots lopt
and fresh stalks bled
       runs the Jerry trench.
And cork-screw stapled trip-wire
to snare among the briars
and iron warp with bramble weft
with meadow-sweet and lady-smock
for a fair camouflage.

Mr Jenkins half inclined his head to them — he walked just
barely in advance of his platoon and immediately to the left of
Private Ball.
   He makes the conventional sign
and there is the deeply inward effort of spent men who would
make response for him,
and take it at the double.
He sinks on one knee
and now on the other,
his upper body tilts in rigid inclination
this way and back;
weighted lanyard runs out to full tether,
         swings like a pendulum
        and the clock run down.
Lurched over, jerked iron saucer over tilted brow,
clampt unkindly over lip and chin
nor no ventaille to this darkening
      and masked face lifts to grope the air
and so disconsolate;
enfeebled fingering at a paltry strap —
buckle holds,
holds him blind against the morning.
   Then stretch still where weeds pattern the chalk predella

– where it rises to his wire[17] – and Sergeant T. Quilter takes over.

Sergeant Quilter is shouting his encouragements, you can almost hear him, he opens his mouth so wide.
Sergeant Quilter breaks into double-time
and so do the remainder.
You stumble in a place of tentacle
you seek a place made straight
you unreasonably blame the artillery
you stand waist-deep
you stand upright
you stretch out hands to pluck at Jerry wire as if it were bramble mesh.

No. 3 section inclined a little right where a sequence of 9.2's have done well their work of preparation and cratered a plain passage. They bunch, a bewildered half dozen, like sheep where the wall is tumbled – but high-perched Brandenburgers
from their leafy vantage-tops observe
that kind of folly:
nevertheless, you and one other walk alive before his parapets.

Yet a taut prehensile strand gets you at the instep, even so, and sprawls you useless to the First Objective. But Private Watcyn takes it with blameless technique, and even remembers to halloo the official blasphemies.[18]

The inorganic earth where your body presses seems itself to pulse deep down with your heart's acceleration ... but you go on living, lying with your face bedded in neatly folded, red-piped, greatcoat and yet no cold cleaving thing drives in between expectant shoulder-blades, so you get to your feet, and the sun-lit chalk is everywhere absorbing fresh stains.

Dark gobbets stiffen skewered to revetment-hurdles and

---

[17]*chalk predella ... his wire*. The approach to the German trenches here rose slightly, in low chalk ridges.
[18]*halloo the official blasphemies*. Refers to instructions given in bayonet-fighting drill. Men were cautioned to look fiercely upon the enemy when engaging him and to shout some violent word – and to not spare his genitals. This attempt to stimulate an artificial hate by parade-ground Staff-Instruction was not popular among men fresh from actual contact with the enemy.

dyed garments strung-up for a sign;
       but the sun shines also
on the living
and on Private Watcyn, who wears a strange look under his
iron brim, like a small child caught at some bravado in a garden, and old Dawes comes so queerly from the thing he saw
in the next bay but one.

But for all that it is relatively pleasant here under the first
trees and lying in good cover.

But Sergeant Quilter is already on the parados. He sorts
them out a bit
they are five of No. 1
six of No. 2
two of No. 3
four of No. 4
a lance-jack, and a corporal.

So these nineteen deploy
between the rowan and the hazel,
go forward to the deeper shades.

# HARRY W. JONES

(British Expeditionary Force)

~

## The Fallen[1]

Cold, still and stark –
A temple with its sacred lights gone dark,
A mansion whence the dweller hath ta'en flight
Into unknown, mysterious, pathless night; –
He lies; a hero fallen for the cause that *he*
  Believed was right.

If khaki-clad or grey,
Ask not. He fell is all we need to say.
His comrades who passed on and left him there
Could only breathe one brief goodbye. No care
Could they bestow on him who fell. To fall
  Was his sole share.

And on the hill
He fell, there yet he lies, cold, stark and still –
  But in the night
When all was calm and silent stars shone bright,
Methought I saw a figure by his side, –
A mother's figure, who shed tears and sighed.
But mother's sighs and tears could not into
  Those eyes bring light.

---

[1]Published in *Welsh Outlook*, April 1919, p. 102.

Harry W. Jones

Can all that War,
Or peace, may bring, bring back to her
A recompense that will tenth part outweigh
Her burning tears, her sorrow night and day?
What gains can fill her emptiness, or charm
   Her grief away?

   Vain powers on high,
The while ye talk and argue, heroes die!

# A. S. JUNIOR

~

## *We exploded a mine . . .*[1]

(SCENE: Common but always impressive, a British Citizen at breakfast, comfort and security personified. His wife is apparently reading her letters, but is really thinking out, an effective costume for the next Flag Day, so that her portrait may appear in the 'Sketch' as a 'Well-known War Worker'. Yet even here there are signs of economy. The British Citizen has given up his 'Times' and come down to the 'Daily Mail'; he has had to be content with one poached egg, and sausages have displaced the customary slices of dead pig.)

British Citizen: 'Another cup 'f coffee, Emma.'

His Wife: 'Yes, dear. Anything in the papers this morning?'

B.C.: 'Butter is up another penny a pound.'

H.W.: 'Dreadful. We'll really have to give margarine to the servants. What about the war?'

B.C.: (With the air of a man who is helping to pay £5,000,000 per day, and doesn't seem to be getting value for his money): 'There's nothin' doing in France as far as I can see. Only "We exploded a mine and occupied the crater."'

H.W.: 'Is that all?'

B.C.: 'That's all.'

There still are people at home who seem to be under the impression that the German front trenches and our own run in parallel lines from the North Sea to Switzerland. Here and

---

[1]Published in *Welsh Outlook*, May 1916, pp. 144–5.

there, near places like Ypres and Verdun, a kind of pitched battle is fought at uncertain intervals; otherwise the two sides are supposed to be sitting quietly in comparatively comfortable trenches perhaps half-a-mile apart, with nothing to do but peep at each other occasionally through periscopes. When we assure the British Citizen that fighting is going on up and down the whole front, night and day, Sunday and Saturday, the British Citizen points with childlike faith to his morning paper: it contains no mention of fighting – therefore no fighting has taken place. Could any reasoning be more conclusive? When we talk of stretches where the average distance between our front line and the Germans' is less than 100 yards, and mention points that are within 15 or 20 yards, we are listened to politely – after all we have been running some risk, and the B.C. feels that certain allowances must be made – but a slight raising of his eyebrows shows that for veracity we are being classed with fishers and golfers.

In the early months of trench warfare a fruitful topic for discussion in dug-outs and billets was, 'Whether do you prefer to be 300 yards from the Germans and shelled, or 30 yards and only bombed?' Bombs in these days were crude, uncertain articles, made out of jam tins or anything that came handy. Sometimes they burst too soon, sometimes they refused to burst at all. But we threw them with a zest unknown to the skilled bomber of today. Occasionally, instead of a jam tin bomb, we threw a tin of jam (plum and apple! My dear Watson, how on earth did you discover that?), and our friends, the enemy, would fling back a tin of (alleged) tobacco. Once I remember meeting a very angry man who had just been hit on the head by a German potato: he did not seem a bit thankful that it was not a live grenade. These irresponsible days are gone, however. We are all very much in earnest now, and into our lives there has come a new type of soldier. He walks with a perpetual stoop; often, on his face and hands and arms there are curious blue marks. (What do you say, Watson? A miner. You grow more wonderful every day.) This gentleman belongs to a Tunnelling Company RE, and in many ways he is quite unique. To begin with, he knows exactly why he is here. 'For to blow the ... up', is how he puts it in his own frank way. He has about as much use for bullets, bombs or bayonets as he would have for a battleaxe. Artillery he respects, but for 'raising a wind' he prefers to rely on 4,000 lbs or so of Poopite, his pet explosive. Before he came, there were areas which had been battered out of all recognition by heavy shells. Now, when certain parts of the front are photographed from aeroplanes, the prints are more like pictures of the moon than of France. The whole ground is pitted with craters as if there had been a violent volcanic eruption. That is all the work of the Tunnelling Company, but the miner does not go about boasting of his power, nor does he keep repeating, 'See what we done!' like certain other branches of the service. Naturally of a retiring disposition, he shuns the public gaze. He cannot understand men who from choice keep on the surface of the ground – where aerial torpedoes and grenades may drop any minute, where trench mortars, or even an oil drum, filled with rusty nails and a bursting charge, are liable to get one in the neck. So he works away in his little tunnel, down and forward, forward and down, and envies none of us our sunlight or fresh air. The trench which we have drained and revetted so carefully, he looks on as a very crude job.

Anyone, he says, could dig a hole and throw the earth about on top, to be seen by every German within miles. The miner's plans are far more subtle. Not even his nearest neighbours know the secrets of his galleries. The 'muck' excavated is put in sandbags and removed as stealthily as a burglar's swag. When nobody is looking, the bags are carefully emptied into old trenches and shell-holes. The tunneller dislikes working in chalk because the debris is so difficult to hide away. For weeks and weeks the human mole burrows on steadily. We have a vague idea that he is trying to get underneath the German parapet, though how he knows his position or the amount of earth above him, we have not the remotest notion. We also hear it rumoured that the Boche is at the same game, and that it is practically a race between the two sets of tunnellers.

One morning a Tunnelling Company subaltern comes into our HQ dug-out with a gleam in his eye. 'Do you want to see something', he says mysteriously. Always open for any new experience, we follow him into the bowels of the earth, first with shoulders bent, then on all fours; lastly, crawling like a serpent into a hole, out of which we feel morally certain we shall never emerge alive. At last the passage widens a little. The guide flashes his torch and demands silence by putting his finger to his lips. Directly overhead can be heard a faint but regular 'tap, tap'. That is enough. Once again in the open-air, the miner allows himself the luxury of a loud chuckle. 'Right below him, by gosh!' he says, thereby letting it be known that in this weird contest of mine and counter-mine his side at this particular point has the bulge on the Boche.

A day or two later, probably while we are at breakfast, a Tunnelling Officer bursts in, and whispers that he is ready to 'poop her off'. He mentions an hour tentatively. It is nothing to him that the time coincides with our relief. We point out that the exploding of a mine is apt to attract undesirable attention to the neighbourhood. That is a mere detail. What chiefly interests the miner is the size of crater that 4,000 lbs of Poopite will make. 'It will be a devil of a hole, anyway,' he concludes, and we are in no mood to contradict him. But delays are dangerous. If he waits the Germans may blow in his galleries, and spoil all his work. So we make our preparations. The artillery are warned to be ready with their barrage of fire on the correct sector; as many men as possible are withdrawn from the danger area; sandbags are doled out, bombers get ready, and machine-guns are trained on selected spots. Then, at the appointed time, the tunneller presses a button, and with a great roar, half of France seems to go up into the air. Immediately every battery in the sector, both German and British, opens fire. The Boches creep forward to the east side of the new crater and throw bombs; we creep forward to the west side and do the same. Shrapnel is bursting over every communication trench; flares go up, trench mortars, canister bombs and rifle grenades rain down. Somewhere within a hundred yards, ten, twenty or thirty strong men are dying horribly, smothered in debris – the lucky ones have been knocked out suddenly and comfortably by the explosion.

Gradually the din lessens, and the flares grow fewer. The 'wind' dies away, and in the morning, except for some scraps of German clothing and a new crater, everything is much the same as before. Aeroplanes come droning overhead, the 'heavies', begin their daily strafe, and twenty-four hours later the British Citizen reads, 'We exploded a mine ...'

That's all!

# M. J. L.

~

## *To one who fell in early youth*[1]

'And so', they say, 'think of his merry ways,
His laughing eyes that never filled with tears,
Tho' fired with passion, never drooped with fears;
The mem'ry of his smiles for ever stays.'
They know not how he loved the long warm Mays,
And talked of joys to come along the years,
As we together walked beside the meres.
'Tis I who know the love of those long days!
Tho' June is here, for me the days are sad;
So frail and fair a life he gave away,
Who freely gave, and joined the Great Array.
And now I sit and look with vacant stare,
And think of long warm Mays and joys we had;
All these to me are now but comfort bare.

---

[1]Published in *Welsh Outlook*, September 1915, p. 356.

120

# SAUNDERS LEWIS

John Saunders Lewis 'was to become the major Welsh literary figure of the twentieth century'.[1] In November 1914 he volunteered, at the age of twenty, for one of the New Army units – the 19th (Service) Battalion of the King's Liverpool Regiment. The following May he was commissioned into the 12th (3rd Gwent) South Wales Borderers, a 'Bantam' battalion[2] being formed at Newport, and went to France in June 1916.

The letters which follow were written to Margaret Gilcriest, whom he was to marry in 1924.[3]

—

**3 June 1916**
My Dear Margaret,
We left our port of landing the very next morning, and after a day and a half's train journey we find ourselves in a little village some twenty-five miles from the firing line. Here we are to spend a fortnight, and then move to another point. It is a little village in lovely country and we look forward to a very easy and pleasant time here. The battalion is in reserve here and we could not wish for a happier spot. I have a very comfortable billet, with a real

---

[1]M. S. Jones, N. Thomas, H. P. Jones (eds.), *Saunders Lewis: Letters to Margaret Gilcriest* (Cardiff: University of Wales Press, 1993), p. xvii. The extracts are taken from this volume.
[2]Bantam battalions were formed of men below the official minimum height.
[3]M. S. Jones *et al.*, *Saunders Lewis*, reproduces many more letters written 'from the day he reported to his local army camp in November 1914 until their marriage in 1924' (p. xvii).

121

bed and white sheets to sleep between. The people are accustomed to English soldiers, and already we have made friends with many.

My men are billeted in the outhouse of a little *estaminet* further up the street and I am firm friends with the little family who keep the place. They are simple, kindly people. There is an old man who does the rough work, his wife who manages, and three daughters – one married has a little boy. Two of us went there this morning, and had a lunch in the kitchen of bread, hard-boiled eggs and light wine, and the little French we had was enough to make us sound friends with the folk. They wanted to know our ages at once and then us theirs.

One of the girls, a sweet girl of twenty, had a miniature of a French soldier fastened to her neck, and told us he was her soldier.

Mingling with us in the kitchen were tiny chickens and hens and the cat, all as friendly as could be. So you see we are in for a very good time.

The only thing needed to improve it is a letter addressed to:
12th S.W.B.
British Exped. Force
France.
c/o GPO.
Give me all the 'hanes' and I'll make time for a real letter shortly.

Saunders.


*7 June 1916*
My Dear Margaret,
I think I told you we were settled now in a little French village about fifteen miles from where the guns begin, and it is here we remain, in billets, very comfortable and enjoying the new surroundings immensely.

The French people are delightful; they are, as you expect, mostly women and children, and old men, as well as a sprinkling of wounded who have been discharged or men unfit. At places we come across refugees from further east, from La Bassée and the places you see mentioned in the newspapers. What I like is their simplicity, the open intimacy of their life. They take us into their kitchens and family circles naturally. This village as one old madame said to me yesterday is governed by the English; it is English troops they have had here from the beginning of war, so that they know our ways and can put up with them.

They are kindly people, their houses are poor as you'd expect of peasants, yet bright and clean, and their food is always appetising. I sleep in a bed – in sheets that are white and sweet. We have all the comforts you have – newspapers, a few books; only the water is undrinkable, and light wines and ales are the staple drinks. *Estaminets* and cafes are everywhere, eggs are cheap and fresh every morning. Daily life is simple, gentle and pleasant. (I have added the pencil details since getting your letter this noon, hence all the particulars in reply.)

We are not working at all hard, as we're supposed to be resting – God knows after what. Nor are we likely to go up to the firing line till well into the end of next week. We get all the news daily, but as you say it is almost better without it, Kitchener gone and the North Sea fight only a very partial success. Russia is again the only bright spot.

Your letter is the best thing that has happened today. I can understand how you feel. But I am learning from these French people. With them the war is a close reality. One break in that line from where we can now hear the guns booming, and the Germans would be living with them, billeted where we are now. Yet day to day is entirely normal; danger and loss are so much closer neighbours than with those who are away; this is all. Every house here has a son or sons or father or brother, either killed, wounded, or fighting. The essentials remain the same with us as with you, and there is very little abnormal or even artificial.

With most of us the causes of anxiety are in England.

Au revoir, Margaret. (Just outside the window a tiny little girl is leading a calf to the stable quite alone.)

Yours, yours,<br>Saunders.

*On 14 June the 12th South Wales Borderers went into the trenches 'under instruction' from the 1st South Wales Borderers and the 2nd Welch Regiment.*

*In early August Saunders Lewis was sent to hospital in Boulogne, suffering from 'trench fever'. At the beginning of September he was with his battalion in a new sector (Maroc) which was graced by the Double Crassier. This was 'an immense slag heap with its butt end in the front line of the Division, from which it projected at right angles towards the enemy'.*[4] *The enemy lines were not far distant and constant vigilance was necessary. Frequent patrols were sent out. On 1 September 'a patrol consisting of Lieutenants J. S. Lewis and Enright, 2/Lt. Wingard and Sgt. Pickett went out at 10.30 p.m. to investigate the state of enemy wire on the right of the line against Crassier. They immediately discovered a strong Boche working party in front, but were able to get near enough to discover that well in front of the wire the enemy had laid a bomb netting about 5ft high and covering their front'.*[5] *Just after eight o'clock on the following evening the Germans exploded a mine and Lt. J. S. Lewis and 2/Lt. Wingard were ordered to take a party of men to Seaforth Crater. 'They did so, and entered and bombed the enemy's sap.'*[6] *Hume Saunders Wingard was to die of wounds on 20 September.*[7]

*3 October 1916*
My Dear Margaret,
    I have very little to say and this morning I'm almost too tired to say it. Being in reserve has this disadvantage that if the front trenches fall into bad condition through rain or shell, the battalion in reserve has to provide the party to repair the damage. It is always night work and a march there and back of some miles, and I was very tired when I came back in the early hours of this morning after being out since the previous evening.
    The rain has broken in on a fine spell of Indian Summer, and now we are having a sort of October mist hanging and drizzling about us like a warm moist blanket steaming. It has a strange effect on the Very lights at night. You see them shoot up from the opposite line and climb out of sight in the fog, then after a moment they fall slowly and dimly on our side and fizzle out dejectedly. There is only a little nervous spasm of machine-gun fire now and again, a trench mortar whistles away and explodes, a rat scurries over the fire-step where the sentry watches and shivers. So we wait for the daybreak.

Yours,
Saunders.

*The night of 23 October found Saunders Lewis and two soldiers out in*

---

[4]*F. E. Whitton, History of the 40th Division* (Aldershot: Gale and Polden, 1926), p. 27.
[5]Battalion War Diary.
[6]Ibid.
[7]*Officers Died in the Great War*, p. 101.

*No Man's Land, investigating the enemy's wire and sap, and gaining information 'which will be of use in the coming raid'.*[8] *During November the Borderers marched southwards by easy stages until, in late December, they went into trenches (in the Rancourt Sector of the Somme) which had recently been taken over from the French. 'Now began three months in the most God-forsaken and miserable area of France, bar, possibly, the salient of Ypres. The whole countryside was a churned-up, yeasty mass of mud, as a result of the vile weather and of the battle which even yet had not petered out. The weather was awful. Constant rain was varied by spells of intensely cold weather and some very heavy snow-falls. Mud and dirt were everywhere.'*[9]

### 4 January 1917

My Dear Margaret,

We have just come out from an eight-day tour in the trenches.

I can't hope to describe to you the mixture of horror and gro-tesque humour of this line. Nothing at all of what I have seen before of trench warfare was at all like this. In the line we held we were in shell-holes waist-high in slime, without even the semblance of a trench; dead men were as common as the living. They had died in all kinds of positions, – numbers had merely drowned, – until your attitude towards them became one of mingled tenderness and sympathy and humorous acceptance. One joked with them and often joined them.

No regiment goes twice in this line to come out more than a quarter strong. More than any fire, exposure and exhaustion drain the battalion. And German and English here cease their fight to join hands against the conditions. I am splendidly fit physically, mentally I suffer also from exposure. It has rained and frozen all thinking out of me.

You are back in Holyhead. Your letter got drowned, and I know your address is Bryngoleu Avenue and there's an Irish name to the house, I cannot remember it. So I trust to this coming your way.

My leave has been drowned also; I expect by this time my father has gone south; and my aunt for the time remains at Wilton St. Ludwig, I'm glad to know, had a week there at Christmas.

---

[8] Battalion War Diary.
[9] Whitton, *History of the 40th Division*, p. 42.

No more news; make the best of your stay home. I should not be bitter to the Sharps, were I you. It calls more for pity.

Yours,

Saunders.

*24 January 1917*

My Dear Margaret,

If it were not for the trenches these would be glorious days, with snow and ice everywhere, and bright sunshine and blue sky. But they are spoilt by this job. Our ears are too frost bitten, snow and ice are too splashed and cut up by shell, and the sky is full of aeroplanes always throbbing and ominous.

Dug-outs are very good in their way, but to think that we must be spending our leisure and finding rest and light in burrows thirty feet underground with only the flickers of candles for seeing by – when sun and snow if left alone would work us such magic ... it's the waste of richness and goodness, the vandalism of it all, even were there no blood spilt, and no actual ugliness, no positive evil or loss. And one gains nothing by it.

I remember how once I was glad to go. Particularly glad to leave you, to leave home, dreaming in my absurd young way of winning strength, character, power, conviction, – and especially depth. Well, it was like most of my dreams, but hollower than most. I have gained no more than if I'd spent three years in the rose garden at Wallasey, discussing Rousseau among the mail-carts.

However, I think I'm writing rot, so I'll shut up.

Yours, as you see, well enough to be ridiculous.

Saunders.

*6 February 1917*

My Dear Margaret,

So my letters smell like a tobacco store. And I am glad that I have been able to give you at last some real taste of the sort of place we live in. Here out of the line the officers' mess is one wood hut heated by two stoves. There is a long table running along the centre and on it candles flicker a shadowy light over the hut at night. A few men are writing letters at one end, two parties are playing bridge at the other; by the stoves, seated on forms, and stooping towards the heat, are small groups singing songs sometimes tender, sometimes indecent (in that all-accepting sort of way only men have), – and everywhere men are smoking, so that with the shadows flicked on the walls by the candle flames, and the slow columns of pipe and cigarette smoke hanging over our heads, everyone looks dim at ten yards interval.

That is our home in the evenings when out of the line, – and though it may not seem as pleasant to you thus described, I shall never forget it, never forget the faces, or the stooping backs, or the songs that express so much men's desires, men's longings and men's grossnesses, – most of them lovable things. We return to the line in four days.

And you have lived to hate Rousseau and mail-carts! Rather unfair to Jean Jacques, I think. After all, he never asked to be read among mail-carts, and he himself was far too natural and loved freedom too well to keep children in a garden where they weren't allowed to walk on the grass or touch the flowers, or run more than fifty yards from a hireling nurse. Then why blame Rousseau for your own sweet folly and my feeble compliances. I'm afraid this letter is getting garrulous, so I'll shut up.

Yours,<br>Saunders.

*The Germans began their retirement to the Hindenburg Line on 14 March. For three weeks the 12th South Wales Borderers worked on building a railway line which was being pushed forward to Péronne.*

18 March 1917
My Dear Margaret,
   I have let your birthday pass without any message at all, which is a piece of frightfulness I should not be capable of if it were not for so many months of close intercourse with the Hun; whose front garden guarded with barbed wire to depths of many yards puts our slender hedges to very shame.

We came out of the trenches two days ago and we are out for a long time. The German has as you may read gone back some way, and for many miles he has left us nor road nor track nor railway by which to supply our troops who are after him. To build these swiftly is as urgent as anything could be and we have been set some of the task.

We should prefer, of course, after having the hunnish countenance peering at us so long to have the chance of chucking things at his back and kissing his hindmost. But that is not given us as our mission, so we must be content with pioneer work.

Yours ever,<br>Saunders.

*After their railway work, the 40th Division found itself at the Hindenburg Line, and was to mount its first substantial assault. The 12th South Wales Borderers' objective was XV Ravine. Saunders Lewis was wounded in the left thigh and calf: two machine-gun bullets went through the knee, and a piece of shrapnel blew the calf of his leg away about an hour later.[10]*

*25 April 1917*
My Dear Margaret,
    Present address is:
        No. 2 Red Cross Hospital
        A.P.O. 2
        B.E.F.
        France.
    Am doing splendidly. Hope to be in England in a few weeks. Hospital's very nice.

Saunders.

---

[10] M. S. Jones *et al.*, *Saunders Lewis*, p. 256.

# OSCAR LLOYD

~

### 'Going West'[1]

(Army euphemism for dying)

I've seen the graves among the trees that used to shade Le
                    Gheer,
The cemeteries that lie around the billets in the rear,
The little mounds beside the trench, the cross upon the wall,
The corpses out in No Man's Land (they lie there as they fall).

The bodies keep the Flanders clay, the chalk pits of the
                    South;
The eyes are closed with heavy earth, there's dust upon the
                    mouth;
The poppies flame above them, but they do not heed the
                    dance
Of English flowers that cover them upon the fields of France.

At night I stare out in the dusk, until I'm almost blind,
And shadows steal long the trench, and fill my empty mind.
With murmuring ghosts who haunt it till the visions
                    disappear,
Of lads who lie in Flanders, but whose hearts are far from
                    here.

---

[1]Published in *Welsh Outlook* January 1919, p.11.

129

*Wales on the Western Front*

A wind blows from the East at dawn, the sunrise holds the
sky,
We stand to arms so silently we hear the souls go by.
They fill the air, and clamour past upon the Western breeze;
They shake the branches as they pass, and ruffle up the seas.

The moor and mountain call to them, they know their ancient
rocks,
The green fields of the valley lands are rich for them with
flocks.

They'll make the sunlight warm for us, and meet us in the
rain
'Gone West' in many an alien land, they all come west again.

# MONMOUTHSHIRE TERRITORIALS

After mobilization, the 3rd Battalion of the Monmouthshire Regiment spent time at Pembroke, Oswestry and Northampton before arriving, 1,020 strong, at Le Havre (on 15 February, 1915). The letters below[1] describe the men's experiences in the trenches of Flanders, the mining of Hill 60, and the decimation of the battalion during the second battle of Ypres (22 April to 25 May, 1915).

—

## Private Harry Roach

I am writing this letter because I have an idea our doings will interest you, and as it may be my last opportunity of writing to you, life is so uncertain, especially out here. Well, I'll come back to our trip across. We were anchored just opposite Netley Hospital[2] for a night, as the sea was too rough for the transport to start out. It was in the night that we finally left dear old England behind. Everything went well for a time, and we all thought we were good sailors. We were not allowed to smoke below deck.

---

[1]The letters were originally published in local newspapers, and have been collected in Janet Dixon and John Dixon (eds.), *With Rifle and Pick* (Cardiff: Cwm Press, 1991). The additional comments are by the original text editors.

[2]Netley – between Southampton and Hamble – was the home of the Welsh Hospital, which was set up on the recreation ground near the Royal Victoria Hospital. The Welsh Hospital had come into being on the initiative of Dr James Robinson, Lord Mayor of Cardiff. The cost was met by voluntary donations from private individuals, villages, towns and various organizations. It received its first patients (104 of them) on 26 October 1914 (B. Owen, 'The Welsh Hospital – The Great War', *Bulletin of the Military Historical Society*, Vol. 43, No. 169 (August 1992), pp. 36–9).

Some very good discipline was carried out in embarking. Well, as we got further out in the Channel the number of men who were allowed to lean over the rails on the deck increased, and some of the boys never reached the top deck. They were lying at all angles between decks, and by now all of them had empty stomachs. We landed at (Le Havre) at quite an early hour on February 15th and a number of little French boys were on the quay to welcome us, and they were singing 'It's a long way to Tipperary', and, mind you, their English was not at all bad. They followed us on our first march on French soil, asking for 'Ingleesh bisceets' and souvenirs. We parted with our first souvenirs here, and the French lasses smiled and shouted out 'Bon-jour, monsieur'. We were marched to a hillside camp where we spent the first night under canvas; we were sixteen in a tent. We woke in the morning to find we were to go on the march again. It was nothing after we had handed in our blankets that we were on the march to the station, where we stayed until 7.30 p.m., when we were herded into ordinary cattle trucks, 40 and upwards in a truck. All this was new experience to us, the first real taste of being on active service. We travelled for 24 hours before we had the order to detrain, but we were now nearer the actual doings.

We could hear the crack of guns. Then again we were on the march. The roads here are paved with square stones, and we marched until we reached Cassel. Our feet were weary of these beastly roads. Then we were put in different billets. Early in the morning we were off again on these terrible roads, and we marched until we could see the town of Steenwoorde. This place had a taste of the Germans early in the war, and some of our soldiers had driven them out. We stayed here about ten days. The churches are really fine, especially the artistic work inside. We were rather sorry to leave this town, but on the 28th February we packed up and were off again. This time we soon got on a good country road, and after five or six miles we had the experience of being picked up by London omnibuses. The Battalion is about a thousand strong and we were 36 in each 'bus, so I leave you to calculate what a sight this was for all of us. One long stream of 'buses, only half a dozen yards apart, pushing on towards the terrible trenches. We were continually passing depots of supplies, and all sorts of petrol driven vehicles, and even wagons, bearing names of English firms. We also passed some of the Canadians. On we went until we had the order to get out. We had reached quite the biggest town so far. This place was full of British Tommies who had come here for a rest, after their turn in the trenches. We were billeted in farm barns, where we heard shameful stories of the enemy's doings. We only spent one night here, and were off again, it now being 1st March, and we were again in barns and near the trenches.

We can now hear the continual rifle fire, while the big guns are all around us and are sending their messages all day to our friends the Germans. It was the 11th March, and we have been in the trenches for the first period of duty. I'll try never to forget that night. The bullets whistled out their notes, yet the sound of these carriers of death is rather bewitching – at least they were to me – but all the same it was with a sigh of relief that we had all got right into the trenches without anyone being hit, which seemed to be a miracle. During the night the Germans kept us quite busy, and at daybreak I had a peep over the parapet to see what was about, when I found their line of trenches was only about 400 yards away. Well, we were ordered to 'stand to', but the crafty and clever Germans had found us out from a range of about 6,000 yards. Their artillery was deadly, and soon a farm occupied by a regiment was hit twice or three times; then their shells came so near that they dropped on our support trenches, which were about 80 yards behind us. I thought every minute my number was up. Then our artillery opened fire on them, and the shells we sent them dropped right in their lines. It was a duel between the guns, and I think I am right in saying that our guns won the duel. The firing got less and less, and, their visit to us was postponed. It was an interesting day, because you mustn't forget it was our baptismal day, and the dear old boys of Aber. behaved like Britons.[3]

(The large town the battalion stayed in for ten days was Bailleul. 1485 Pte Harry Roach was wounded in action on 5th May 1915 and died the following day.)

---

[3]*Abergavenny Chronicle*, 14 May 1915.

## *Private D. C. James, to his home*

We went in all right with a few narrow escapes. Next day the Germans shelled us terribly. The shells were dropping about a hundred yards from us then a bit to our right, which was worse; then they came nearer the trenches, afterwards into a village which was all in ruins, and all that was left standing was the poor church steeple, and that has been knocked down now. The officer who was in charge of us asked for a volunteer to guard from six to six while the other fellows were digging trenches. Well about midnight something started the Germans and they let go rapid fire and as I was walking down the trench a bullet caught my bayonet which gave me a bit of a fright, I own. After it had stopped one of the regulars who was in the trenches with us came in and I told him; he said that very likely it was my bayonet shining over the parapet that had done it, because I had my rifle slung over my shoulder so after that I did not. It is nothing to hear a bullet whizz and then fall with a plop in the mud in front of you. We were mixed up with the Regulars that forty-eight hours; it was only 'A' Company that went up that time.[4]

## *Private William Dallimore, to his parents*

I suppose you have heard about us being in the trenches. I can tell you it is a funny experience the first time, but you soon get used to it. We don't mind the bullets so much as the shells. I can tell you they make you feel a bit creepy as you are waiting, not knowing where the next one is going to drop. We have lost a couple of men but I suppose we must expect that out here, but thank God, I am safe so far, and I hope to continue the same so that I can come back to spend a day or two with you again. The weather gets a little warmer out here and a good job too as it is very cold in the trenches by night.[5]

(Private William Dallimore was killed in action on the 11th May 1915. He had been living in Cwm at the time of his enlistment into the 3rd Monmouths.)

---

[4] *Abergavenny Chronicle*, 2 April 1915.
[5] *Abergavenny Chronicle*, 9 April 1915.

## Sergeant-Major T. E. Banks

(Letter dated 19 March 1915)

We have just come out of the trenches. We went in last Friday, so we have had our fair share of it ... I am pleased to tell you I have just been congratulated for bringing a wounded man out of the trenches and taking him back to the dressing station – a mile back – in broad daylight and above all who do you think it was – Young Pocock. He was with another sergeant in a support trench, behind my fire trench and he got shot right through – the bullet passing through his lung. This was in the morning, 9 a.m. He would have died if he had been left until night, so I crawled out under fire to where he was, dressed his wound and crawled to let my Captain know ... a chap belonging to the King's Own volunteered to come back to the support trenches with me. We had no stretchers, so we took a brush wood fascine from one trench back with us ... the task was to get him out. So two more of the boys – Dan Skinner and Sullivan – volunteered to come back to our headquarters with us, so we started out. We had not gone far when the Germans opened a heavy fire on us, so we dropped down in a ditch and the fascine being so heavy, we made a stretcher out of two branches and our putties, and managed to get him away all right.[6]

(Private George Pocock died of his wounds on the 28 March; he was just sixteen. Private William Sullivan was killed in action during 2nd Ypres. The Captain of 'B' company at the time was Captain R. O. Gardner who was also killed during 2nd Ypres.)

## The Mining of Hill 60

(Letter from an NCO of the 1st Battalion (believed to be Sergeant D. Evans).)

It was a cold raw morning in February when a party of Monmouthshire 'Terriers' left 'Somewhere in France' in motor omnibuses, under the command of Lieutenant W. B. Burnyeat and

---

[6]*Abergavenny Chronicle*, 30 April 1915.

Lieutenant Lancaster to undertake the difficult task of mining the now historic Hill 60. After a few hours run we were dropped a few miles from the town of Ypres to which we had to march. We moved into our billet and made ourselves as comfortable as circumstances allowed. The same night ten selected NCOs and men proceeded to the hill to survey the position under the guidance of the Northumbrian Engineers who were commanded by Major Pollard DSO. The soil was of a soft sandy clay, giving off a good deal of water. After some discussion Major Pollard selected the site for our first mine. It was arranged to work in shifts and the party was divided accordingly. The idea was to sink a vertical shaft in our trench from which we were to tunnel under the German lines.

To accomplish this it was necessary to go down to a depth of about 16 feet. Owing to the soft nature of the soil and the amount of water this proved a very difficult and tedious operation.

The whole of the party were Monmouthshire miners and were accustomed to working in a small space, but this task proved a severe test of our ability.

Our first attempt proved a failure, but Lieutenant Burnyeat who, by the way, has a good deal of experience in the South Wales Coalfield, selected another site, and we set to work determined to succeed. Our second attempt was brought to a successful issue, with the aid of good pumps which enabled us to overcome the water. The work was rendered more difficult owing to the continual bombardment of our trenches by the German artillery.

Every description of shell was hurled over our heads but luckily our mines were not damaged. When we were ready to commence tunnelling Lieutenant Lancaster was wounded and Lieutenant Burnyeat took charge of the whole party.

The tunnelling proved a difficult operation, but with skilful workmanship it was overcome. To enable the men to work in atmosphere free from gas, a small fan was rigged up, from which the air was conveyed by means of small pipes.

On March 12th the enemy exploded a mine in the vicinity of our abandoned mines. Anticipating a rush, the men were withdrawn from the mines to assist the Liverpool Scottish to repel the attack. The experience gained in first aid in the Welsh mines now stood the miners in good stead, as they were able to render yeoman service to the stretcher bearers in attending to the wounded. Thus we worked and fought alternately.

On March 16th we were informed that the Germans were counter mining. Three shifts were arranged, and the situation made clear to the men. This put us all on our mettle and we put forth every effort to get there first. The result is now a matter of history.

On March the 18th Colonel Robinson, who commanded the first Battalion Mons., came to inspect our work. He congratulated all concerned and impressed upon us the importance of the work. While relieving the same night Lieutenant Burnyeat was badly wounded in the thigh and I was left in charge of the party. About the 20th Lieutenant Hill took over command of the party under the direction of Major Pollard DSO. We had several officers, after this, among whom was Major Griffiths of the 171st Company RE who very cleverly directed operations.

On April 1st we found that the enemy's mines were in close proximity to ours so our efforts were increased in our endeavour to outpace them. From the 1st to the 10th was the most exciting period of my life, coupled with anxiety. The men worked like Trojans, knowing the tremendous issue at stake. We had the tunnels completed by the 10th and then we were busily engaged in carrying explosives to charge them.

Tons of explosives were carried up through the communicating trenches from the dumping ground in the rear. The nature of our work may be better realised if I state that a regiment going into the trenches to relieve another considered themselves fortunate if they didn't lose more than 50 men.

The approaches to our communication trenches were being continually shelled, and a few points were under machine gun fire. The officers carried the detonators in their pockets, and the men the explosives on their shoulders. One mishap, and we should all be hurled to eternity.

The strain during this period became almost unbearable, but with the tenacity of the British bulldog we stuck to it. By the 15th the chambers were charged and the wires laid ready for the order to let them off.

During the period of waiting for the orders the mines were zealously guarded, the wire and fuse were examined every two hours. This meant a man having to get into the mine, thereby running the risk of being buried alive in the event of the enemy finding our mines and exploding them. We could now hear them working overhead, which made us anxious to see our mines off.

In all there were six mines laid under the hill, and at 7 p.m. on April 17th the first mine went up, to be followed in rapid succession by the remaining five. What was once a German trench was now a mass of broken earth, among which were the mangled bodies of the German brutes.

Never will I forget the feeling of relief which I felt when the hill went up, and the satisfaction it caused among the men who had laboured so hard and faced so many dangers to destroy one of the strongest positions in the German line. Each man proved himself a hero, and when the full history will be written by an abler pen than mine, the collier boys of Monmouthshire will receive the credit which up to the present has not been published.[7]

## Corporal G. C. Powis, Regimental Bootmaker

(A letter to a friend in Northampton describes events at Ypres.)

It is enough to make anyone bad out here. It is hell on earth. We are at a point in the line I should term the death trap of the Western Front. We were in a bombardment for two days and nights last week. It was like hell let loose. I thought my time had come, but God was good. The first night the shelling seemed to tear the sky to pieces. It was awful to see the horses lying dead about the streets during the first two days. There were about two hundred killed and wounded in the town. One piece of the German shrapnel cut one of our boys clean off the back of a limber that had just come back from the trenches, and one of their shells also killed two of the 1st Mons. that were guarding a canal bridge. It is a sight to see some of the holes their 17 inch shells made, you could put a whole house in one. It must have been a lovely place before the war, now it is one mass of ruins. Our boys are still in the trenches; this is the 14th day in for them this time. I am expecting them out tomorrow night. Up to now the last 14 days we have lost about sixty killed and wounded. We have just received some cigarettes from the 'Abergavenny Chronicle' fund.[8]

---

[7]*South Wales Daily News*, 15 November 1915.
[8]*Abergavenny Chronicle*, 14 May 1915.

## *Private E. H. Peake, Stretcher Bearer*

(Letter dated 21st June 1915.)

I can claim by this time I have had considerable experience of active service. I must also say that we have been highly praised as regards our behaviour. After we left England, and crossed the Herring pond we disembarked at ... and spent one night in a rest camp. Next day we took a first class cattle train for the front, and it shook us up a little, but we were none the worse for that. We had not long to wait until we were in the trenches for the first taste. We were put in with the Welsh – a regular regiment, for training, and it was then that we received the name of 'the Mad Mons'. Our casualties during our first time were only slight. The following Sunday was Palm Sunday, and with the help of Sergeant Major Baxter we got some roots from a deserted priest's garden and kept the day good by decorating our comrades' graves in such a manner that they were equal to any graves in the old country. We left for a rest in a town in northern France. It rained in torrents and we were inspected by General Smith-Dorrien, who, after the inspection commended us on our work. He told us we were to be attached to the Brigade and were to leave and proceed to Egypt; but our Egypt turned out to be our present situation, which we were taken to in some London motor-buses, and we were again landed in the trenches. On this occasion we relieved the French. After this we left for a large town in Belgium where we stayed in an asylum – which suited our name of 'Mad Mons' well. This was the town which the Mons defended and where they won honours that will stick to them for ever. We proceeded to the trenches under a heavy bombardment. We had a very hot time of it on May the 8th. We were bombarded from 2 in the morning until the night. It was the heaviest bombardment in the world's history. Well, on the morning we were having a rest from carrying our comrades down, when all of a sudden they discovered our dressing station and landed a few of their shells into the roof, which set on fire, and we had our work cut out clearing the wounded out in the open. We had to carry on our work of dressing the wounded out on the road, which was very rough, as Fritz was sending his Jack Johnson's and coal boxes all down the road.

We continued our work there until it became too hot and then we retired to a lower dressing station. It was then that our medical officer himself got wounded, but he wanted to get off

the stretcher to bandage some of our boys up. He was brought
down to the dressing station, and we had not been there half
an hour before they sent some of their poisonous gas shells
over us. I must say in closing that the Germans seem to be
delighted in doing anything which is inhuman. When General
French inspected us he said he was more than pleased with us,
as we had been engaged in the thickest fighting.[9]

(The forward dressing station had been at Verlorenhoek and the
MO was Lieutenant McLean. The nick-name of the Mad Mons
was given to the battalion early in their service and although
the above letter suggests it was given by the Welch Regiment
it has also been suggested that it arose as a result of the successful mining of Hill 60 by Monmouths after the RE had met
with little success.)

## *Private W. H. Badham*

(A letter to Private R. Jones, who had been wounded and was
in hospital in Leeds.)

Glad to hear you have come through all right. Sorry for poor
Ish, but he had it bad, poor chap. I expect you know about Will
Bevan; he was always with me. Well, he got killed the same
day as you were wounded. He was near you when you got hit.
He ran right into one of the 'whizz bangs' and got killed with
another man. Well, old pal, you say that the people of Northampton and Tredegar think a lot of the 3rd Mons. Yes they do.
We had orders from the General. The Germans broke through
the French lines on our left and just got to Ypres – that was a
few days after you got wounded; but we drove them back. Then
we had the orders to retire in the night and the Germans did
not know that we had gone. You know the dugouts – the two
big ones that were timbered. Well, we went further back than
that, up to the railway line, so we gave them about two miles or
more. We did not go into the trenches there but the East Yorks
did, and we went back to the dugouts, but we only stayed one
night, because the Germans, after they found out that we had
gone, came down; but they lost hundreds of men, and when
they got about 500 yards away they used their gas. That was

---

[9]*Abergavenny Chronicle*, 16 June 1915.

where we lost a lot of our men. We had orders to go up and reinforce the East Yorks owing to their being gassed. Our boys had to go up in daylight, right in the open, so you can tell that they lost a lot. The shells were dropping amongst us like hailstones, and they had their maxim guns on us, but that did not stop the gallant 3rd Mons. We got to the trenches and the gas was all but coming over us. The sight we saw there was awful. The trench was full of dead, and we had to bury them in the night – not a very good job. That would be about the 2nd and 3rd of May. We lost about a company in that advance, and then the fight started in the morning. Their guns opened fire at about half past 4, and shell after shell came all but in the trenches. They put all the shells you could think of, from the 'whizz bang' to the Jack Johnson. We had a lot of men buried in the trench, and had to dig another one behind, because we could not get the fellows out. We could see reinforcements coming up to them, and I expected an attack, but it did not come off; that was the 7th of May. The 8th was the day I shall never forget.

They started bombarding the same time in the morning, and about half an hour afterwards we could hear a long blast of a whistle, and the attack started. We were only a handful of men, and they came on in thousands, but we kept them at bay; but I knew we would have to give way before long. The fellows on our left and right were retiring and we had orders to do the same, but we did not go until we put some more shots into them. It was in the retirement that we lost a lot of men. They were bayoneting our wounded that we had to leave behind. Well, we got back to our second line of trenches, and reinforcements came up. After that I don't know what happened. I went to hospital with shrapnel in my back and a big bruise on my shoulders and the gas in my eyes, but I heard that our fellows drove them back with heavy losses until they shouted for mercy. Well old pal, I hope you will get your discharge and get home. If you should go up and see my mother, she will be glad to see you. Keep the letter and show it to her. Well, about myself. I am coming on all right. I expect I shall be home next week. I am in a fine place – a big gentleman's house.[10]

(W. H. Badham was killed in action on 24th March 1918. He was then a sergeant serving with the 9th Welsh. Private William

---

[10]*Abergavenny Chronicle*, 16 July 1915.

Bevan was killed in action 26.4.15. The reference to 'Ish' is thought to refer to 1362 Private Ishmael Evans who died of wounds on 28.4.15.)

## *Lance-Corporal J. McCarthy to his mother in Tredegar*

This is after 22 days of solid fighting. We have had it this time I can tell you. We went into the trenches and you know what happened: I thought that was 'hell upon earth', but what we have been through since is heartbreaking. It started like this. We had been in the trenches 17 days when we had the order to go to another part. We had about seven hours' rest, when we had the order to go up to the trenches to help another regiment in broad daylight. Our company went up. We had not gone far when the Germans spotted us. They shelled us and used that rotten gas on us and their Maxim guns. Our poor fellows fell like sheep. The Captain and I got to the trenches, and we had it hot and heavy, I can tell you. Little did we think we were coming through all that. When we got to the trenches we made up for our poor fellows. We gave them all they gave us and a lot more, but that was not the last of it. On the 7th they opened fire on us at 6.30 a.m., and if ever 'hell was on earth' it was that day. Our poor fellows were gassed first; then they were driven out of the trenches; then it was God help us − our poor fellows were falling all around us. They stuck to it to the last, until we could go no longer. The sight I shall not forget. You could see nothing but masses of fire all along the line. Fancy about 200 guns playing on you for about twelve solid hours. How we got back alive God only knows. I have thanked him I can tell you. Then they were not satisfied at gassing, as they were sticking bayonets in our wounded. Our major and about fifty men tried to take them but we failed. But it was only for a time. We got reinforced by a couple of thousand men and we gave them what they wanted. By God you should have seen them running. I can tell you there were heaps of their dead lying about, as we took no pity on them. If I was to tell you all of our boys that have gone under it would take up a lot of paper. The two Gravenors are wounded.[11]

---

[11]*South Wales Argus*, 20 May 1915.

# SIEGFRIED SASSOON

After an education at Marlborough and Clare College, Cambridge, Siegfried Sassoon hunted, played cricket and wrote poetry. In August 1914 he enlisted in the Sussex Yeomanry, being commissioned into the Royal Welch Fusiliers in May 1915. In November he joined the 1st Battalion in France where he became known as 'Mad Jack' because of his disregard for his own safety, and was awarded the Military Cross. He became increasingly disillusioned with the war and, whilst convalescing in Britain in the summer of 1917, formulated a statement which included the words: 'I believe that the War is being deliberately prolonged by those who have the power to end it ... I believe that this War, upon which I entered as a war of defence and liberation, has now become a war of aggression and conquest.' Copies of the statement were sent to several well-known people; it was read out in the House of Commons and printed in *The Times*.

He was not brought before a court martial but was persuaded, by Robert Graves, to attend a medical board which sent him to a hospital for shell-shocked officers. On 26 November 1917 he was deemed to be fit for further service and was sent first to Ireland, and then to Palestine. On 13 July 1918 he was wounded in the head, leaving the army officially in March 1919. *Memoirs of An Infantry Officer* appeared in 1930, and is the source of the two following passages.[1] People appearing in the book were all given a *nom de guerre*, and his regiment became the 'Flintshire Fusiliers'.

~

## Corps Rest

Although the War has been described as the greatest event in history, it could be tedious and repetitional for an ordinary Infantry Officer like myself.

---

[1]Published by Faber and Faber, 1930.

From Corbie Station the War had started me on my home journey in a Hospital Train. Rather more than seven months later, at midnight, it again deposited me at Corbie Station after eight hours in an unlit and overcrowded carriage which had no glass in its windows. My valise was on a truck and though I made a scrambling attempt to get it unloaded the train clanked away into the gloom with all my belongings on board. We slept on the floor of the Field Ambulance Hut outside the station; my companions grumbled a good deal, for several of them were out again after being wounded last year, and one of them claimed to have been hit in both lungs. Two cadet-officers were going with me to the Second Battalion, but I had little in common with them except our lost valises, which were returned to us a week later (with one sample of everything abstracted by someone at the Army Service Corps Dump). Next morning, after glumly congratulating myself that I'd packed my safety razor in my haversack, I walked to my new unit, which was seven miles away. I was wearing my best friends, a pair of greased marching boots whose supple strength had never failed to keep the water out; how much those boots meant to me can only be understood by persons who have shared my type of experience; I can only say that they never gave me sore feet; and if this sounds irrelevant, I must remind the reader that a platoon commander's feet were his fortune.

The Second Battalion of the Flintshire Fusiliers had recently returned from two months in the Cléry sector of the Somme Front, where they had endured some of the severest weather of the War. Battalion records relate that there were no braziers in the trenches, fuel was so scarce that wooden crosses were taken from casual graves, and except for the tepid tea that came up in tins wrapped in straw, food was mostly cold. Major-General Whincop, who commanded the Division, had made himself obnoxiously conspicuous by forbidding the Rum Ration. He was, of course, over anxious to demonstrate his elasticity of mind, but the 'No Rum Division' failed to appreciate their uniqueness in the Expeditionary Force. He also thought that smoking impaired the efficiency of the troops and would have liked to restrict their consumption of cigarettes. General Whincop had likewise demonstrated his independence of mind earlier in the War by forbidding the issue of steel helmets to his Division. His conservative objection (which was based on a belief that this new War Office luxury would weaken the men's fighting spirit – 'make them soft', in fact) was, of course, only a flash in the pan (or brain-pan) and Whincop's reputation as an innovator was mainly kept alive by his veto on the Rum Ration. GOCs, like platoon commanders, were obliged to devise 'stunts' to show their keenness, and opportunities for originality were infrequent. But since 1918 Generals have received their full share of ridicule and abuse, and it would not surprise me if someone were to start a Society for the Prevention of Cruelty to Great War Generals. If such a Society were formed, I, for one, would gladly contribute my modest half-guinea per annum; for it must be remembered that many an unsuccessful General had previously been the competent Colonel of an Infantry Battalion, thereby earning the gratitude and admiration of his men.

Anyhow, the frost had been intense, and owing to the rationing of coal in England the issue to the Army had been limited and coke-issues had caused many cases of coke-fume poisoning where the men slept in unventilated dug-outs. After this miserable experience (which had ended with a thaw and a hundred cases of trench-feet) the Second Battalion was now resting at Camp 13, about two miles from Morlancourt. The huts of Camp 13 had been erected since last summer; they disfigured what I had formerly known as an inoffensive hollow about half a mile from the reedy windings of the Somme. No one had a good word for the place. The Battalion was in low spirits because the Colonel had been wounded a few weeks before, and he had been so popular that everyone regarded him as irreplaceable. His successor was indulgent and conciliatory, but it seemed that greater aggressiveness would have been preferable. Contrasting him with the rough-tongued efficiency of Kinjack, I began to realize that, in a Commanding Officer, amiability is not enough.

Meanwhile we were in what was called 'Corps Reserve', and Colonel Easby had issued the order 'carry on with platoon training' (a pronouncement which left us free to kill time as best we could). No. 8 Platoon, which was my own compact little command, was not impressive on parade. Of its thirty-four NCOs and men, eight were Lewis gunners and paraded elsewhere. Eight was likewise the number of Private Joneses in my platoon, and my first difficulty was to differentiate between them. The depleted Battalion had been strengthened by a draft from England, and these men were mostly undersized, dull-witted, and barely capable of carrying the heavy weight of their equipment. As an example of their proficiency, I can say that in one case platoon training began with the man being taught how to load his rifle. Afterwards I felt that he would have been less dangerous in his pre-existing ignorance.

It was difficult to know what to do with my bored and apathetic platoon. I wasn't a competent instructor, and my sergeant was conscientious but unenterprising. *Infantry Training*, which was the only manual available, had been written years before trench-warfare 'came into its own' as a factor in world affairs, and the condensed and practical *Handbook for the Training of Platoons* was not issued until nearly twelve months afterwards. One grey afternoon, when we had gone through all our monotonous exercises and the men's eyes were more than usually mindless, I had a bright unmilitary idea and ordered them to play hide-and-seek among some trees. After a self-conscious beginning they livened up and actually enjoyed themselves. When I watched them falling in again with flushed and jolly faces I was aware that a sense of humanity had been restored to them, and realized how intolerable the ordinary exercises were unless the instructor was an expert. Even football matches were impossible, since there was no suitable ground.

The main characteristics of Camp 13 were mud and smoke. Mud was everywhere. All the Company officers lived in one long gloomy draughty hut with an earth floor. Smoke was always drifting in from the braziers of the adjoining kitchen. After dark we sat and shivered in our 'British Warm' coats, reading, playing cards, and writing letters with watering eyes by the feeble glimmer of guttering candles. Orderlies brought in a clutter of tin mugs and plates, and Maconochie stew was consumed in morose discomfort. It was an existence which suffocated all pleasant thoughts; nothing survived except animal cravings for warmth, food, and something to break the monotony of Corps Rest routine.

## On the March

We had halted on some high ground above Pont Noyelles: I can remember the invigorating freshness of the air and the delicate outlines of the landscape towards Amiens, and how I gazed at a line of tall trees by the river beyond which not two miles away, was the village of Bussy where I'd been last June before the Somme battle began. At such a moment as that the War felt quite a friendly affair and I could assure myself that being in the Infantry was much better than loafing about at home. And at the second halt I was able to observe what a pleasant picture the men made, for some of them were resting in warm sunlight under a crucifix and an old apple-tree. But by midday the march had become tedious; the road was dusty, the sun glared down on us, and I was occupied in preventing exhausted men from falling out. It was difficult to keep some of them in the ranks, and by the time we reached Villers-Bocage (nearly fourteen miles from Corbie) I was pushing two undersized men along in front of me, another one staggered behind hanging on to my belt, and the Company Sergeant-Major was carrying three rifles as well as his own. By two o'clock they were all sitting on dirty straw in a sun-chinked barn, with their boots and socks off. Their feet were the most important part of them, I thought, as I made my sympathetic inspection of sores and blisters. The old soldiers grinned at me philosophically, puffing their Woodbines. It was all in the day's work, and the War was the War. The newly-joined men were different; white and jaded, they stared up at me with stupid trusting eyes. I wished I could make things easier for them, but I could do nothing beyond sending a big batch of excruciating boots to the Battalion boot-menders, knowing that they'd come back roughly botched, if anything were done to them at all. But one Company's blisters were a small event in the procession of sore feet that was passing through Villers-Bocage. The woman in my billet told me in broken English that troops had been going through for fifteen days, never stopping more than one night and always marching towards Doullens and Arras. My only other recollection of Villers-Bocage is the room in which our company's officers dined and slept. It contained an assortment of stuffed and mouldy birds with outspread wings. There was a stork, a jay, and a sparrow-hawk; also a pair of squirrels. Lying awake on the tiled floor I could watch a seagull suspended by a string from the ceiling; very slowly it revolved in the draughty air; and while it revolved I fell asleep, for the day had been a long one.

Next day's march took us to Beauval, along a monotonous eight-mile stretch of the main road from Amiens to St Pol. Wet snow was falling all the way. We passed into another 'Army area'; the realm of Rawlinson was left behind us and our self-sacrificing exertions were now to be directed by Allenby. Soon after entering the Allenby Area we sighted a group of mounted officers who had stationed themselves under the trees by the roadside. Word was passed back that it was the Corps Commander. Since there were only three Corps Commanders in each Army they were seldom seen, so it was with quite a lively interest that we put ourselves on the alert to eyes-left this one. While we were trudging stolidly nearer to the great man, Colonel Easby detached himself from the head of the column, rode up to the General, and saluted hopefully. The Corps Commander (who was nothing much to look at, for his interesting accumulation of medal-ribbons was concealed by a waterproof coat) ignored our eyes-lefting of him; he was too busy bellowing at poor Colonel Easby, whom he welcomed thus. C.C. 'Are you stuck to that bloody horse?' Col. E. 'No, sir.' (Dismounts hastily and salutes again.) As Leake's Company went by, the General was yelling something about why the hell hadn't the men got the muzzles of their rifles covered (this being one of his 'special ideas'). 'Pity he don't keep his own muzzle covered,' remarked someone in the ranks, thereby voicing a prevalent feeling. The Corps Commander was equally abusive because the 'Cookers' were carrying brooms and other utilitarian objects. Also the Companies were marching with fifty yard intervals between them (by a special order of the late Rawlinson). In Allenby's Army the intervals between Companies had to be considerably less, as our Colonel was now finding out. However, the episode was soon behind us and the 'Cookers' rumbled peacefully on their way, brooms and all, emitting smoke and stewing away at the men's dinners. Very few of us ever saw the Corps Commander again. It was a comfort to know that Allenby, at any rate, could be rude to him if he wanted to.

We started from Beauval at four o'clock on a sunny afternoon and went another eight miles to a place called Lucheux ... There is nothing in all this, the reader will expostulate. But there was a lot in it, for us. We were moving steadily nearer to the Spring Offensive; for those who thought about it the days had an ever intensifying significance. For me, the idea of death made everything seem vivid and valuable. The War could be like that to a man, until it drove him to drink and suffocated his finer apprehensions.

Among the troops I observed a growing and almost eager expectancy; their cheerfulness increased; something was going to happen to them; perhaps they believed that the Arras Battle would end the War. It was the same spirit which had animated the Army before the Battle of the Somme. And now, once again, we could hear along the horizon that blundering doom which bludgeoned armies into material for military histories. 'That way to the Sausage Machine!' some old soldier exclaimed as we passed a signpost marked *Arras, 32 k.* We were entering Doullens with the brightness of the setting sun on our faces. As we came down the hill our second-in-command (a gentle middle-aged country solicitor) was walking beside me, consoling himself with reminiscences of cricket and hunting.

Thus the Battalion slogged on into an ominous Easter, and every man carried his own hazardous hope of survival. Overshadowed by the knowledge of what was ahead of us, I became increasingly convinced that a humble soldier holding up a blistered foot could have greater dignity than a blustering Corps Commander.

That night we were in huts among some wooded hills. I can remember how we had supper out in the moonlight sitting round a brazier with plates of ration stew on our knees. The wind was from the east and we could hear the huge bombardment up at Arras. Brown and leafless, the sombre woods hemmed us in. Soon the beeches would be swaying and quivering with the lovely miracle of spring. How many of us will return to that, I wondered, forgetting my hatred of the War in a memory of all that April had ever meant for me ...

On Good Friday morning I woke with sunshine streaming in at the door and broad Scots being shouted by some Cameronians in the next hut. Someone was practising the bagpipes at the edge of the wood, and a mule contributed a short solo from the Transport Lines.

On Saturday afternoon we came to Saulty, which was only ten miles from Arras and contained copious indications of the Offensive, in the form of ammunition and food dumps and the tents of a Casualty Clearing Station. A large YMCA canteen gladdened the rank and file, and I sent my servant there to buy a pack full of Woodbines for an emergency which was a certainty. Canteens and *estaminets* would be remote fantasies when we were in the devastated area. Twelve dozen packets of Woodbines in a pale green cardboard box were all that I could store up for the future consolation of B Company; but they were better than nothing and the box was no weight for my servant to carry.

149

# EDWARD THOMAS

Although Philip Edward Thomas was born in London, his parents were Welsh – his father from Tredegar and his mother from Newport.[1] He was brought up in a Welsh atmosphere 'where Welsh servants and mother's helps came and went'[2] and spent a good deal of time in Wales and the Marches, with his mother's relatives in the border counties and his father's at Pontarddulais. Edward Thomas was at Oxford from 1897 to 1900, marrying Helen Noble in June 1899. Apart from a short period as assistant secretary to the new Royal Commission on Ancient Monuments in Wales, he earned a living by writing and reviewing, becoming a friend of W. H. Davies, Robert Frost, Walter de la Mare and Arthur Ransome. Twenty-seven of his poems had been published before his death.

On 14 July 1915 he joined the Artists' Rifles.[3] He was almost thirty-seven years old and married, with three children aged fourteen, twelve and four. Edward Thomas became a Lance-Corporal instructor at Hare Hall Camp near Romford until July 1916 when he was accepted for a commission and began his training with the Royal Garrison Artillery. In the New Year of 1917 he was posted to No. 244 Siege Battery in

---

[1]The information about Edward Thomas's life is from R. G. Thomas, *Edward Thomas: A Portrait* (Oxford: Oxford University Press, 1985).
[2]Ibid., p. 8.
[3]The 2/28th (County of London) Battalion (Artists' Rifles) of the London Regiment. Formed in August 1914, by March 1916 it was at Hare Hall where it became No. 15 Officer Cadet Battalion. During the war over 10,000 officers were commissioned after training with the Artists' Rifles. The Royal Artillery alone received nearly 1,000 (E. A. James, *British Regiments, 1914–1918*, 1978, p. 116).

France, where he found himself 'three years older than the Commanding Officer and twice as old as the youngest'.[4]

∼

## *Letter to Robert Frost, 11 February 1917*[5]

I left England a fortnight ago and have now crawled with the battery up to our position. I can't tell you where it is, but we are well up in high open country. We are on a great main road in a farmhouse facing the enemy who are about two miles away, so that their shells rattle our windows but so far only fall a little behind us or to one side. It is near the end of a three weeks' frost. The country is covered with snow which silences everything but the guns. We have slept – chiefly in uncomfortable places till now ... I have enjoyed it very nearly all. Except shaving in a freezing tent. I don't think I really knew what travel was like till we left England.

Yesterday, our second day, I spent in the trenches examining some observation posts to see what could be seen of the enemy from them. It was really the best day I have had since I began. We had some shells very near us, but were not sniped at. I could see the German lines very clear but not a movement anywhere, nothing but posts sticking out of the snow with barbed wire, bare trees broken and dead and half-ruined houses. The only living men we met at bends in trenches, eating or carrying food or smoking. One dead man lay under a railway arch so stiff and neat (with a covering of sacking) that I only slowly remembered he was dead. I got back, tired and warm and red. I hope I shall never enjoy anything less. But I shall ... I am now just off with a working party to prepare our gun positions which are at the edge of a cathedral town a mile or two along the road we look out on. We are to fight in an orchard there in sight of the cathedral.

*In February he was made Assistant Adjutant of the 35th Artillery Group (to which his own battery belonged) at Arras, where he worked on the artillery plans for the forthcoming battle.*

---

[4]R. G. Thomas, *Edward Thomas*, p. 279.
[5]The letters to Robert Frost are reproduced from R. G. Thomas, *Edward Thomas: A Portrait* (Oxford: Oxford University Press, 1985), pp. 282–5.

## Letter to Robert Frost, 23 February 1917

I am temporarily thrust out of my Battery to assist some head-quarters work with maps, etc. We are living in rather a palace – a very cold dark palace – only 2,000 yards from the Hun, in a city which is more than half in ruins already. It is full of our men and no doubt one night we shall know that the Hun knows it. I woke last night thinking I heard someone knocking excitedly at a door nearby. But I am persuaded now it was only a machine-gun ... But I am very anxious to go back soon to my battery. They are only three miles away and when I walk over to see them it is something like going home. I am in a way at home there, but here I have a Heavy Artillery Group Commander to hang about after and do as he pleases and my soul is less my own. You know the life is so strange that I am only half myself and the half that knows England and you is obediently asleep for a time. Do you believe me? It seems that I have sent it to sleep to make the life endurable – more than endurable – really enjoyable in a way. But with the people I meet I am suppressing practically every-thing (without difficulty tho' not without pain).

## Letter to Robert Frost, 8 March 1917

You sound more hopeful than most people are here. Not that they are despondent, but that they just don't know what to think. They know that the newspapers are stupid and the 'Hun wise', and there practically is the end of their knowledge. We are still fairly quiet here except for brief raids on the enemy ...

I know some things about houses now that you don't know. The houses I observe from, for example, are all modern small houses, the last left standing before you come to the front line trenches. In front of them no houses for about 1,500 yards, that is to say about the same distance behind the enemy as we are behind our troops. No Man's Land is 150 yards wide. These modern houses have all been hit and downstairs is a mixture of bricks, mortar, bedsteads and filth. Upstairs you spy out through tiles at the enemy, who knows perfectly well you are in one of these houses and some day will batter them all down. One of the houses is at the edge of a suburb of the city. One is at the edge of a pretty old village. It was being finished when war overtook it. If a shell hits it it will fall to pieces, not in huge masses of masonry like the old brickwork at the citadel. But it is not so much individual houses as streets. You can't paint death living in them. – As I went to the village house today I heard a very young child talking in another equally exposed house in the same street. Some are too poor or helpless or what to leave even these places. But I positively am not going to describe any more except to make a living . . .

I already know enough to confirm my old opinion that the papers tell no truth at all about what war is and what soldiers are – except that they do play football close to the fighting line and play instruments of brass too – here we often hear the bagpipes.

*Edward Thomas returned to the 244th Battery on 9 March, where he continued the preparations for the offensive. Towards the end of the month the gunners began a systematic programme of firing to destroy enemy batteries, telephone exchanges and observation posts, leading up to 'the greatest barrage ever seen'.[6] Edward Thomas recorded events in his diary:[7]*

## April

1. Among the ragged and craggy gables of Beaurains – a beautiful serene clear morning with larks at 5.15 and blackbirds at 6 till it snowed or rained at 8. All day sat writing letters to Helen, Father and Mother by the fire and censoring men's letters, etc., an idle day – I could not sleep till I went to bed at 10. Letters from Helen, Baba and Deacon. A fine bright day with showers.
2. Letter to H. K. Vernon. Another frosty clear windy morning. Some sun and I enjoyed filling sandbags for dug out we are to have in battery for the battle. But snow later after we had fired 100 rounds blind. Snow half melting as it falls makes fearful slush. I up at battery alone till 9.30 p.m. Writing to Helen and Frost. Rubin and Smith sang duets from 'Bing Boys' till 11.

[6]M. Farndale, *History of the Royal Regiment of Artillery: Western Front 1914–1918* (Woolwich: The Royal Artillery Institution, 1986), pp. 165, 166.
[7]R. G. Thomas (ed.), *The Collected Poems of Edward Thomas* (Oxford: Oxford University Press, 1978), pp. 480, 481.

## Letter to Robert Frost, 2 April 1917

I have seen some new things since I wrote last and had mud and worse things to endure which do not become less terrible in anticipation but are less terrible once I am in the midst of them. Jagged gables at dawn when you are cold and tired out look a thousand times worse from their connection with a certain kind of enemy shell that has made them look like that, so that every time I see them I half think I hear the moan of the approaching and hovering shell and the black grisly flap that it seems to make as it bursts. I see and hear more than I did because changed conditions compel us to go up to the very front among the infantry to do our observation and we spend nights without shelter in the mud chiefly in waiting for morning and the arrival of the relief. It is a 24 hour job and takes more to recover from. But it is far as yet from being unendurable. The unendurable thing was having to climb up the inside of a chimney that was being shelled. I gave up. It was impossible and I knew it. Yet I went up to the beastly place and had four shell bursts very close. I decided that I would go back. As a matter of fact I had no light and no information about the method of getting up so that all the screwing up I had given myself would in any case have been futile. It was just another experience ... but it was far less on my mind, because the practical result of my failure was nil and I now see more from the ground level than I could have seen then from 200 feet up the factory chimney.

Otherwise I have done all the things so far asked of me without making any mess and I have mingled satisfaction with dissatisfaction in about the usual proportion, comfort and discomfort. There are so many things to enjoy and if I remember rightly not more to regret than say a year or ten years ago. I think I get surer of some primitive things that one has got to get sure of, about oneself and other people, and I think this is not due simply to being older.

*Diary*
April 3. Snow just frozen – strong south east wind. Feet wet by 8.15 a.m. Letters from Gordon and Freeman. The eve. Letters to Gordon, Freeman, Helen. A fine day later, filling sandbags. MACBETH.
4. Up at 4.30. Blackbirds sing at battery at 5.45 – shooting at 6.30. A cloudy fresh morning. But showery cold muddy and

slippery later. 600 rounds. Nothing in return yet. Tired by 9.15 p.m. Moved to dug-out in position. Letter from Helen. Artillery makes air flap all night long.

5. A dull morning turns misty with rain. Some 4.2s coming over at 10. Air flapping all night as with great sails in strong gusty wind (with artillery) – thick misty windless air. Sods of f/c's[8] dugout begin to be fledged with fine green feathers of yarrow – yarrow. Sun and wind drying the mud. Firing all day, practising barrage, etc. Beautiful pale hazy moonlight and the sag and flap of air. Letters to Mother and Helen. HAMLET.

6. A lazy morning, being a half day: warm and breezy, with sun and cloud but turned wet. Billets shelled by 4.2: 60-pounders hit. In car with Horton to Fosseux and Avesnes and met infantry with yellow patches behind marching soaked up to line – band and pipes at Wanquetin to greet them, playing 'They wind up the Watch on the Rhine' (as Horton calls it). After the shelling Horton remarks: 'The Bosh is a damned good man, isn't he, a damned smart man, you must admit.' Roads worse than ever – no crust left on side roads. Letters from Helen, Mervyn, Mother, Eleanor.

7. Up at 6 to OP.[9] A cold bright day of continuous shelling. N. Vitasse and Telegraph Hill. Infantry all over the place in open preparing Prussian Way with boards for wounded. Hardly any shells into Beaurains. Larks, partridges, hedgesparrows, magpies by OP. A great burst in red brick building in N. Vitasse stood up like a birch tree or a fountain. Back at 7.30 in peace. Then at 8.30 a continuous roar of artillery.

8. A bright warm Easter day but Achicourt shelled at 12.39 and then at 2.15 so that we all retired to cellar. I had to go over to battery at 3 for a practice barrage, skirting the danger zone, but we were twice interrupted. A 5.9 fell two yards from me as I stood by the f/c post. One burst down the back of the office and a piece of dust scratched my neck. No firing from 2–4. Rubin left for a course.

*The next day, Easter Monday, the infantry began their assaults in rain and snow. Edward Thomas was directing the guns from his forward*

---

[8]Forward controller.
[9]Observation post.

*observation post when he was killed, at just after 7.30 a.m., by an enemy shell.*[10]

*Shortly before his death he had written to his son, aged seventeen.*[11]

## Letter to Merfyn

I brought back a letter from you in the mail bags today and also a new battery for my torch. Thank you very much. Do you know I have been so careful that the first one is not exhausted yet. It must have been a very good one. It is most useful in crossing this dark street when crowded with lorries or columns of horses and limbers on all sorts of occasions.

I was so glad to hear from you and how much you were earning for Mother as well as yourself. At the same time I am more anxious for you to learn than to earn at present and I hope you will soon be moved to a new shop. You haven't found an OTC[12] yet, have you? I wish you could, though I hope you will not have to go further than that for a very long time! I don't think war would trouble you. I see lots of infantrymen no bigger or older than you. There was one machine gunner doing sentry over the parapet the other night when I was in the very front trench. He had to stand up there behind his gun watching for an hour. Then he was relieved and made some tea for me and himself and turned into his comic little shanty and slept till his next relief. He looked ever so much older as well as dirtier when morning came. He was a very nice bright Scotch boy. Well, I expect you could do just the same. His officer was the same age and very much like him so that I think he had to look unduly severe to show the distinction.

I wonder could you climb that chimney?[13] There were iron rings all the way up and one I knew was loose, but I didn't

---

[10]The following year his friend W. H. Davies published his poem 'Killed in Action (Edward Thomas)' which included the words:

> But thou, my friend, art lying dead:
> War with its hell-born childishness
> Has claimed thy life, with many more.

[11]R. G. Thomas, *The Collected Poems of Edward Thomas*, p. 287.

[12]Officers' Training Corps.

[13]Cf. the letter to Robert Frost, dated 2 April. Edward Thomas's diary for 15 March records: 'Tried to climb Arras chimney to observe, but funked. Four shells nearly got me while I was going and coming.'

know which. One bad feature was that you were always hanging *out* a bit, because the chimney tapered. It has been hit three times but only with small stuff. Now I suppose it is likely to survive as the enemy is further off. The crossroads round it became known as Windy Corner because everybody got the wind up as he came near it. Thousands had to go that way and yet very few were injured and only about two killed. Isn't it wonderful how some men get hit and some don't. But it is the same with trees and houses, so that I don't see why it makes some people 'believe in God'. It is a good thing to believe. I think brave people all believe something and I daresay they are not so likely to be killed as those who don't believe and are not so brave.

You would have laughed to hear the machine gunners talking to one another and chaffing the infantrymen as they came along the trench tired and dirty.

The men all think we are fast-winning the war now. I wonder if we are: I hope so. Of course I am not a bit tired of it. I want to do six months anyhow, but I don't care how much so long as I come back again. It is going to be Spring soon. Are you glad? Are you often happy and usually contented, not often in despair? Try never to let despair at any rate make you idle or careless. But be as idle and careless as you can when you are happy and the chance comes. If you are troubled, remember that you can do what perhaps nobody else will be able to do for Mother, and Bronwen and Baba: only don't let that make you anxious either. All will come well if you keep honest and kind.

Upon my word, this sounds like a sermon and I do hate sermons, of which it is not true to say that it is more blessed to give than to receive, but it is more easy to give a sermon than to receive.

Do you have time to read now? I only read for 10 minutes in bed, Shakespeare's sonnets, with a pipe which I smoke about a quarter through and then put out the light and forget the flash of the guns across the street and the rattle of the windows, everything except the thud of a shell in the marsh behind, but that seems to have stopped now. Goodnight. Ever your loving Daddy.

# C. H. DUDLEY WARD

Second Lieutenant Dudley Ward joined the Welsh Guards (from the London Regiment) on 20 October 1915. The battle of Loos was still going on, and his new unit was at the 'Hohenzollern Redoubt'.

~

## The Hohenzollern Redoubt[1]

On 3rd October 1915 the battalion marched back to Vermelles and relieved the 9th Battalion Highland Light Infantry in support trenches a mile east of the village. Battalion HQ was at Notre Dame de Consolation.

The Guards Division was now operating on the left of the great battle and was concerned with that mass of trenches and wire and machine guns called the Hohenzollern Redoubt. This place was thrust forward between the Quarries and Fosse 8, but nearest the latter. It had been taken in the first rush on September 25th, together with Fosse 8 and the Quarries. But on September 27th the Germans succeeded in regaining Fosse 8 and the Quarries and nearly the whole of the Hohenzollern Redoubt. The 85th Brigade (28th Division), under General Pereira, restored the situation as regards the Redoubt (both he and his Brigade-Major John Flower being wounded in the fight); but, although some of them got on to Fosse 8, they could not hold it.

The Hohenzollern Redoubt, dominated by Fosse 8, was now a most unpleasant place. It was part of the 3rd German Line which included Fosse 8, so that British and Germans were not

---

[1]Extracts reproduced from C. H. Dudley Ward, *History of the Welsh Guards* (London: John Murray, 1920).

only within fifty yards of each other, but connected up by old communication trenches. Bombing attacks were fierce and frequent. By October 3rd the enemy had succeeded in getting into part of the Hohenzollern Redoubt. The Guards Division then took over from the 28th Division.

Much work was done by the battalion while in support at Notre Dame de Consolation connecting up the old British and German trenches. They went back to rest in Vermelles on the night of the 5th.

The billets in Vermelles were anything but comfortable. The gunners with their cheering weapons were all over the ruins, and, although one likes to hear the sound of British guns, no one wants to lie down by the side of them to rest. The Germans had a naval gun which fired armour-piercing shells with what seemed a retarded action, and they searched with this gun for the British batteries amongst the ruins. This went on all day and night, and there were a good few casualties.

There were several other reasons why Vermelles was not thought much of by the battalion, and the gas fatigue was one of them. This consisted of carrying cylinders of gas up to the front line. Gas was not very popular at that time, a feeling due no doubt to the many casualties caused by our own gas to the troops on September 25th. But, in any case, it was a dangerous fatigue. Three parties, of 184 men each, did this job under Bradney, Bulkeley and Roberts. Dene had the worst part of the business, having to direct the unloading and handing over of the stuff to the fatigue parties at the entrance of the communication trench. 'Bullets', he said, 'came flipping round the corner pretty frequently, and if one of them had punctured a heap of cylinders there was an end of me.'

The maze of trenches, too, which led up to and round about the Hohenzollern Redoubt was most confusing, and several parties got lost in them. It is not pleasant to be lost with a cylinder of gas on your shoulder.

On October 8th the Germans launched a big attack stretching from the Hohenzollern Redoubt to Loos, with a special effort against the former. But the situation was 'well in hand', and the Welsh Guards were not required and took no part in it. As regards the line held by the Guards Division Lord Cavan wrote: 'The battle ended in the complete repulse of three German battalions by handfuls of bombers of the Guards Division.'

The night of the 12th saw the battalion back in billets at Sailly la Bourse, but on the 13th it was hurried into Lancashire Trench, on the north-east of Vermelles, to be in reserve to a fresh attack by a Line Division from the Hohenzollern Redoubt.

The fighting was very severe. The confused state of affairs may be gathered from the orders received on the 14th, which were that the 3rd Guards Brigade would take over the front line held by two brigades of the 46th Division, but when the 1st Battalion Grenadiers and the 2nd Battalion Scots Guards arrived they found that half the line they were supposed to take over was in the hands of the Germans.

The Welsh Guards did not move, but provided heavy fatigues digging in the front line and carrying material.

On the night of the 15th, 25 bombers from the 4th Battalion Grenadier and 25 from the Welsh Guards were rushed up to help a battalion of the Sherwood Foresters who had lost all their bombers.

But the German was not to have all the say in the matter of attack. The Brigade HQ had been organising all the detonating and carrying of bombs, but this work was now handed over to the Welsh Guards. During the day the men detonated 9,000 bombs, and 7,200 were carried up to a reserve store between 10.45 a.m. and 5.30 p.m.; each journey took one and a half hours, and a party of 25 men set out every quarter of an hour. Basil Hambrough was looking after the detonating and was sitting in a cellar with Charles Greville (4th Battalion Grenadier Guards) and a corporal when a shell hit the house and penetrated the cellar. The corporal was killed (Daniels) – Hambrough and Charles Greville got out. There were about 10,000 bombs in the cellar but none of them went off.

At 5 a.m. on the 18th a bombing attack by the 1st Battalion Grenadier and the 2nd Battalion Scots Guards commenced (in conjunction with the 2nd Brigade) with the idea of straightening out the line. The Welsh Guards HQ and No. 2 Company bombers went forward to support the 2nd Scots Guards. Together they won about 160 yards of 'Big Willie'. Sergeant Wheatley, one of the best battalion bombers, was wounded in the hand. The battalion was again thanked by Lieutenant-Colonel Cator.

Trenches were made to bring the part of Big Willie which had been gained into the system we held, and while engaged on this Claud Insole was approached by one of his men who told him there was a dead man in the shallow bit of trench he was working on. Insole, who knew that a lot of the men had a dislike of handling dead bodies, told him abruptly to throw this one out. He then overhead the following conversation:

'You heard what the officer said, Dai – we are to throw the man out.'

Inaudible mumbles.

'Come on, Dai – you take the man's legs and I will take his shoulders. Now then . . .'

'Oh, damn! Ianto, the man has no legs! What shall we do?'

Inaudible conversation.

'The officer said so. Come on, now, take hold of him any where and let us throw him out.'

Which was at last accomplished. This finer feeling, which was very prevalent when the battalion first arrived in France, soon disappeared.

The comparatively safe, if not comfortable, Lancashire Trench was left on the 19th, when the battalion went to Vermelles, and occupied, for the most part, cellars. The village was still a mark for German gunners, with their infernal armour-piercing shells, mixed up with others, so that, although they were called rest billets, it was preferable to be nearer the front line. During the four ensuing days casualties crept up. But another draft arrived on the 20th. Five officers – Captain Aldridge, Lieutenant Windsor Lewis, Lieutenant Williams Ellis, Second Lieutenant Crawford Wood and Second Lieutenant Dudley-Ward straight from England – and late in the evening Captain Allen with fifty men from the base at Havre.

On the 23rd the battalion relieved the 1st Battalion Coldstream Guards in the Hohenzollern Redoubt, of which the following account was written at the time:

'We started in bright moonlight – a ghostly business, especially when in a perfectly flat country of chalky soil and rank grass, dug all over with trenches which appear to be grey banks and mounds inhabited by men. As one walks along voices come from the ground, and lights glint between cracks in so-called dugouts. Now and then you come across a group of men sitting silent on one of these heaps and you realise, with a queer feeling, that they live inside it. We arrived at a hedge where there was an entrance like a gateway sloping into a communication trench. Then in single file we started what seemed an endless twisting and turning along a narrow deep ditch. Finally we came to troops

161

and dugouts – this was the third line, they said. And so we came to the second, and so to the firing line. The men were posted without too much confusion, relieving the Coldstream – and then followed a long, cold, and sleepless night ... The trenches are good and bad mixed. We hold about half new and half old German. The Hun trench stinks and has lots of Hun bodies built into the parapet, and there are a good many of our dead, men who took the place, lying outside. The chief method of warfare is bombs, which we hurl at each other all night, fortunately with small effect so far as we are concerned, but much fearful noise. It seems to die away by mutual consent about four in the morning, when the regular sound is shelling from our guns. My job is chiefly to patrol the trench, which I seem to have done cease-lessly – I have also inspected rifles ... When the early morning mist had cleared I peered at the German trench and the nasty ground in between through a periscope. The position is very odd, as we share one trench with the Hun and others face all sorts of ways. It is as though we had captured part of a maze. I wonder if we shall get the other part! There is at least some truth in describing the noise here as continual thunder.

*October 25th*
The Hun made a lively bomb display last night after dark, but of the many hundreds they threw only five fell in our trench and wounded two men slightly. They were more successful in other ways. Aldridge's company and some Grenadiers were sent out last night digging in front with the object of straightening our line and bringing it all close to the Hun. The Engineers went in front of them to put up wire and it was a good sight to see the Sappers work. The young fellow in charge led them down the trench and 'hoiked' a few sandbags off the parapet to make a step, up which they all went over the top, strolling along as though there were no Huns there and laying out their wire as calmly as though they were demonstrating in a field. When they had nearly finished the Huns saw them and opened fire wildly. But they went on until machine guns started on them and were then ordered back. One fellow came lounging up to the traverse where I was, and, instead of jumping in as I expected, leaned over the sandbag parapet much as he would over a bar in a public-house. He jingled coins in his hand. 'That b– Fritz out there', said he, 'has only got tuppence in his pocket. Oh, I beg pardon, sir.' And he climbed in the trench. The Sappers lost

three men. Aldridge and his men got under cover and were able to carry on till four this morning. Aldridge no casualties, Grenadiers one.'

(*Diary of C. H. Dudley Ward*)

But the Hohenzollern Redoubt cannot be adequately described. No. 2 Company held West Face, the sides of which were composed of dead men, equipment and a little loose earth. A brawny tattooed arm was found to belong to a Highlander of the gallant New Army, but most of these dead were Germans. Outside the trench were British dead on either side. On what was now the rear, formerly the German front, they clustered where the wire was uncut, and there was a nobility in the positions of these men which, unless it has been seen, cannot be communicated.

An enormous hand stuck out of the bottom of the trench at one place, and Dick Bulkeley was curious about it. 'I wonder', said he, 'who that hand belongs to?' and tapped it with his stick. He had a portion uncovered and found it was a huge officer of the Prussian Guard. Everyone has a story of some fearful sight in the Hohenzollern Redoubt.

In spite of the heavy rain which fell on the night 24th/25th the battalion did good digging work, connecting saps which had been thrown out. But soon the main trench began to fall in and their efforts had to be confined to clearing it.

The justifiable anxiety of the higher command proved to be unfounded, as the expected German attack did not develop; indeed it was thought by the officers of the battalion that a relief was taking place in the enemy lines. The sniping and general truculence of the enemy seemed to die down and it required rifle grenades to stir them up.

On the night of the 26th the trench was handed over to the 6th Battalion Queen's and the battalion marched to Allouagne.

The relief was very slow and difficult. Men could not pass each other in the trench, and companies had to go out the same way as the Queen's were coming in. Men had to take off their packs and squeeze past the incoming troops. The way out was very long and wearisome, ankle deep in clay mud which went 'chuck-chuck' as the men pulled their feet out of it. The battalion left at 6.30 p.m. and did not get out of the communication trench till about 9 p.m. Companies were very exhausted when they arrived at Bethune. A little farther on some intelligent person had posted sentries along the road so that battalions might not miss the way, but he put them on the wrong road. This was discovered by the Commanding Officer, who sent orderlies to try and stop his companies. The Prince of Wales's Company was warned and sent back; the others, however, went on and eventually arrived at this correct destination, having done five miles too much. The last four miles were the devil. We arrived at 4.30 a.m.

## Welsh Guardsmen

Every soldier who fought and fell in the Great War has his reward in the memory of his friends; but an adequate monument, worthy of his sacrifice, can only be erected by the future action of his countrymen – men whom he never saw.

While writing of gallantry we have the deeds of some men at Mortaldje always in our mind. It was easy on this occasion to describe, we will say, 1189 Private W. Jones advancing alone with only the flickering, shadow-raising flare from Verey lights dispersing the dark of a moonless night. We can see him stumbling along the strange trench, we can see the walls of earth on either side of him, his bayonet flashing, the sharp turn in the trench and the jumping light throwing a shadow like a black wall from the angle of the turn. We appreciate the courage which led him through the shadow and round the turn in the trench. We realise that he knew he might meet the enemy at any moment, and was deliberately seeking him – he was a determined man looking for his enemy. But what are we to say of Corporal David James? He was not looking for Germans. He grasped no weapon, his mind was not worked up to the frenzy of killing. He slipped into treacherous shell-holes, tripped over unseen stakes, tore his clothes on rusty bits of wire that rose out of the earth like brambles, and over his shoulders was a coil of the same kind of wire, scratching his face and hands, clinging to his legs, his coat, his sleeve, catching at everything he passed and jerking him back. He led his party of men into the open and commenced to lay out his wire.

Mud, mud, mud comes as a kind of chant through every account of the war. Slimy mud, green mud, blue mud, brown mud, black mud, hiding sharp bits of tin, old bayonets, rifles, caps, clothes, dead men. Shell-holes one can understand; they are just holes of varying sizes – and the mud at the bottom of them. There are lots of shell-holes; the ground is pitted with them, like smallpox – bad smallpox; and the ridges of earth, separating one from the other, are ridges of soft, crumbling earth into which your feet sink, and it sticks to your boots. There is no grass. The whole thing is destruction – the earth is destroyed, pounded, smashed, blown up for miles, making a long belt of devastation where the two great armies face each other. This is the open.

At any time you would hate to walk over the open; you would hesitate to touch an open, bleeding wound, how much more would you hesitate to touch this wounded, festering, putrid earth? Corporal James did not think about it. All he thought about was laying out his entanglement of barbed wire.

But we have not yet finished with the 'open'. In the open you are exposed – you might as well be named – you feel so naked. And you seem to tower above everything, you are gigantic, and the only covering you think of is a small, deep shell-hole in the ground. It is because you hear sounds all round you which you know may kill or maim.

A man was blown up at Mortaldje, flung twisting in the air amongst a shower of mud. He began to run about in an aimless manner, with short pauses to take off some portion of his garments. After a while he ran about naked until another shell killed him. He was mad and felt naked. This is the open.

Corporal James worked at his wire in the open. Something infinitely more vicious in sound than thunder was crashing all round him. The explosions cut one another like the shell-holes in the ground. But Corporal James made a good job of his wire. He had six men with him. One was smashed – then another. He worked with Private Viggers. Viggers was smashed, and Corporal James was alone. All his men were broken and scattered like bits of old stakes, and mixed with other shattered fragments in the mud. This was the result of the sound all round him, crashing sound and flashes of light. The sound was still there, shaking the air, and making the earth stagger. Corporal James had put out all his wire. There was more to be got out, but he had no men to fetch it. If he had more men could he put up more wire, or would they all be killed too? No one was supervising his work; he was all alone. The Verey lights enabled him to see that everyone else in the open was apparently engaged on some work, so it was extremely unlikely that he could get more men to carry wire. Corporal James asked for more men; said his job was unfinished.

Of course he was only doing his duty. He was not supposed to be killing Germans, and there is no story of valour attached to him. He was killed at the battle of the Somme.

In a dim kind of manner these acts were sometimes recognised, and Corporal James received a Military Medal; he might well have been given more. On the other hand, the conditions of fatigues at the battle of the Somme and the third battle of Ypres were very similar to this incident at Mortaldje and differ principally as to the proportion of casualties – also the casualties were picked up and the fatigue carried out – yet no one received even a Military Medal, and no one is mentioned for carrying out these fatigues in this account of the war. Hard as it is to raise a thrill over Corporal James's duty while a minor operation is in progress, it is still harder where the everyday duty of the battalion is concerned.

What are we to say of a man like G. E. Randall, who, rather than fall out when the battalion was on the march because the sole of his boot came off, tramped into billets with a track of blood behind him? He might be called a gallant fellow. We can feel for Randall – many people have suffered from a sore foot, and imagination can supply the muddy, cut-up road and maybe the shell-pounded track. But can many people, without the experience, imagine the sentry in the trench?

The sentry has marched there, four or five miles, carrying his rifle, a hundred and twenty rounds of ammunition, a heavy pack, a spade and a bag of rations. It is cold and it is raining, but he is sweating under his load. And he arrives at the trench. The trench is perhaps six feet deep, and he cannot see over the top, but, as he tramps along it, he brushes the muddy sides with his sleeves. If there are no trench-boards his feet sink over the tops of his boots in thick, glue-like mud. His post is a step cut in the side of the trench, a step which will allow seven or eight men to sit on it. He stands on the step, his rifle in hand, his bayonet fixed, and his head over the top of the parapet and about eighteen inches above the level of the ground. He stares into the night, and each bump in the ground, each tuft of grass, each stake holding the barbed wire in front of him looks big and moves. His eyes are always playing tricks. At times he gets dazed, so that he sees nothing at all. He hears movements of rats, or birds, or the wind. He gets cold and is relieved after one hour, and then sits cold and drowsy for two hours – or perhaps he has to work at digging or revetting. Bullets crack about his ears like whips. Sometimes the shells blow up the trench near him. Everyone stands to arms an hour before daylight, and then he eats his breakfast. During the day he gets six men in his post, one only is on sentry by day and two at night. It rains all the time. His feet are wet, his clothes are wet, he is blue with cold. This goes on for two or four nights, and on the third or fifth, as the case may be, he is relieved by another unit and marches back to billets with his load, minus the rations, but plus a considerable weight of mud and water. He rests in a dilapidated barn with holes in the roof, and frequently water on the earth floor, or else he rests in another trench with the added luxury of several bits of tin as a roof. He is probably bombed or shelled during the nights and days that follow, but possibly does one hour only each night as sentry. And then he goes back to the 'Line' again. And this goes on for months. He has only one suit of clothes at a time and one pair of boots at a time. There is no story of valour, but what are we to say of the man who did it, and sang while he did it?

But, it will be said, certain men mentioned have done all this and more – they have been noted as having done more than their duty? For all we know, so has every other man. The nominal roll of the Welsh Guards is the list we give of gallant men, and the deeds of the battalion are their deeds.

# MORGAN WATCYN-WILLIAMS

Morgan Watcyn-Williams was a Calvinistic Methodist minister, as were his father and grandfather. After attending a Board school in Grangetown, Cardiff, Morgan Watcyn-Williams went to the West Monmouth Grammar School in Pontypool and thence to University College, Cardiff. He read philosophy, was president of the Literary and Debating Society and represented his college at water-polo. In September 1914 he preached for the last time as a civilian at Trinity Church, Canton, before joining the 21st (Public Schools) Battalion of the Royal Fusiliers, at the age of twenty-three.

He went 'into the line' for the first time in November 1915 before being sent (in March 1916) for officer training at Corpus Christi College, Cambridge. He was posted to the Royal Welch Fusiliers at Kinmel Park, Rhyl, and returned to France in September 1916 with the 10th Battalion. He 'went over the top' at Serre and was involved in several other actions, being awarded the Military Cross. In 1917, at Zonnebeke, he was wounded by a shell splinter in his left eye. Convalescing at Parc Wern Hospital, Swansea, he began his work on behalf of ex-servicemen – in particular for the 'Bit-Badge League', a forerunner of the British Legion. Discharged from the army as unfit in July 1918, he wrote newspaper articles, studied theology at Aberystwyth and campaigned for Sir Alfred Mond in the general election of November 1918.

Morgan Watcyn-Williams began his ministry at Nolton Presbyterian Church, Bridgend, moving to Merthyr Tydfil in 1923. He wrote *The Beatitudes in the Modern World, Creative Fellowship* and *Where the Shoe Pinches* as well as teaching in adult education classes and working for the unemployed. His autobiography *From Khaki to Cloth* (1949)[1] contains this account of his experience of the battle of Arras.

~

---

[1]Published in 1949 by the Calvinistic Methodist Book Agency at Caernarvon.

# Arras: Easter 1917

On parade we underwent intensive training for the battle of Arras. The trenches and wood which we were to attack were reproduced for us from aeroplane photographs, so day in, day out, during six weeks of strenuous work, we traversed its length and breadth. Scarcely a contingency was unforeseen and the final capture of the wood, a very pretty piece of drill, came off in the actual event.

The men toiled at the rifle ranges, or at their bombing schools, while the officers practised revolver shooting, and pored over maps and photographs. Never was there a more concentrated effort, for in addition to purely military exercises we organised a splendid series of games and sports. My only regret was that we had no swimming bath, as it was still too cold to allow of bathing in the open. Unable to swim, I rode more miles on horseback than at any other period of my life, realising physical joy to the full. By Easter, 1917, we were as fit as fiddles.

In the evenings I lectured to the NCOs and men, or galloped off to listen to talks by Staff Officers whose rank varied from that of major to lieutenant-general. Returning from one such conference, Compton-Smith said to us, 'It would be a good stunt, if at the end of the war, all Army and Corps commanders had to attend a lecture by Private Jones. They'd learn a hell of a lot.' My only quarrel with the proposition was that I saw no reason for postponing it until the war was over. Private Jones could have told them many things which would have saved hundreds of lives and thousands of casualties. He at least would have had the sense not to proceed with an attack when all the circumstances for which it was planned had changed. Only a person sitting in safety behind his chateau door could expect troops, unsupported by a barrage and wading through snow to carry out a scheme dependent on fine weather and strong artillery support.

My mail was unusually heavy, but I could do little except reply with Field Post Cards. I reserved longer answers for Janie and Dad. A letter from him contained a word which I have always treasured. It is almost too intimate for these annals, but I mention it because it illustrates his generosity, and the tie which binds us. 'Whatever happens, I shall have nothing to think of in our relationship but that which is sweet. You have never given me any pain.' During a friendship which lasted for forty years we had no misunderstandings and even the slight differences which occasionally troubled us were due to natural and inevitable divisions of loyalty. On our own fellowship no cloud or shadow ever fell.

For days I walked on air, not stopping to ask why that which made living so urgent also made it easier to die. At Serre, and later at Bullecourt and Passchendale I was often half-crazy with apprehension, but going up to Arras I was almost completely poised and calm. It was our brigade custom to send company commanders into every other attack, alternating battle and rest (so short were we of experienced officers), but owing to casualties the exemption due to me was impossible. On April 5th I had a pow-wow with Brigadier-General Porter, a fine leader, Lieutenant-Colonel Compton-Smith, and Captain Don Quin, our adjutant. They decided that I should be in charge of forward operations, with A and C Companies leading the way to Devil's Wood.

In the evening I strolled through the dusk into an orchard where my men were camping. I could not help contrasting its peace with all that lay before us, for the earlier trees were in bloom and the air was touched with a hint of fugitive fragrance. Suddenly my thoughts were interrupted by a harsh, strong voice saying, 'The only good Boche is a dead one.' The speaker stood by a brazier, talking to a group of his fellows, and as the flames shot up I could see the hate in his eyes. I knew Jones' story. He was the sole survivor of three brothers who had joined the army. 'You remember Bill,' he continued, 'a cheerier kid never left Wales, and the devils watched him shrieking on the wire at Ypres until he died. Bert was blown to hell at Loos. I'll get even with the swine yet.' With a smothered curse, which was half a sob, he turned abruptly away, hurrying off into the darkness with his sorrow. Not for the worlds would I have been eavesdropping, but I had to wait a moment or two, lest any movement on my part should give rise to anxious thoughts as to how long I had been there. The group took up the story, fact and fiction rivalling each other in horror and brutality. Some of them spoke quite cheerfully of killing prisoners, but the majority protested, both on military and humanitarian grounds.

I slipped away quietly, and sauntering to my quarters found myself on the old, eternal treadmill. To butcher prisoners was to break faith, but was killing anyone more justifiable? Sleep came at last, deep and heavy, and if it brought little peace to my soul, it revived and refreshed me.

On the road to Arras the guns were howling in fury, and night and day we could hear the mutter of machine-guns, high on the clouds, as our men fought their duels with German aeronauts. They were making a desperate effort to control the skies before the attack was launched. In underground cellars we rubbed shoulders with half-a-dozen other regiments, and on the night of April 7th I talked to the men of British ideals and justice, pointing out the wisdom and the rightness of taking as many prisoners as possible. Only one man remained completely sceptical. Jones told me frankly that if he came across them they were as good as dead. It was useless arguing with him, but I chatted with him for a short time and hoped that all would be well. Easter Sunday found me on a reconnaissance with my NCOs in the front line. From an observation post we could see the four lines of trenches and the wood, scarcely a tree of which remained undamaged. The position looked formidable enough, full of sinister threatenings. On the way back I ran into Lieutenant F. C. Thompson of the RFA 'spotting' for his battery. He was the Latin lecturer at Cardiff when war broke out, and I had spent Boxing Day with him in Calais, on our return from leave, sharing the only bed we could obtain in a pleasant little hotel. Now we could hardly hear each other because of the roar of the guns, and after a few minutes' conversation, we had to part. It was our last meeting, as a day or two later he was killed in action. He was a very perfect gentleman.[2]

On the morning of Easter Monday, April 9th – what a Bank Holiday – we walked into the dawn, going through the Gordons, who had taken their objective at a stride. I was too busy to feel afraid, as every now and then a runner left my side, here to hold up a hurrying section and there to hasten a little group which tended to hang back. The men swarmed over the ground at a fine pace, preferring the risk of splinters and back-bursts from our own guns to the certainty of machine-gun murder. It was a beautiful morning, with the most weird colour effects. Behind us were miles of pin-points of flame, where our guns were firing, and in front the sunrise, and the 'golden rain'

---

[2]Francis Clement Thompson died of his wounds six months later, on 3 October 1917.

and green and red lights of the enemy, conveying their message to the artillery. Almost lying on top of the barrage, we swept through Devil's Wood without a hitch, giving the Germans no elbow room. Out of a vast dug-out underneath a ruined house in the middle of the wood, eighty-three prisoners poured, and down the steps we found two machine-guns ready for action. Had we allowed time for them to be mounted, they would have spelled disaster to the battalion, but as it was we captured them and their crews without loss.

Our casualties were very light, two men killed and twenty-three wounded, but until the enemy had been cleared out of Tilloy by the 37th Division, who were waiting to go through us, we had to watch for snipers from the village just beyond. One of our Lewis guns exposed a nest of them hiding behind some tumbled-down brickwork. For the time being I was happy, although my mouth was parched and dry, with a curious taste of iron on my tongue. I had a drink, lit my pipe, and began to move about seeing to the work of consolidation. We built four strong points for our Lewis-gunners and bombers, and a fifth for the Machine Gun Corps, wiring them all securely.

Then odd things began to happen. I found a poor fellow in a green uniform, obviously a hopeless case, who begged of me to put him out of his misery. Our own doctor had been killed by a shell, and even had I possessed a pellet of morphia, I could see that the man was in no condition to swallow it. Was I to kill a prisoner and at his own request? I felt I ought to − wrong though the feeling may have been − and I knew that I couldn't. His wounds were beyond description. In a moment or two kindly death solved his problem and mine. A few minutes afterwards, Jones came down the trench, pushing before him a very small German. 'What shall I do with this, sir?' he asked grimly. The question was jerked out, the harshness of the voice trying in vain to conceal the humour that danced in his eyes. I told him he'd better feed it, so without more ado he sat the little prisoner on the firestep and plied him with biscuit and beef. All the time Jones stood over him, shouting, 'Now tell us your blasted submarines are starving us.' We gave the boy, for that is what he really was, a cigarette and sent him down to the Corps cage. A long silence ensued, broken by my question, 'Well, Jones, what about killing prisoners now?' He looked straight at me, his face set and white, but his eyes laughing still, 'Not in cold blood, sir. I couldn't do it in cold blood. Besides, he was such a kid.' So the temptation passed and the poison gas which had descended upon his soul lifted for ever.

Reaction began to set in, now that the excitement was over, and all sorts of strange ideas came into my head as I sat down on an old tree stump. An occasional shell from a long-distance gun fell on the far edge of the wood, and I could see its final passage through the air, like a cricket ball dropping to the boundary. I was filled with memories of torn and bleeding men and dying eyes that yet gleamed with hate, or quivered with fear, or were too tired to express any emotion. The one blessed thought in the whole business was that the company, for the first and last time in its fighting career, had escaped serious loss. We had been told that after taking Devil's Wood we should be relieved, but our very good fortune vetoed the proposition. I turned in with Harry Curran, and together we settled down to sleep.

During the night of April 9th a heavy snow-storm surprised us, and when we 'stood-to' in the morning the wood presented a most lovely sight to the eye, the trees and hummocks of earth all covered with a vesture of white. We had little heart for its beauty. Snow meant cold feet, and wet garments, and cooking difficulties, with movement reduced to a snail's pace in the thick and heavy mud. Happily I made a marvellous discovery. Parry, my orderly, and I were exploring a number of dug-outs and underneath a pile of sacking which no one had disturbed we came across a thousand Tommies' Cookers. There were enough for all of us to have two each, and to hand over a few dozen to the stretcher-bearers for special work. The Colonel was as delighted as I at our good luck, for these little tins, with their solidified methylated spirits, guaranteed hot food and drink. What we should have done without them I do not know, as all the wood we found was wet and sodden.

Late on the afternoon of the tenth of April Compton-Smith sent for his company commanders, and explained that we were to attack the village of Guemappe the next morning. A heavy creeping barrage would support us, and with the King's Own and the Suffolks to lead the way through the few trenches that were left, all would be well. He was gay and confident in manner, but I detected a good deal of anxiety in his eyes. It seemed to me that he knew in his bones that it was doomed to be a rotten show. Before I went to sleep a young Swansea officer, Second

Lieutenant James, reported for duty. It was his first experience of the line, so I resolved that my runners and I should go over with the platoon he was to command. I felt far sorrier for him than he did for himself, so full of pluck and energy was he at the prospect of his baptism of fire. The rest of us were utterly fed-up, relief denied and another sticky job in front of us. At 2.45 a.m. on April 11th we marched up to Feuchy-Chappelle to our assembly positions, where a considerable amount of enemy shelling made the work intensely difficult. Most of it came from 5.9's, and the German gunners kept searching the ground in a most uncanny and uncomfortable manner. Our own reply was feeble in the extreme, and before we attacked I knew why the colonel had looked so anxious. He must have had serious doubts from the first regarding the support we were to get. I think he had done his best to indicate the almost insuperable barriers we should be expected to overcome. Luckily the men knew nothing of all this – 'theirs not to reason why, theirs but to do and die,' and as I moved along our line I was amazed at their good humour and morale.

When we moved off to support the attack on Guemappe at 7 a.m. there were no pin-points of flame behind us, no yelling and barking of our guns like hounds reaching out to their prey. Everything was curiously quiet and at most I saw twenty or thirty shells fall on the village. Our left was on the Arras-Cambrai road where many hundreds of yards ahead lay Les Fosses Farm, which a part of the men in front of us seemed to think was their objective.

A squadron of cavalry passed us racing on to Monchy, and in a few minutes we could see riderless horses scampering up and down in torture and in fright. The sweeping, searching shelling of the German guns continued relentlessly, increasing in tempo with every yard of our advance, while the tendency of the line to swerve to the left made me very anxious indeed.

We were now walking into a hell of machine-gun fire, heavier even than at Serre and the air was alive with the 'ping-pong' and the 'zip-zip' of bullets. Second Lieutenant James was rubbing elbows with me when he fell with a bullet through his arm, the one that was brushing my side, as I was telling him to keep well to the right. His was the most rapid entry and exit I knew. Happily he got back safely and although maimed continues to pursue his work at Swansea. By half-past seven there were no troops in front of us, for the King's Own and Suffolks were smashed by the appalling fire. How they hung on as long as they did is a mystery to me. All that I could do was to re-form the line and occupy shell-holes until we received ample artillery support to continue the attack. A short cut of trench near the farm afforded some shelter, but that was half-a-mile away to my left, and although we had advanced some fifteen hundred yards, the value of the ground covered seemed to me exactly nil.

The casualties were terrible, and any attempt to get them away was almost suicidal. For all that the stretcher-bearers stuck to their job magnificently, wonderfully helped by Captain Allcock, the medical officer of the 11th Warwicks. Finding that the right consisted largely of Suffolks and King's Own, I handed that part of the line over to the one remaining Suffolk officer I could see, so heavily had they suffered, and then proceeded to link up our own men to the left. Whenever I dropped into a shell-hole it was to discover a little group, puzzled and wondering, with no idea of what was happening, except that movement was impossible. Several times they begged me not to try to go further, but I could see that the effort was inevitable.

I have never been 'spooky' and my premonitions and intuitions in the realm of fact are negligible. None the less Parry and I shared one queer secret. He believed that neither of us would ever be hit unless the other fell at the same time, and on this particular morning I was caught by the aura of his faith. I felt certain that I should escape from the situation, and in that mood I managed at last to reach Les Fosses Farm and to establish contact with Captain Murray of our battalion and Captain Manlove of the King's Own. At 8 a.m. we were pegged down to our line of shell-holes, so I sent a message through to the colonel telling him how we were fixed.

I gave him a sketch of our position with as much information as I could collect regarding the number of the men, the supply of water and ammunition and the points held by the few officers who had not been struck down. No obvious duty remained except that of preparing for counter-attack and succouring the wounded. By the early afternoon the farm was full of casualties where Captain Allcock worked incessantly until midnight. At 2.30 p.m. the 1st Gordons tried to reach the village but though they received a little more artillery support than was accorded us they withered away before the barrage of shells and bullets which the Germans put down. Whoever ordered them to make the attempt must have been stark staring mad in the light of the experience which had befallen the rest of the brigade. They, at least, might have been saved until once again our guns were able to blaze a trail forward.

I sat in a shell-hole fuming at the callous stupidity which directed our slaughter. How stupid it was can be deduced from the fact that cavalry were used and that a young officer with two Hotchkiss guns and seven men, their horses all shot from under them, attached themselves to me as reinforcements. Throughout the day we were engaged with enemy snipers and machine-guns, several of which our picked men succeeded in silencing.

Shortly before dusk I received a message from Compton-Smith[3]: 'You have done simply splendidly. Get ready 8 platoon guides, I tried to reach you but got held up in a shell-hole and could not move for MG fire; three with me were shot. My love and congratulations to the men. I personally asked the Div. Cmmr. that you should be relieved – and I think it is practically a cert. I am about done. Have lived in shell-holes all day. G. C.-S.'

Slightly wounded two days before, he had kept in touch with us the whole time, in addition to having a couple of hurried conferences with his seniors regarding further developments. When the Middlesex relieved us I was completely exhausted and wet through from lying about in the snow, but I managed to crawl back with the company to the old dug-outs in the captured German front-line. Before I went to sleep I wrote our recommendations of those whose gallantry had caught my eye, of whom Parry, my orderly, received a Military Medal and Lieutenant Curran and Captain Allock no reward at all. Decorations were always scarce in a 'dud' show though bravery was much more common then than in success.

The medical officer discovered that I was running a temperature 103°, and without hesitation he ordered me to hospital. Because the fighting round Monchy continued unabated and every Casualty Clearing Station was full or waiting to be filled, I got as far as Camieres within sight and sound of the sea. It was good to be

---

[3]G. L. Compton-Smith (who was Morgan Watcyn-Williams's battalion commander) was one of a number of hostages killed in Ireland in April 1921.

in a bed again, good to eat decent food and above all good to see the faces and to enjoy the ministrations of kindly women. Sister Jackman and Nurse Davidson gave me every care and attention, and the whole ward was ready to rise up and call them blessed. At the end of a fortnight I moved on to the Infantry Base Depot at Rouen.

# WYNN WHELDON

Wynn Powell Wheldon, born in Blaenau Ffestiniog, became an officer in the Royal Welch Fusiliers at the age of thirty-five. Before the war he had read law at Cambridge, subsequently joining Lloyd George's firm of solicitors in London. After the war, in which he was awarded the DSO, he was appointed Registrar of the University College of North Wales at Bangor. His son, Huw, thought that his father 'looked like a soldier among academics, and an academic among soldiers'.[1]

In June 1933 Wynn Wheldon became Permanent Secretary of the Welsh Department of Education in London and was knighted in 1939. He died in November 1961.

—

## The Canal Bank at Ypres[2]

The public fame of the Welsh Division in France rests mainly on its achievements on the Somme in 1916 and 1918 – particularly the latter year – but those who know the Division best, will agree that its powers of determination were most tried in the long and weary trench fighting on the Ypres Salient from August, 1916 to September, 1917, culminating in the capture of Pilckem Ridge (the resting place of Hedd Wyn) on the 31st July, 1917.

The sector was at first held by the Division on two Brigade fronts; the 114th Infantry Brigade was usually on the right, just clear of the town of Ypres on the north side, and

---

[1]Paul Ferris, *Sir Huge: The Life of Huw Wheldon* (London: Michael Joseph, 1990), p. 5.
[2]Extract reproduced from W. P. Wheldon, 'The Canal Bank at Ypres', *The Welsh Outlook* (March 1919), pp. 65–6.

holding two Battalion fronts – one in a sector called Irish farm, and the other in the Turco farm sector, and with two Battalions in support on the canal bank. The next Brigade, usually the 113th Infantry Brigade, also had two Battalions in the front line, holding the Lancashire farm sector and the Zwanhof farm sector, again with two Battalions in support on the canal bank.

When the Division first came into the area, the French were on our left, but we eventually took over their ground, and this sector, called the Boesinghe sector, was usually held by the 115th Infantry Brigade. In this part of the line, the canal alone divided the combatants, so that the canal bank was a very important place indeed, and if the salient was to be held at all, the enemy must not cross the canal. On the left (Boesinghe Front), the canal bank was the fighting front line, not the support line, and its chief interest by now lies in some highly successful raids made, despite the canal, both by our own men and by the enemy, and the splendid crossing of the canal by the Guards on the 30th July, 1917.

On the right, the canal and its two banks, have much more permanent interest. It will be gathered from what has already been said that there were four battalions of men resting there in turns. In addition, there were many more permanent troops: the Staffs of the Brigades, the troops of the RE Field Companies, and other oddments, such as tunnelling companies. It was a town with all the variety and interest of a densely populated industrial area, which in many respects it greatly resembled.

The accommodation was at first very bad – it improved later – affording little comfort or safety to its harassed population. The death rate was heavy, despite the abundance of fresh air, and minor casualties frequent, but there was no birth rate. Its cemeteries were an obvious reminder to all of the terms and conditions of existence in that neighbourhood. It had its church, which again like its prototype at home, was the one building in a crowded area, rarely over-crowded. It had its hospitals, – noble concrete edifices, which defied the best efforts of the enemy, – and its shops, which did a roaring trade, earning profits which would make any profiteering grocer green with envy.

The canal itself was shallow with a bottom of slimy filth, strewn with bully beef tins and empty jam tins; some derelict barges there were too, – one proudly named the Duke of Wellington, – all of which only made it abundantly clear that it was no longer a canal, but a drain in which rats alone of all living things found life and pleasure. The stream running parallel to the canal, and called the Yperlee, in times of flood flowed muddy and strong. To behold it in drier seasons, it was incredible that any man could have drunk of its waters and lived, but many did, or if they died, the cause of death was something more drastic, if really less nasty, than its waters.

In the canal bank community there were also reproduced the nice distinctions found at home in classes of houses. The best dug-out mansions were occupied by Brigade Headquarters. Even these would not probably survive any test of our local housing inspectors, but they did combine some security with comfort – fuggy but safe. Close on their heels came the dug-outs of the Royal Engineers (buildings which explained the mysterious disappearance of much RE material), and some of the battalion headquarters, the most famous in the area, perhaps, being Fusilier House in the Zwanhof sector. The erection of St Paul's Cathedral aroused no more pride in its architect, than did this structure (Fusilier House) in its builder, though mockers from among the RE's did say that the weight of the concrete in the roof was such that a blow of a shell which did not penetrate, would break its inadequate support and bring the whole roof down on its occupants. Colonels and adjutants proved mathematically that this was not so. Happily no heavier shell than a 4.2 ever attempted a solution of the problem and so far as I know Fusilier House still stands. There was a considerable drop from these 'desirable residences' to the dug-outs of the company officers and men. They did eventually become less dangerous, and in the later months, it rarely happened that a shell entered a canal bank dug-out, killing or wounding all those therein, though in the later months casualties outside the dug-outs were very numerous in the canal bank.

To carry the resemblance to an industrial district further – there was a strong social life on the canal bank. No one could walk along the trench boards on the old tow path, or behind the western bank, without meeting friends and acquaintances, both among officers and men alike. Visits to neighbouring dug-outs were frequent, and many a happy meal has been shared in those melancholy surroundings. During those months, Welsh was heard everywhere in greeting, in denunciation, in warning, and in snatches of Welsh hymns.

180

The bridges of the canal have become historic. They were wooden structures, some strongly built to carry heavy traffic, and several footbridges of more flimsy construction. The more famous of these were bridges 4, 6 and 6d. Bridge 4 was the principal and biggest bridge and at night was always crowded with traffic, men, and trucks incessantly coming and going. Bridge 6 was a less pretentious structure, but equally busy. The principal RE and ration dump was at its western end, and any night there was an indescribable scene of apparent confusion at this place, especially if there was much wiring in the front line afoot. Mules, horses, wagons, trucks, ration parties, carrying parties, working parties, fiery RSM's, loud-voiced sergeants, profane and angry men, all made one mad medley of uproar, where seemingly, the only law was the survival of the fittest – the fittest being the most over-bearing. Still all the rations, RE material, and all else did, as a rule, reach their appointed destination each night.

Bridge 6d was called Blighty Bridge. It gave access to the northern part of the Zwanhof sector, and was probably so called because those who were hit in crossing it, and they were not few in number, did not as a rule get to Blighty.

I do not know whether I have given the reader any glimmering of the intense and vigorous social life of this place – the constant movement of large bodies of troops in single file, troops relieving, troops being relieved, men coming to and fro from working parties, men going to hospital, men going on leave (most rare birds), men going to baths (in the catalogue of our amenities I omitted the baths). It must be remembered that once the canal bank was left, no other infantry troops would be encountered except a few at the Chateaux of Elverdinghe and Trois Tours, until a mournful trudge of seven miles brought the muddy and probably lousy warrior to the dismally jolly town of Poperinghe, or its outlying camps which were entirely dismal.

Of the front line, I have said nothing. To reach this every three, four or six days, each battalion in its turn wandered round La Brique, wearily crawled past La Belle Alliance (a crowded headquarters where the indignation of a Brigadier at finding one entire dug-out set apart and marked 'RSM's Latrine' was not without warrant); sploshed up Huddersfield trench or climbed in and out of the debris of Skipton, each in turn to occupy posts more or less isolated in groups of six or eight men to all seeming arbitrarily dotted here and there on a flat desolation of shell holes, mud and a few splintered trees, pollards and the inevitable ruined farmhouse with its noisome pond.

There were 'strong points', notably Hill Top. This presented itself to the imagination of the distant 'brass-hat' as a steep and inaccessible fastness whose doughty garrison would fight to the last cartridge, biscuit, and drop of blood. No doubt they would, but it would require a native of flat Cambridgeshire to detect there the existence of a hill without the assistance of a large scale map.

Turco was another stronghold sure, but to the ignorant observer, it might have contained a shrine of some great holiness, so precipitately and incessantly did all those who approached it prostrate themselves into the mud around. But these devotees did reverence only to a German machine gun.

Fargate, too, with its old French dug-outs shared rank with Gibraltar, and was filled like a mediaeval fortress with quantities of food, water, and munitions of war. It also had its portcullis, loop-holes, and other pleasant devices. It narrowly escaped destruction by one of our 'flying-pig' trench mortars falling short, but no doubt it still survives. There were other areas each famous in its way. For instance, a trench called Headingley, – the paradise of tin-pickers, – so packed was it with accumulation of old bully beef tins and jam tins. One Brigadier, whose particular hobby was 'tins', found this an easy vent for his enthusiasm, and did prodigies of valour for an unheeding Empire by causing thousands of tins to be collected and buried. Who again who has ever been there can forget Lancashire Farm, The Nile, and Skipton?

Lancashire Farm, where the pleasant smell of a soup kitchen fought unavailingly against the stench of the old farm pool, the sickly stink of blue clay ladled about by mysterious tunnellers, and the universal trench combination smell of brazier, sandbag, chloride of lime, creosote, latrines and fried bacon. The Nile also, beloved of our Trench mortar batteries, tin stricken like Headingley, whereto armies of working parties, and tons of material went to construct dug-outs of great safety and dryness, and yet somehow no safe or dry dug-out ever seemed to exist there.

Skipton, most loathsome of spots, where our line ran almost into the point of the German salient, called by us Caesar's Nose – the most battered nose in all history this surely was, and then, as if in sudden alarm at this proximity our line ran back a couple of hundred yards up Colne Valley to White Trench.

Colne Valley was no place to stay in, with its broken dug-outs and its problem never solved, namely, how to get the water which gathered there to run out of the trench and its dug-outs, and not always into the same. From here many brave men adventured on patrol into No Man's Land, making for Huddlestone Cross Road, there supposedly to rendezvous with Bosche, similarly brave, but the Bosche was rarely at the rendezvous or else he timed his visits badly.

Of Zwanhof Farm, there was no wall or part thereof standing, nothing but mouldered bricks and the skeleton of a cow to mark it, but its bricks made excellent dug-outs for us in Welsh Harp, a spot not so convivial as its name suggests. On the extreme left of the Zwanhof sector there was a very isolated front post close to the canal and to the enemy, which was at one time the left post of the British line. To this post the garrison and visitor usually marched, as Napoleon said of every army 'on its belly', but when a good trench made it accessible to a General of high rank it aroused him to great enthusiasm. It was for him, the left post of the left platoon of the left company of the left division of the left corps of the British Army, and he warmly shook the Platoon Commander by the hand, and congratulated him on this great post. The platoon commander, on the retirement of the General, inquired of the sentry if he had listened to the General, and realised the amazing importance of his situation. The sentry said 'Yes'. Thereupon the platoon commander gravely said 'Then if Sir Douglas Haig gives the order: 'British Army – Left form', you, sentry, will make a smart turn to the left and mark time till the end of the war!' Happily there was no need to make this remarkable manoeuvre, but it did seem often during those months on the Salient that we were merely marking time laboriously until the end of the war, though we now know that the Britisher emerged through the trench-warfare period full of spirit and vigour, while the German did not.

# ANEURIN WILLIAMS

Aneurin 'Dick' Williams joined the Royal Field Artillery at the age of fifteen. A Dinas Powys boy, he enlisted at Penarth: 'The officer and sergeant had a quick look at us and signed us all on ... The doctor walked past and when he came to me he said, "You're a bit young aren't you?" "I'm eighteen, sir." "Good, off you go then and the best of luck." ' He was sent to Preston and then to Deepcut in Hampshire, where he was to join the 285th Battery of the 91st Field Artillery Brigade, which was part of the New Army 20th (Light) Division. Dick Williams was pitched into an organization stretched to its limits:

'The divisional artillery was started by sending to Deepcut two officers and two drafts of nearly 2,000 men each. The available artillery accommodation, which had been built for two brigades with a total peace-time strength of 700, was strained to its utmost: rooms originally intended for 20 men had now to accommodate about 50. By December, in the Artillery, the men were clothed partly in full dress blue uniforms, partly in canvas suits, and partly in shoddy thin blue suits. By this time a few horses had also arrived, and the available saddlery was made up of civilian-pattern snaffles, regulation bridles, hunting saddles, and colonial saddles. Each artillery brigade also possessed enough harness for one six-horse team, and each brigade also had four guns (two French 90mm and two 15 pounders) but no sights. In February 1915 twelve old 18 pounders arrived from India and each 18 pounder battery received one gun, henceforward proudly known as "our battery's gun".

Later on in February 1915 the Division moved to Witley, Godalming, and Guildford; but part of the divisional artillery had to go by train as there was not enough harness to move all the vehicles. The issue of khaki now began, additional horses and harness arrived, and the divisional ammunition column was completed with mules.'[1]

In April 1915 the Division, including Dick Williams, marched to

---

[1]A.F. Becke, *History of the Great War: Order of Battle of Divisions: Part 3a* (London: HMSO, 1938), p. 100.

Salisbury Plain, covering the sixty-three miles in four days. It embarked for France at the end of July, concentrating in the area west of St Omer. In his eighty-sixth year Dick Williams made a tape recording of some of his memories.[2]

~

## The Somme, 1916

At last we started off for the Somme. After a long march we got there in August and our troubles started again. We were now six gun batteries; our first position was in front of Combles. The guns and gunners were in the open. Now the rank and file did not know much of what was happening – only in your own unit. So we had to guess a lot and that was not always right. Of course the wagon line was as far back as possible but we had to be handy because we had to move the guns sometimes at a moment's notice, but I think the Guinchy Ridge was the worst place of all. We had a lot of casualties there. We could not get to the gun line with ammunition wagons so we had to take it up by pack horses, four rounds on the rider and eight rounds on the off horse, and they went through it I can tell you. Up to their bellies in mud and water most of the time. We had a rough passage, but the poor old infantry, they were in a terrible plight, bodies of men and horses all over the place. We were there until about Christmas 1916, I should think.

While we were on the Somme, Ianto Evans, from Llanhilleth, the lead driver of No. 4 section, won a MM. The guns were near Guillemont and as the ammo was being taken there a shell killed Cowin the centre driver. Now Ianto unhitched the centre horses, put Cowin on the limber, and with him leading one horse and the wheel driver the other, they brought Cowin back. Cowin was from the Isle of Man and had always been getting into trouble. He had once given Corporal Logue a real shiner and that had kept the battery talking for a week. Ianto's MM didn't do him much good though. Later, when we were at Bullecourt, he was killed. At this time the guns were in a sunken road and firing so much it was difficult to keep them supplied with

---

[2]The transcript, provided by Dr John Dixon, was published in the *Journal of the Western Front Association* (Summer, 1990).

ammo. Ianto was made officer's groom and when the officer took him up to the sunken road, Ianto was killed by shellfire. Two of Ianto's mates, Harry Davies and Ginger Pritchard, also from Llanhilleth, were killed at about the same time ...

Another incident happened while we were here in this position. We were on pack ammo and old Jerry was using 5.9s firing at random looking for the heavy batteries in the vicinity, and he dropped one about forty yards in front of me and one of my horses shied and backed back into this old shell hole. All I could see of him was his little head sticking out of the hole. I must explain here that this type of shell he used, we called delayed action shells. They used to penetrate the ground and explode leaving a small hole in the surface. I believe they were used for blowing up dugouts and the like. Now don't forget the horse had eight rounds of ammo on its back and there was I one horse above ground and the other below ground, and me with the wind up. I don't know what would have happened if it had not been for some gunners of a nearby 6 in. battery who saw my plight and came over with some drag ropes and one gunner went down and put a rope around the horse's hind quarters and pulled him out all brand new. We carried on up to our battery.

## Beaucamp

Our next position was at Beaucamp. It was here at Beaucamp that I had my narrowest squeak of the war. About eight of us drivers were detailed to take ammo up to the guns by pack horses. We got up there all right and I was last in the convoy, so was the last to be unloaded and so was the last to get away from the battery. Now the other drivers had got about 500 yards up the track and everything was nice and quiet. But all of a sudden Jerry started shelling the battery with his light field guns, whizzbangs we used to call them. So I got my skates on and was away up the track and he seemed to follow me, he was dropping shells all around me and when I got about fifty yards from the battery, bang! he dropped two, I should think, right by my horses and down they went and me between them. The horses scrambled up and were away up the track leaving me on the floor and Jerry was still shelling. So I got up and made a dive into an old trench that was handy and that no doubt saved my skin. After a short while he stopped shelling, so I got out of the trench and went looking for my horses. A driver must not lose his horses on any account; horses were more valuable than men. So I went up the track as quickly as I could and eventually found them both together. I was sure they were waiting for me. The blood was pouring out of poor old Rufus's many wounds. He bled to death. I will never forget that horse as long as I live, he was almost human. I had had him a long time and he and Kitty had got me out of many a scrap. Kitty had several flesh wounds, but she got over them.

## The German Offensives, 1918

On the early morning of 21 March Jerry started belting us with a vengeance and we had plenty of open warfare in reality. No sooner had we put the guns in action and fired a few rounds than it was limber up and off again.

We were on the move there all right – and we were retreating. There was one occasion we were limbering up and old Jerry's infantry were coming out of a wood about a couple of hundred yards away. He thought he had us; but we were too quick for him, thanks to good horses. There were many times we would put the nosebags on the horses and before they had half finished we would have to take them off and away again. It went on like this for some time. To us it seemed weeks, but of course it was not. Sometimes food was short for the horses and us, but what could you expect on the retreat. It went on like this for days and I well remember crossing a bridge near Guiscard and it collapsed just as we had got over. We were very lucky again.

It was about now we had come under the French, but it did not make much difference to us, it was still all go. It was hard on the horses as they were, like us, very short of rations. I do not know how long we were with the French Army but we left them and after four or five days' march we joined the British Army and put the guns in the open in a little valley near Villers Bretonneux. I remember quite well, Jerry got the range of our guns perfect – one just in front and one just behind – before we could get away with the horses. We were now made up with men and horses to full strength and things had gone quite well for a while.

Our commander, Price-Williams, must have smelled a rat.

All the gun limbers and gun teams were always ready harnessed to move at a moment's notice. So one night it was as black as the Ace of Spades and we went up with the limbers and withdrew the guns back to another small valley about 500 yards away. Next morning Jerry started for Villers Bretonneux. He used a lot of tanks, our battery knocked out one by open sights at close range, but the battery had a lot of casualties. The valley we withdrew from was plastered with shells so we were very lucky we got out of it. But Jerry did not hold Villers Bretonneux long. Our infantry and the Australians soon got it back. We drivers had a very hot and busy time supplying the guns with ammo. The gunners were at it all the time. Some of them were awarded the MM, Major Price-Williams the DSO and Sergeant Major Brierly the DCM and the poor old horses got a good feed.

## Cherisy

We moved to Cherisy in the beginning of October and where we did a lot of training and cleaning up.

At Cherisy a cruel thing happened and I had a piece of luck. Let me explain. The area around Cherisy was captured ground, badly knocked about and full of shell holes. The entire section was sleeping under a big canvas sheet, supported by a pole covering a large shell hole. Every morning our sergeant would come and kick the pole to get us up and was usually greeted by a barrage of swear words and shouting. Luckily our sergeant always took it in good part. One morning a sergeant called Gladstone came but was not amused when he was greeted this way. He put Driver Slater on a charge for 'answering back'. We all knew Slater as 'Sailor' because before the war he had been a seaman for years. Anyway, it was Slater's turn to go on leave but that was stopped because of the charge. I went instead. While I was on leave Slater and two others were cooking up burgoo (porridge) in the shell hole when the heat from the fire caused a buried dud to explode. It killed all three of them. We had all done it often and it could so easily have been me.

Then I got another stroke of luck. While I was sent home on leave, with fourteen others, Driver Barr took over my job as leader of the gun. The battery went back up the line a few days after I went on leave and coming back with the limbers they lost two drivers killed, five wounded and about twenty-eight horses. This must have been very hard going for the drivers. Driver Barr was killed on 7th November; he was an only son. He went out with the battery like myself.

## Creature Comforts

I never read much about the Salvation Army or the YMCA but they were very often up quite close to the lines with their little shacks dishing out tea and biscuits which we thought a lot of, especially on cold and wet nights, and of course there was the Expeditionary Force Canteen. They were a big concern and when our QM had a chance he would take the GS wagon down and get a lot of stores of all sorts, tinned milk, custard, cocoa, cigarettes, whisky for the officers and sometimes bottles of beer which we could purchase from him. I think he made a good thing out of his journeys down to the EFC. The EFC was always near a railhead where they used to get everything for the battery such as harness and spare parts of all sorts. It was a different thing with the rations. There was an ASC driver who had his own wagon with a pair of heavy horses driving them with long reins from the box of the wagon. It was an everyday job for him.

As I said before, drivers in the artillery had plenty to do, whatever the circumstances. Our grooming kit consisted of a body brush, a dandy brush, main and tail comb, curry comb and a small sponge and a hoof pick, all wrapped up in a horse cloth. In ordinary circumstances there were two sessions of grooming which included mouth inspection, cleaning the hooves out and sponging eyes, noses and docks, and in cold weather ear pulling and the horses loved it. And what time we had left it was harness cleaning.

I think most divisions had concert parties for entertaining the troops, when they were out at rest. Ours had a very good one called the 'Very Lights'. There were some good singers and they got hold of some of the latest songs like 'Sister Suzy Sewing Shirts for Soldiers', 'Itchy Coo', 'When the Midnight Choo Choo Leaves for Alabam', 'Tipperary', 'Trumpeter', 'Keep the Home Fires Burning'[3] and 'If You Were the Only Girl in the World' and lots of others. They had a portable stage but I don't know where they kept it and the other gear when they were up the line. They also performed sketches of the officers and Jerry and they were very good.

I remember the 20th Division holding a grand show but I can't think where it was held. All the units of the division took part; there was tent pegging, boxing, peg driving, horse jumping and VC races and all the sports you could think of, best turned out gun teams, tug of war, and lots of foot races. There were also events for the French civilians such as milk carts drawn by dogs, horse and donkey drawn vehicles. It was a grand turnout all round. There was a small grandstand which was full of nurses and officers and French civilians. It was a small racecourse and very well kept and the show lasted four or five days. I must not forget the big canteen, which was quite handy.

We Dinas Powis boys were well treated by the Dinas Powis Red Cross. They sent us a parcel intermittently of various things such as socks, handkerchiefs, balaclava helmets, khaki shirts and vests and pants. Some of the underclothes that were issued were very thick and fleecy-lined and a great attraction for body vermin, especially when we were in the line. The things we used to do to try to keep clean. There was an ointment called Harrisons Pomade which used to burn my skin terribly. The thing I found best was what the Red Cross sent out. It was a thick sort of string soaked in some sort of ointment to tie around the body. It was very effective, but the best thing was to go around the seams with a hot iron. That used to bake them. Did you hear about the driver who put his shirt out on a bush one frosty night hoping to freeze them to death? But when we went to get the shirt next morning there they were dancing up and down on the branches of the bush to keep warm. Have you ever read the book 'The Story of the Blood Stained Thumbnail' by Crunch and Crackem?

There was one advantage the infantry had over the artillery, and that was their field kitchens. They were drawn by a pair

[3]'Keep the Home Fires Burning' had been written early in the war by the 22-year-old Ivor Novello (real name Davies) who came from Cardiff. He wrote the tune and the first line; the rest of the words were written by Lena Guilbert Ford, an American. She and her son were killed in an air raid in 1918.

of horses and the food was being cooked while they were on the march. We carried ours in our haversacks – it depended on what was going. It could be cheese and bread, or biscuits, corned beef and bread or biscuits, water in our water bottles. When we got to our destination the cooks would make a fire and drum-up tea and stew. It could be corned beef, mutton or beef or bully beef, usually corned beef. If it was mutton you could soon tell by the lumps of half cooked fat floating on the top, and it did not look very appetising. A good ration was Maconochies, it was a full feed in a round tin, but we did not get much of that. I think most of that went to the infantry and they deserved it. There were several brands of corned beef but the most popular were Fray Bentos and Libby's. One disadvantage was, when the keys on the tins failed we had to resort to the old jack knife and it was a very poor patent. Many a finger was poisoned by being cut by a slip on the tin. A better knife was issued later. Of course, there was Tickler's jam and pork and beans. Each tin of pork and beans had a piece of pork fat floating on the top and I liked them very much. They were a different taste all together to today's beans ...

There was the rum issue, but we did not get it all that often, about three tablespoons full per man but it was surprising how many of the lads did not care for it and used to swap it for a few fags with us who liked it.

There was a young officer in charge of us at one time, and he came to us as a signal officer. He was a proper toff and a pain in the ... head for the OC as he was always larking about with us in the ranks, which was not done in those days. But he turned out to be a brilliant observation officer and by all accounts the signallers loved to be down at the observation post with him. When he was ranging the guns he was always dead on target. When he was serious you had to watch out. The signallers always had something to say about his pranks. One was about the old Jerry infantryman who used to go to the bog about the same time every morning. So this morning he spotted him through his binoculars. He said 'That old Jerry is going to light a fire, he's got some paper in his hand. Oh gosh! Damn! He must not do that, what would my mother say.' So he laid one gun on the bog and the signaller said you should have seen old Jerry run. His name was Gilby or Gillespie but we knew him as 'Gosh Damn'. He was awarded the MC later in the war.

# W. G. SWEET

Sergeant Sweet, from Usk, joined the 2nd (Pontypool) Battalion of the Monmouthshire Regiment (Territorial Force) in 1912, and served throughout the war. In 1921 he wrote up a memoir, from notes which he had made at the time.[1]

~

## October 1918

We moved up to the outskirts of Lille at La Madeleine, and were billeted in an asylum where we had mattresses and cots, and at the top of the place were three padded cells for which our police tried to find occupants, but no one had the chance to run wild. The main road bridge at La Madeleine was blown up at both ends and dropped neatly across the lines, so we had to help the Royal Engineers to cut it up, clear the sections and rubble, then relay the lines getting at least one part working. The steel rails were beautifully made and weighed 60 lbs per foot, so we had some heavy handling to do. It took as many hands to lift it as could crowd on.

Whilst there, three of us had quite a sharp lesson. The evening we arrived, after settling in the men, Sergeant Whits, Smith and myself went out to have a look at Lille. Along the railway, and then on the canal footpath we got into the industrial area. Rows and rows of houses, just like a town in Lancashire. We saw only an occasional person, and some distance ahead we saw troops pass across the top of a road in formation, which, as

---

[1]The memoir, edited by Barry Johnson, appeared in the *Journal of the Western Front Association* (Winter, 1990).

they had soft caps, we took to be Portuguese, knowing that they were somewhere in the area. A little farther on, a woman spoke to us in English. She was Irish, married to a Frenchman, and asked us where we were going.

'Only into the town, to have a look around', we said.

Her reply was, 'Go back, the Germans are not yet gone – didn't you see them march across the top of the road a few minutes ago?'

'Good gracious! Were they Germans?'

'Yes', she said, and we took her advice and quickly made our way back. If we had been a couple of minutes earlier we would have walked into them, and probably have been shot on the spot.

(The last Germans left Lille at 5 a.m. on 17 October. Three days later, the crossing of the River Lys took place, with the battalion laying pontoon bridges and clearing the approaches to them.)

From La Madeleine we were moving up again, and found ourselves near Courtrai. We were billeted in a brickworks where we had a few bombs most nights. One day we had to go up in the town to help the REs build a pontoon bridge with the enemy on the other side of the canal. Captain Comley told me that it was likely to be a sticky job, and he was with us that morning, leading the company. Not far from the site, we were going along a street taking as much cover as possible against the walls, when the Captain said to me, 'Halt the men here, Sergeant, and we will go along and see what all the firing is about.'

Going up the street, we both looked around the corner and saw the RE wagons with the pontoons all smashed up and smouldering. The Germans had seen them coming and smashed them up at near point blank range.

'Oh', said the Captain, 'It looks as if our job this morning is off.' So we returned to camp, and the job was done two nights later.

The Germans were shelling the town and Hallin, the tile-making part. As the civilians were all there, they started streaming out. We were on patrol and saw the people coming over an open space, when an enemy plane swooped down and started machine gunning. A tall woman with two little boys about eight years old, gathered the boys to her and bent over them, sheltering them with her body. I am glad to say none of them were hit. We all shouted out to her, 'Bravo, Madame!' It was a mix-up, with the civilians in cellars, the enemy had one half of the town and we the other. Right up in front we were handed bottles of wine out of the cellars. This lasted for about a week, and the enemy were again on the retreat and we followed up.

(After this, the Battle of Courtrai, 29th Division were withdrawn for rest on 24 October. Tourcoing had been liberated on 18 October, and by the 24th was some 15 km behind the front, which was along the River Scheldt.)

On 5 November we marched into Tourcoing and we billeted in the Rue de Roubaix. It was the fourth anniversary of the battalion coming to France (5 November 1914). Sailing from Southampton we had landed at Le Havre four long years ago.

The sergeants set themselves up in a cafe, 'Le Cheval Blanc', just below the railway bridge where the main line crosses the road – our people were just in time to stop it being blown up. We were entertained by the daughter of the landlord, and had a nice evening and good beds. She told us that the people were crying and saying the Germans will never go. Out in the streets the people were rounding up the women who had been friendly with the Germans, sitting them on chairs in the middle of hostile groups and cutting off their hair. One man was swinging a woman around by her hair, but our boys stopped that. Marching out next day, the people were giving us loaves of bread, like round paving stones – these were soon cut up and put in our haversacks. We were ordered not to accept them, but as they insisted we thought it a pity to disappoint them.

The enemy stuck on a part of the Scheldt and we moved up for a big attack to be on 14 November. Our job was to get into the water and fix footbridges of planks on floats made of four feet cube boxes covered with canvas and pitched.

With other NCOs we went to see the site where the river like a canal passed through a large village. Peeping around the corner we could get occasional glimpses of the enemy who did not seem to take much notice of us. On the way up we passed through a town with very tall houses and had our halt there right opposite an Army Group HQ, and a staff officer came out and told us the news! *The Germans had crossed the lines at*

*Valenciennes and asked for an armistice!* That was good news and the next few days were all rumours. If a shell pitched some distance away, we ran for cover and avoided the area being shelled. At ordinary times we would have taken little notice if not too close, but now the end was near we were taking no chances of being pipped at the last lap.

(On 7 November, the division crossed the Scheldt, encountering no opposition. The village of St Denis is 3 km west of the river, so Sergeant Sweet did not go across until the 11th, when he marched to Celles, a village 5 km east of the Scheldt.)

A couple of days before the 11th we moved into St Denis, a small town with the street sloping down to the river and the main railway line. The sergeants fixed themselves up in a gendarme's abandoned house! Nice little place with tiled floors and a small new cooking range. The front part was intact but the back had caught a shell and was smashed in.

The town generally was badly knocked about, but there were plenty of billets for the troops. The place had only been evacuated a few days earlier, and bedding, etc. was still in place. We got a couple of mattresses from upstairs and put them on the floor of the living room, and were very comfortable with the stove. Someone scrounging found a nice clean pan of fresh lard, another a dump of potatoes. I volunteered to cook some chips if someone peeled the spuds, so that took about three hours, and we all had a good feed and settled down for the night.

All day rumours were going about that the war would finish at 11 o'clock, and at 11 o'clock that night we could hear our lads going up and down the street beating tins and cheering.

'Come on', said my pal. 'Let's go out, the war is over – can't you hear the cheering?'

It was very cold and I was comfortable so I told him, 'Don't be a fool. Haven't you been told the first seven years will be the worst? We have only had just over four up to now.'

We went out, and no sooner had he gone than the enemy who no doubt could hear the cheering sent over a couple of salvoes of shells which burst behind the houses. The cheering and tin bashing stopped at once, and my pal came back in saying, 'Something wrong – did you hear those shells?' We all laughed at him for being so optimistic and got down to a night's sleep.

Early in the morning the old gendarme and his wife returned and made themselves comfortable on a bed upstairs, and we found them a couple of blankets. As we had to be ready to move off at 8.30 a.m., we were about early, and took the old couple a mug of hot tea.

The morning of 11 November was very cold with a sharp white frost. Moving off, we marched down the village to the bridge which the REs had just completed. They had had a rough time, and we saw several of their lads dead on the roadside. I could not help thinking what bad luck to get it now that the end is so near. We moved on and came to a village called Celles, where we waited for a time, and thought that we would be billeted there. I was in a barn getting my platoon settled in when Colonel John Evans came in, wished us good day, looked at his watch and said, 'Men, I am pleased to tell you that in one hour's time the War will be over and you will be able to return to your homes again. The Armistice comes into force at 11 a.m. today.'

Well, after all the rumours, here it was from the horse's mouth, as one of the boys remarked – our CO has told us himself. This time it was true. We did not cheer, just stood, stunned and bewildered. All we had to do was to stay alive for the next hour and then we were going home.

Soon after, we had to move again, and about 10.50 a.m. were halted and told to fall out for a rest. Then just before 11 a.m. we had to fall in again. My platoon was leading and just in front was the Colonel. With the HQ detachment of wagons, he had joined up with our 'C' Company for the march. He was looking at his watch, and on the stroke of 11 a.m. he raised his hand, and told us that, at long last, THE WAR WAS OVER. We cheered, and with our tin hats on our rifles held aloft, cheered again. After four long years the day had come at last, with our reprieve, and now we should have a chance to live our lives, instead of living with the knowledge that we only had less than a 50/50 chance of getting through. Just a matter of time with the odds against us!

Next came the shock. We had to continue the march. We thought we had to stay put wherever we happened to be, but as it was drizzling rain and there was nothing in sight but muddy fields, we were more pleased than sorry. The old hands plodded on, their thoughts miles away, hardly realising that the long awaited day had come at last! The noisy section of the new reinforcements who had joined up only a few months ago, started shouting that everyone should throw away their picks and shovels that we were carrying to repair the blown up parts of the road, and called the officers everything they could think of. A corporal and I went back along the platoon, and threatened to bash with the butts of rifles anyone who threw any kit away. We soon had order restored.

# VIVIAN DE SOLA PINTO

Vivian de Sola Pinto was eighteen when war broke out. Brought up in the suburbs of London, he left University College School, but was rejected at the recruiting office because 'the British Army had no use for spectacled officers in August 1914'. He went up to Christ Church, Oxford, where he joined the Senior Division of the Officers' Training Corps. After several attempts to join up, he managed to enlist as a Rifleman in the Inns of Court OTC.[1] In April 1915 he was offered a commission (in the 2/6th Royal Welch Fusiliers) through the influence of a friend of his father's: Major Marvin 'a stout, genial red-faced person in the wine trade'. The Commanding Officer of this Second Line Territorial Battalion was 'in civil life a Welsh country doctor ... a kind and humane person'. Vivian de Sola Pinto's company commander was Dick Hughes, 'a tall fair haired Welsh gentleman farmer, very jolly and easy going', while his fellow subalterns 'were chiefly sons of Welsh squires and professional men, who drank fairly heavily ... Our men were chiefly farm labourers and quarrymen from North Wales and Anglesey. A fair proportion only spoke Welsh and a very large number were called Jones. The Joneses were often distinguished by the names of the villages or districts where they lived and were known as Penmaenmawr Jones. Ffestiniog Jones and so forth.[2] They were for the most part rather short, sturdy, tough, hard-bitten fellows.'

Pinto volunteered to be one of a draft of eight junior officers sent to reinforce the 1/6th Battalion, which had suffered heavily in the Gallipoli landings. By the end of November 1915 he was suffering from exposure and dysentery and was collected by the 1st Welsh

---

[1]During the war over 11,000 men received commissions after initial service with the Inns of Court OTC. In September 1916 it became No. 14 Officer Cadet Battalion.

[2]*Soldiers Died in the Great War (Part 28)* lists 50 soldiers called Jones from the 1/6 Battalion (out of a total of about 200).

Field Ambulance for evacuation to Cairo. In April 1916 he took part in operations in Egypt and Sinai, but by August he was back in Britain for more medical treatment. He joined the 19th Royal Welch at the time of the German withdrawal to the Hindenberg Line, and was wounded twice more, before being posted to the 25th (Montgomery and Welsh Horse) Battalion of the Royal Welch Fusiliers in June 1918.[3]

~

## The Montgomery and Welsh Horse Yeomanries: 1918[4]

On the following day I arrived at the headquarters of the 25th RWF. I sensed at once an entirely different atmosphere from that of the other two fighting battalions in which I had served. These men had taken part in Allenby's triumphant advance to Jerusalem; they were big, bronzed fellows for the most part, with something of the swagger of cavalrymen. Many of them still wore their puttees wound in the reverse way from that of the infantry and carried their haversacks hitched up, cavalry style, under their arms. The divisional sign was a broken spur, and the very smart divisional flash was a green diamond with a vertical white stripe, which I had sewn on to the shoulders of my tunic as soon as possible. Battalion Headquarters was in a partly ruined chateau, and there I reported to the adjutant, a stout dark man with a row of decorations, who, I afterwards learned, had been a sergeant-major in the 1st Royal Welch. He said, 'You know our CO is a real lord', and ushered me into the presence of Lieutenant-Colonel Lord Kensington, a courtly, rather frail-looking old gentleman, who looked as if he would have been more at home in a West End drawing room than in these scenes of desolation.[5]

'You're to go to "A" Company as second-in-command to Captain Sassoon.'

---

[3]The 25th Battalion had been formed at Helmia in Egypt, on 4 March 1917, from the dismounted Montgomery Yeomanry and Welsh Horse Yeomanry.
[4]These extracts are reproduced from V. de Sola Pinto, *The City that Shone; An Autobiography (1895–1922)* (London: Hutchinson, 1969).
[5]An Old Etonian, the 6th Baron Kensington was formerly a Lieutenant in the 15th (The King's) Hussars and had served in South Africa (1900–1) as ADC to Lt.-General Sir Leslie Rundle. The 'old gentleman' was in fact forty-five years old, and had commanded the Welsh Horse since 18 August 1914.

I pricked my ears at these words. Could it really be possible that I should have the incredible luck of serving under the author of *The Old Huntsman*? . . .

### 6 October 1918

I found the battalion in a new front line, consisting of fortified posts and 'pill-boxes' near La Bassée, and I was given command of 'A' Company once more, but was told that a yeomanry captain of the Welsh Horse, who had been serving on the staff in England for the last three years, was coming out to supersede me.

On 11th October I brought the company out of the line to reserve billets in the cellars of the usual smashed village in 'country which British troops had not occupied since 1914'. On the 13th I was playing in a football match in a muddy field in a side of officers against NCOs of the battalion. The officers were winning by 4 nil, when the game was stopped by a shower of German 'whizz-bangs' and both teams had to take cover. In a letter to my father written on that evening I ask him to send me 'an indelible pencil, candles and the works of Petronius in the Loeb edition'. On the next day Captain Wood of the Welsh Horse arrived and I reverted to my old position of second-in-command.

During the next few weeks the kaleidoscope of the war seemed to be shaken violently and life for front-line troops became a kind of phantasmagoria, a series of quite incredible happenings, succeeding each other with bewildering rapidity. On the night after Captain Wood's arrival our company was taken up to the line in lorries. To soldiers of the Second World War this will seem a perfectly normal proceeding, but to us, who were used to a long, weary march when we went to relieve another battalion, it was little short of a miracle. Our staff had at last realised the possibilities of motor transport! Memory recalls an evening meal eaten by the company mess consisting of Captain Wood, two subalterns and myself in a dug-out in the support line. This meal had the quality of a sort of farewell feast, because we knew that at dawn we were to go 'over the top'. Our mess cook had just returned from a cookery course and produced a remarkably succulent repast of which, he told us proudly, the sole ingredients were bully beef, army biscuits and some tinned vegetables and fruit.

A few hours later in a grey, misty October dawn we scrambled through our wire in fighting equipment with 'iron rations' for three days. In front of us was a smoke barrage through which we could dimly see the shapes of some tanks. When we reached the enemy wire we found that it had been flattened most effectively by these monsters and the German trenches were deserted. Going gingerly for fear of booby-traps, we managed to get clear of the German trench system by the late afternoon and I shall never forget the thrill of breaking through that barrier, which had resisted Allied attacks for four years, and arriving at long last in the almost mythical country behind the enemy lines. We seemed to have penetrated 'through the looking glass' into a world where anything might happen.

It was already getting dark when we reached the first inhabited building, a farmhouse with a light in the window. When Captain Wood knocked at the door it was opened by an elderly Frenchwoman and she and her daughter made us some coffee on their stove. Looking pale and ghostly in their black dresses, they seemed half-dazed and were obviously suffering from lack of sleep. They told us that the Germans had left the night before.

Till pretty late that evening we marched by moonlight along a road of a kind to which we were to become accustomed in the next few weeks. The telegraph posts which had run along it were all chopped down and at each cross-road newly dug earth revealed the presence of mines. That night I slept in a sinister-looking deserted house overlooking one of those mined cross-roads. Two shapes huddled against a wall close by were revealed by my electric torch to be dead Germans. Very early the next morning our brigade formed a column of route on the main road and orders were passed down that we were about to enter the great city of Lille and that we were to march to attention through the city and not to speak to any of the inhabitants. When we reached Lille at about 5 a.m. on a grey, misty morning the whole population seemed to be in the streets, at the windows or on the balconies of the houses, from many of which Tricolors and an occasional Union Jack were flying. The people all seemed to be dressed in dark clothes and to look pale and ghostly like those first two Frenchwomen whom we met. They watched us in silence as we marched through the city with fixed bayonets and drums beating.

It is broad daylight in the suburb of Tourcoing and our men are resting by the roadside and eating some breakfast. Now comes a remarkable manifestation of French courtesy. The street where we are is called Avenue de Wet. I am sure none of us took any particular notice of that name and we certainly should never have thought it an insult to the British Army. Some of the local residents, however, thought otherwise, and we saw several of them solemnly approaching with a big board which they hung over what seemed to them the offending name. With another officer I strolled up to see what was on this board and found the name Avenue Haig roughly painted on it in large black letters. This act seemed to me at once rather charming and slightly ridiculous. These good citizens of Tourcoing had ascribed to us a touchy nationalism like their own. Still, it was an exquisite piece of courtesy and I am afraid that the inhabitants of an English town would never have thought of changing the name of a Bismarck Avenue or a Moltke Street so as not to offend the susceptibilities of French troops.

We spent a night in billets in Tourcoing and the next morning Captain Wood left us to go on a course, so I was again in command of 'A' Company. There followed a period of several days in which the dream of all the generals on the Western Front was at last realised and we were able to take part in 'open warfare'. In a letter dated 'about 18th October' I write that 'I have been walking or riding for thirty-six hours without a wash, change, sleep or anything to eat except army biscuits washed down with an occasional cup of *ersatz* coffee supplied by the liberated inhabitants who turn out to cheer us'. At this time we had to drink a terrible lot of this curious liquid, made chiefly of acorns and chicory.

I wrote that I was 'walking or riding'; I had, of course, inherited the company charger, a brown horse called Caernarvon. Siegfried, who is a hunting man and an expert in horseflesh, was rather contemptuous of the qualities of this animal, but I found him a good, faithful friend, quiet, patient and docile. I did not usually ride him when we were marching along roads except when I wanted to get quickly along the line of march. I liked to walk beside the men, and when I saw any of them looking particularly tired, I would relieve them of their rifles (a most unsoldierlike proceeding and, I believe, contrary to regulations) and hang them on Caernarvon, who would often plod along carrying five or six Lee Enfields.

A curious thing happened to us early one morning which I have never been able to explain. We were advancing 'in open order' across ploughed fields when a biplane with RAF markings swooped down low over our heads. We could see the pilot clearly, and following instructions, the men took off their 'tin hats', put them on the end of their fixed bayonets and waved them. Then a gun, apparently from a wood quite close behind us, started firing shrapnel at the aeroplane. The pilot fired several bursts from his machine-gun and flew off. I reported the incident that evening and was informed that no Allied aeroplane had been in the vicinity that morning and that there was no gun anywhere near us. I cannot help thinking that what we saw in the ghostly dim light of that early October morning was something that happened months or perhaps even a year or two before when some British aeroplane had flown over the spot and had been fired at by a German AA gun.

One day I arranged with Captain Miller, who commanded 'C' Company on my right, that we should 'take' a village in the style of the old manual of 'Infantry Training'. Both company commanders were on horseback throughout the 'action', riding from one platoon to another with bullets whistling round us as the Germans fought a half-hearted rearguard action and the inhabitants waved to us from the windows of the houses shouting, *'Vivent les Anglais!'*

We are marching along the road to Tournai and approaching a village. I halt the company and decide to go ahead and explore, accompanied by John Barton and a gunner officer from a battery that is following us. The village is silent and seems deserted. At the end of the main street there is a huge barn with a great door. We knock at it with the butts of our revolvers. It is opened very cautiously by an old man who stares for a moment in amazement at our uniforms and then cries: *'Anglais ou Americains?'* We answer *'Anglais'* and are promptly surrounded by a crowd of excited villagers of both sexes who embrace us and we have to endure being kissed dozens of times on both cheeks. The whole population of the village seems to have taken shelter in the barn. We then go back and fetch the company for a triumphant entry during which the embarrassed British Tommies are kissed by villagers of all ages and even have wreaths of flowers hung round them.

When we reach the Belgian frontier we are warned to be cautious in our dealings with the inhabitants, as some of the Flemings are said to have pro-German sympathies. However I never noticed any sign of this and our reception in the Belgian liberated villages was quite as cordial as in the French. On 25th

October we halt at a village outside Tournai and I am billeted with my two subalterns at the house of the Curé. This good man has hung over his front door a large Belgian flag which he tells me he has hidden throughout the occupation. It is King Albert's birthday and we are invited to dine with him to celebrate the occasion. Before dinner he leads us with an air of mystery to a pond at the end of his garden and begins probing the muddy bottom with a long rake. At last he finds what he wants and pulls to the surface a big tin case. We help him to bring it to the bank, and when he opens it we find that it contains several dozen bottles of wine. 'My best burgundy', the Curé explains. 'I hid it here when the Boche arrived in 1914; it was far too good to be drunk by those pigs.' It is, indeed, an excellent wine and we drink King Albert's health in it that evening and delight our host by showing him a *communiqué* announcing that the King has landed from a British destroyer at Ostend and that the left wing of the Allied armies is now on the Dutch frontier. He tells us that he used to collect the leaflets dropped by our aeroplanes and distribute them to his parishioners and that the Germans threatened to shoot him for his pro-Ally activities.

We were told that we were going to make a state entry into Tournai as it would be the first important Belgian town to be liberated by our division. As I wanted 'A' Company to shine (literally) on this occasion, I wrote home to order fifty tins of Brasso and fifty of khaki Blanco. However, the capture of Tournai proved to be less easy than we anticipated. When we advanced to the banks of the Scheldt we were heavily shelled from German positions on the other side and all the bridges were blown up. So we settled down to build posts in the old style and wondered if the enemy really were going to make a determined attempt to hold the line of the river. Meanwhile our artillery put down a cleverly selective bombardment round the city, and we learned afterwards that only one small pane of glass in the cathedral was damaged.

During the days which I spent at the house of the good Curé I was studying the excellent manual recently issued by the War Office called *The Fighting Platoon*. As I was reading this booklet one evening, my eye happened to fall on a newspaper which had just arrived from England and I noticed the phrase 'the ennobling effects of war'. The juxtaposition of this piece of claptrap with *The Fighting Platoon* produced the following lines:

## The Fighting Platoon

The Lewis-gunners first, twelve men, two guns:
They'll do for any amount of close-cropped Huns;
Those two squat barrels pumping streams of lead
Can make a green field hideous with dead.
Then bombs, pin out, a blinding flash, a roar,
And where a dozen healthy lads before
Sat smoking fags with faces red and fresh,
There'd be an ugly mass of bleeding flesh.

The rifle-bomb, that deadly shooting-star,
Has much the same effect but from afar.

Enchanted by these toys, do not forget
The short Lee-Enfield and long bayonet,
A level sight, two pressures does the trick:
A man's brains scattered – or the cold steel stick
Into his guts the good old-fashioned way.

'War is ennobling': so the papers say.

At last, on 30th October, our Intelligence reported that the Germans were evacuating the line of the Scheldt. On 1st November, a bright autumn morning, we crossed the river on a temporary bridge hastily erected by the Sappers. Various explosions and columns of smoke on the far bank indicated demolitions carried out by the retreating enemy. When we entered the ancient city of Tournai, however, we found it completely intact and were surprised to notice that various provision shops were well stocked with such luxuries as cream cakes and pastries which it would have been difficult to obtain at that time in most French or English towns. We were told that the explanation was that Tournai had been kept as a kind of pleasure city for German officers on leave.

When we left Tournai my company with a detachment of cyclists was sent forward as an advance guard. A solitary German aeroplane dropped some leaflets on us as we set out on the road to Ath and Brussels. They were headed 'The German People Offers Peace' and expressed the willingness of the new German democratic government to evacuate Belgium and make peace on the basis of President Wilson's Fourteen Points. When Sergeant-Major Evans handed me one of these documents I remarked, 'When the Devil was sick, the Devil a monk would be.' My advance guard, covering fifteen to twenty miles a day, soon left the main body of the brigade far behind. Our company signallers had some carrier pigeons and we sent back one of these birds every evening with a message containing the map-reading of our position. Each village that we entered was adorned with Allied flags and a malicious and probably apocryphal story was circulating that these flags had been sold to the peasants by enterprising German business men before the enemy left. The Belgian villagers seemed in much better shape than the inhabitants of the liberated French territory and we were now regaled not only with the everlasting *ersatz* coffee but also with stronger liquids and cigars. I have a Brueghel-like memory picture of an evening at a little inn where a *kermesse* was organised in our honour. After supping on sausages, rye bread, and cakes, and drinking quantities of beer and schnapps, we danced with strapping Flemish wenches to the music of a bagpipe into the small hours of the morning.

When we halted for the night at a village on 6th November I received a visit from the Brigadier. It was a rainy evening and I remember squatting with him in a shed and looking at a map by the light of our electric torches. I said, 'Can I push on and take Brussels, sir?' I always regard this question as the highlight of my military career. The great man, however, said that we were to stop where we were and await the arrival of the rest of the brigade. He told me that he had information that a mutiny had broken out in the German army in Brussels and that the mutineers were besieging their officers in one of the main railway stations.

On the next day the rest of the battalion caught us up and we now continued our march along the main road, passing hastily over the mined cross-roads. The great stream of British troops moving eastwards was now met by other human streams going in the opposite direction. These consisted of ragged, footsore German deserters, and British prisoners who had walked out of the prison camps now deserted by their mutinous guards. We all knew now that German envoys were at GHQ and that the terms of an armistice were being discussed. On the evening of 10th November the Divisional General passed us in his car on the road and shouted to us that the armistice had been signed. Later that evening a cavalry regiment overtook us. It was the 2nd Dragoon Guards, who were supposed to be our 'cavalry screen', but had only just caught us up! They were greeted with ribald shouts from the infantry.

On the morning of the 11th we were still being shelled and machine-gunned occasionally by German rear-guards and one of our captains was killed by a direct hit on a latrine. Our objective that day was Perquise, a village on the Tournai–Brussels road and we were probably further east than any unit in the British Army. That morning, as we were on the march, the elegant Captain Lord Chevington (once more arrayed in beautiful white breeches) galloped along the column shouting, 'No firing after eleven o'clock.' We halted at eleven o'clock outside Perquise on that misty November morning and at midday some German officers came to show us where the road had been mined. Soon after, as we approached the outskirts of the village, we were met by a crowd of peasants, headed by a little hunchback with an accordion who led us in triumph into Perquise, playing the Marseillaise. That evening copies of the armistice terms roughly printed on broadsheets by the famous secret press of the *Indépendance Belge* in Brussels were distributed among the troops. The weather was cold and rainy. No wine was available in Perquise but I managed to obtain a chicken for the evening meal of 'A' Company mess and we washed it down with some rum and water. Walking round some farm buildings where our men were billeted, I heard a voice complaining about 'the bleeding weather' and another voice answering, 'Put a sock in it. After what we've heard today I could sleep like a bird in a tree.'

# SELECT BIBLIOGRAPHY

The bibliography lists the works from which this anthology was compiled (they are marked '*'), together with some suggestions for further reading on the subject of 'Wales on the Western Front'.

*Adams, B., *Nothing of Importance: A Record of Eight Months at the Front with a Welsh Battalion October 1915 to June 1916* (London: Methuen, 1917).

Allinson, S., *The Bantams: The Untold Story of World War I* (London: Howard Baker, 1981).

Atkinson, C. T., *The History of the South Wales Borderers, 1914–1918* (London: Medici Society, 1931).

Atkinson, C. T., *The South Wales Borderers, 24th Foot, 1689–1937* (Cambridge: Regimental History Committee / Cambridge University Press, 1937).

Beckett, I. F. W. and Simpson, K., *A Nation in Arms: A Social Study of the British Army in the First World War* (London: Tom Donovan, 1990).

*Bowden, W. G., *Abercynon to Flanders and Back* (Risca: Starling Press, 1984).

Brereton, J. M., *A History of the Royal Regiment of Wales (24th/41st Foot) and its Predecessors 1689–1989* (Cardiff: The Regiment, 1989).

*Clayton, C. P., *The Hungry One* (Llandysul: Gomer Press, 1978).

*Davies, E., *Taffy Went to War* (Knutsford: Knutsford Secretarial Bureau, 1976).

*Dixon, J. and J., *With Rifle and Pick* (Cardiff: Cwm Press, 1991).

*Dunn, J. C., *The War the Infantry Knew 1914–1919* (London: Sphere Books, 1989 edn.).

*Evans, M. St H., *Going Across, or with the 9th Welch in the Butterfly Division: Being Extracts from the War Letters and*

*Diary of Lieutenant M. St Helier Evans*, ed. Frank Delamain (Newport, Mon.: R. H. Johns, 1952).

Falls, C., *The First World War* (London: Longman, 1960).

Farndale, M., *History of the Royal Regiment of Artillery: Western Front 1914–1918* (Woolwich: The Royal Artillery Institution, 1986).

Glover, M., *That Astonishing Infantry: Three Hundred Years of the History of the Royal Welch Fusiliers (23rd Regiment of Foot) 1689–1989* (London: Leo Cooper, 1989).

*Graves, R., *Goodbye To All That* (London: Cassell, 1957 edn.).

*Graves, R., *Poems about War* (London: Cassell, 1988).

*Griffith, L. W., *Up to Mametz* (London: Faber and Faber, 1931).

*Gurney, I., *Selected Poems of Ivor Gurney* (Oxford: Oxford University Press, 1990).

Haythornthwaite, P. J., *The World War One Source Book* (London: Cassell, 1992).

*History of the Corps of Royal Engineers: Vol. 5 – The Home Front, France, Flanders and Italy in the First World War* (Chatham: Institution of Royal Engineers, 1952).

Hughes, C., *Mametz: Lloyd George's Army at the Battle of the Somme* (Norwich: Gliddon Books, 1990).

*Jones, D., *In Parenthesis* (London: Faber and Faber, 1963 edn.).

*Jones, H. W., 'The Fallen', *Welsh Outlook* (April 1919), p. 102.

*Jones, M. S., Thomas, N., Jones, H. P. (eds.), *Saunders Lewis: Letters to Margaret Gilcriest* (Cardiff: University of Wales Press, 1993).

*Junior, A. S., 'We exploded a mine . . .', *Welsh Outlook* (May 1916), pp. 144–5.

*M. J. L., 'To one who fell in early youth', *Welsh Outlook* (September 1915), p. 356.

*Lloyd, O., 'Going West', *Welsh Outlook* (January 1919), p. 11.

Low, G. and Everrett, H. M., *The History of the Royal Monmouthshire Royal Engineers (Militia)* (Pontypool: Griffin Press, 1969).

Macdonald, L., *Somme* (London: Michael Joseph, 1983).

Marden, T. O., *The History of the Welch Regiment: Part II, 1914–1918* (Cardiff: Western Mail and Echo, 1932).

Middlebrook, M., *The First Day on the Somme* (London: Penguin, 1971).

Moore, W., *A Wood Called Bourlon: The Cover-up after Cambrai, 1917* (London: Leo Cooper, 1988).

Munby, J. E. (ed.), *A History of the 38th (Welsh) Division* (London: Hugh Rees, 1920).

*Officers Died in the Great War 1914–1919* (Polstead: J. B. Hayward & Son, repr. 1988).

Owen, B., *Owen Roscomyl and the Welsh Horse* (Caernarfon: Palace Books, 1990).

*Pinto, V. de Sola, *The City that Shone: An Autobiography (1895–1922)* (London: Hutchinson, 1969).

Putkowski, J. and Sykes, J., *Shot at Dawn* (Barnsley: Wharncliffe, 1989).

*Richards, F., *Old Soldiers Never Die* (London: Faber and Faber, 1933).

*Sassoon, S., *Memoirs of an Infantry Officer* (London: Faber and Faber, 1930).

Simkins, P., *Kitchener's Army: The Raising of the New Armies, 1914–1916* (Manchester: Manchester University Press, 1988).

Smithers, A. J., *Cambrai: The First Great Tank Battle 1917* (London: Leo Cooper, 1992).

*Soldiers Died in the Great War 1914–1919: Part 28, The Royal Welch Fusiliers* (Polstead: J. B. Hayward & Son, repr. 1988); *Part 29, The South Wales Borderers* (repr. 1989); *Part 45, The Welch Regiment* (repr. 1988).

Strange, K., *Wales and the First World War* (Mid Glamorgan County Council Education Department, n.d.).

*Sweet, W. G., 'A memoir of the final advance 1918 by Sergeant W. G. Sweet', ed. Barry Johnson, *Stand To! The Journal of the Western Front Association*, No. 3 (Winter 1990), pp. 13–16.

Terraine, J., *The First World War* (London: Leo Cooper/Secker & Warburg, 1983).

*The Times Diary and Index of the War* (London: Times Publishing, 1923).

Thomas, E., 'War Diary', *Anglo-Welsh Review* (Autumn 1971), No. 45, pp. 8–31.

*Thomas, R. G. (ed.), *The Collected Poems of Edward Thomas* (Oxford: Oxford University Press, 1978).

*Thomas, R. G., *Edward Thomas: A Portrait* (Oxford: Oxford University Press, 1985).

War Office, *Statistics of the Military Effort of the British Empire during the Great War* (London: HMSO, 1922).

*Ward, C. H. Dudley, *History of the Welsh Guards* (London: John Murray, 1920).

*Watcyn-Williams, M., *From Khaki to Cloth* (Caernarvon: Calvinistic Methodist Book Agency, 1949).

Welsh National Executive Committee, *Report* (Cardiff: *Western Mail*, 1921).

*Wheldon, W. P., 'The Canal Bank at Ypres', *Welsh Outlook* (March 1919), pp. 65–6.

Whitton, F. E., *History of the 40th Division* (Aldershot: Gale and Polden, 1926).

*Williams, A., 'An artilleryman's war, 1914–19', *Stand To! Journal of the Western Front Association*, No. 29 (Summer 1990), pp. 23–9. Transcript provided by Dr John Dixon.

Williams, W. A., *The VCs of Wales and the Welsh Regiments* (Wrexham: Bridge Books, 1984).

# APPENDIX A: THE ARMY OF 1914

The *Regular Army* provided troops for the imperial garrisons, as well as holding units in readiness for an expeditionary force which could be deployed rapidly to any part of the world. The role of the *Special Reserve* was to supply drafts for the expeditionary force. Each regimental depot was the headquarters for a Special Reserve battalion whose members, recruited directly from civilian life, undertook six months of full-time training, after which their obligation was to attend for three to four weeks training a year.

The *Territorial Force* was intended for home defence. It was organized into fourteen infantry divisions and fourteen brigades of yeomanry cavalry. The part-time soldiers agreed to serve only in the British Isles, unless they volunteered for overseas service.

## Infantry

A typical infantry *battalion*, going on active service, consisted of about a thousand men. It was commanded by a lieutenant-colonel and contained four companies (200–50 men), each commanded by a major or captain. A company was divided into four platoons of fifty or sixty men.

Battalions were, usually, brigaded together; an *infantry brigade* had four battalions, and was commanded by a brigadier-general. Three brigades made up an infantry *division*, which was a major-general's command. It consisted of eighteen thousand men and about 5,500 horses. As well as infantry there were artillery and engineers, together with medical and other support services. On the march, the division occupied about fifteen miles of road.

212

The disposition of the Welsh infantry regiments at the outbreak of the war was:

### The Royal Welch Fusiliers*
Depot: Wrexham

*Regular Army*
| 1st Battalion | Malta |
| 2nd Battalion | Portland |

*Special Reserve*
3rd Battalion — Wrexham

*Territorial Force*
| 4th (Denbighshire) Battalion | Wrexham |
| 5th (Flintshire) Battalion | Flint |
| 6th (Caernarvonshire & Anglesey) Battalion | Caernarvon |
| 7th (Merioneth & Montgomeryshire) Battalion | Newtown |

### The South Wales Borderers
Depot: Brecon

*Regular Army*
| 1st Battalion | Bordon, Hampshire |
| 2nd Battalion | Tientsin, China |

*Special Reserve*
3rd Battalion — Brecon

*Territorial Force*
The Brecknockshire Battalion — Brecon

### The Welch Regiment*
Depot: Cardiff

*Regular Army*
| 1st Battalion | Chakrata, India |
| 2nd Battalion | Bordon, Hampshire |

---

*Welsh or Welch?* Until 1920 the official War Office spelling was 'Welsh'. The regiments, however have always preferred the more ancient 'Welch' which has almost invariably been used in their own writings and regimental histories.

*Special Reserve*
3rd Battalion                      Cardiff

*Territorial Force*
4th Battalion                      Carmarthen
5th Battalion                      Pontypridd
6th (Glamorgan) Battalion      Swansea
7th (Cyclist) Battalion          Cardiff

## The Monmouthshire Regiment

*Territorial Force*
1st Battalion                      Newport
2nd Battalion                      Pontypool
3rd Battalion                      Abergavenny

The Territorial Force battalions were all part of the 53rd (Welsh) Division (TF).

# Cavalry

A cavalry regiment contained fewer men than an infantry battalion, having twenty-one officers and something over five hundred 'other ranks'. In August 1914 there were three regiments of Household Cavalry, and twenty-eight other cavalry regiments – ten regiments of dragoons, twelve regiments of hussars, and six of lancers – although there was by this time no real difference between the role and equipment of the three branches (except that lancer regiments still carried their lances). In addition to the thirty-one regular regiments of cavalry, there were three of the Special Reserve (the North Irish Horse, South Irish Horse, and King Edward's Horse) and fifty-four regiments of Territorial Force Yeomanry Cavalry, which were formed into fourteen mounted brigades. The Welsh Yeomanry regiments were brigaded as follows:

*South Wales Mounted Brigade*
Headquarters: Barracks, Carmarthen
Glamorgan Yeomanry          Bridgend
Montgomeryshire Yeomanry    Welshpool
Pembrokeshire Yeomanry       Tenby

*Welsh Border Mounted Brigade*
Headquarters: High Street, Shrewsbury
Cheshire Yeomanry          Chester
Denbighshire Yeomanry      Wrexham
Shropshire Yeomanry        Shrewsbury

*1st South Midland Brigade*
Headquarters: St John's, Warwick
The Royal Gloucestershire
Hussars                    Gloucester
which contained a Monmouthshire Squadron

The *Welsh Horse* was formed in south Wales on the outbreak of the war.

# Artillery

The Royal Regiment of Artillery consisted of three main branches: the *Royal Field Artillery* (RFA) operated guns and howitzers to provide support for the infantry, whilst the *Royal Horse Artillery* (RHA) had a similar role with the cavalry although, with the advent of trench warfare, it came to perform the same function as the RFA. The *Royal Garrison Artillery* (RGA) was equipped with medium and heavy guns and howitzers which were usually commanded directly by Divisional, Corps, or Army headquarters. It embodied a division of mountain artillery – nine batteries, transported by mules.

The guns in use by the regular army were of four types. Both the *13-pounder* and the *18-pounder* could deliver up to twenty rounds a minute over a maximum range of three to four miles. The *4.5-inch howitzer* fired a 35-pound shell up to four miles. (A howitzer fired a heavier shell than a gun of similar calibre, with a larger bursting charge, and steeper angle of descent.) The *60-pounder* gun, employed by divisional batteries, had a range of nearly six miles. Territorial Force gunners had to make do with more antiquated types.

The *Welsh Territorial Force Artillery* of 1914 consisted of:

*Royal Horse Artillery*
 The Glamorgan Battery          Port Talbot

*Royal Field Artillery*
| | |
|---|---|
| *1st Welsh (Howitzer) Brigade:* | Swansea |
|   1st Glamorgan Battery | |
|   2nd Glamorgan Battery | |
|   1st Welsh Ammunition Column | |
| *2nd Welsh Brigade:* | Cardiff |
|   3rd Glamorgan Battery | |
|   4th Glamorgan Battery | |
|   The Cardigan Battery | |
|   2nd Welsh Ammunition Column | |
| *4th Welsh Brigade:* | Newport |
|   1st Monmouthshire Battery | |
|   2nd Monmouthshire Battery | |
|   3rd Monmouthshire Battery | |
|   4th Welsh Ammunition Column | |

*Royal Garrison Artillery*
| | |
|---|---|
| The Welsh (Caernarvonshire) Heavy Battery | Bangor |
| Glamorgan RGA | Barry, Cardiff, Swansea |
| Pembrokeshire RGA | Milford Haven |

The Royal Horse Artillery unit was part of the South Wales Mounted Brigade (Yeomanry). The Royal Field Artillery belonged to the 53rd (Welsh) infantry division (Territorial Force) as did the Heavy Battery.

# Royal Engineers

To the army in the field, the Royal Engineers (RE) contributed 'Field Companies' (in 1914 each division had two, but by 1915 this had been increased to three – one to each brigade). Commanded by a major, a Field Company contained at least 200 men: carpenters, bricklayers, blacksmiths, masons, tailors, engine-drivers and many other craftsmen. The only Special Reserve units of the REs were located in Wales: the *Royal Anglesey* and the *Royal Monmouthshire Royal Engineers* (which traced its existence back to the sixteenth-century trained bands of Monmouth). Both units were composed of Siege and Railway Companies. Siege Companies were employed on general engineering work, including road-building and maintenance, and providing piped water supplies for men and horses. The task of the Railway

Companies in wartime was to survey, build, repair and operate railways overseas.

The Royal Engineers were also responsible for a good deal of the inter-communication systems between the various units, including 'field airlines' (wire erected on poles) and 'field cable' (which was laid along the ground). The Territorial Force was also involved in these activities, with the *Welsh Field Company* and the *Welsh Division Telegraph Company* being part of the 53rd (Welsh) Division.

## *Medical*

The first stop for an injured man was the Regimental Aid Post, controlled by the battalion medical officer, after which he would arrive at a Field Ambulance. This was a mobile unit, working immediately behind the fighting troops, which could be split up into three independent Advanced Dressing Stations. (The *1st, 2nd and 3rd Welsh Field Ambulances* of the Territorial Force were part of the 53rd (Welsh) Division.) From the Field Ambulance men could be sent to a Casualty Clearing Station – a mobile tented unit – and from there, perhaps by ambulance train, to Stationary or Rear Hospitals. The Territorial Force Nursing Service was responsible, in Britain, for organizing twenty-one General Hospitals, which were based on existing civilian hospitals.

# APPENDIX B: KITCHENER'S ARMIES

The need for more manpower was quickly foreseen by Lord Kitchener, who had been made Secretary of State for War on 5 August. Predicting a lengthy conflict, he sought parliamentary approval to expand the army, and wrote immediately to the lords lieutenants of counties and to the chairmen of the Territorial Force county associations: 'It is intended to enlist as soon as possible 100,000 men, and I would ask you to use your influence ... to secure the necessary recruits as soon as possible.' He emphasized: 'It is not an ordinary appeal from the Army for recruits, but the formation of a second army.' Late August saw the Battle of Mons, and the subsequent retreat, impelling the prime minister to write to the lord mayor of Cardiff (and others) that 'the time has now come for a combined effort to stimulate and organise. public opinion and public effort in the greatest conflict in which our people has ever been engaged'. Asquith proposed that a start should be made by holding meetings throughout the country 'at which the justice of our cause should be made plain and the duty of every man to do his part should be enforced'. Recruits flocked to the Colours – in August 298,973; in September 462,901.

The following table shows the new, volunteer, battalions of the Welsh infantry regiments raised in the first two months of the war. They were all designated as 'service' battalions – for example, '8th (Service) Battalion, The Welch Regiment' – and were formed for the duration of the war:

**Service Battalions formed before 30 September 1914:**

'K1' (August 1914)
| | |
|---|---|
| 8th Royal Welch Fusiliers | Wrexham |
| 4th South Wales Borderers | Brecon |
| 8th Welch Regiment | Cardiff |

'K2' (early September)
| | |
|---|---|
| 9th Royal Welch Fusiliers | Wrexham |
| 5th South Wales Borderers | Brecon |
| 9th Welch Regiment | Cardiff |

'K3'
| | |
|---|---|
| 16 September: 10th Royal Welch Fusiliers | Wrexham |
| 18 September: 11th Royal Welch Fusiliers | Wrexham |
| 3 September: 13th Royal Welch Fusiliers | Rhyl |
| 12 September: 6th South Wales Borderers | Brecon |
| 14 September: 7th South Wales Borderers | Brecon |
| 19 September: 8th South Wales Borderers | Brecon |
| September: 10th Welch Regiment | Rhondda Valleys |
| 11th Welch Regiment | Cardiff |

It was estimated that (up to 30 September) a total of 50,000 men had been recruited in Wales for the Navy, Regular Army and Territorial Force of Great Britain. (Many, of course, had joined formations outside Wales, just as Englishmen had joined the Welsh regiments.) They had been drawn from a limited pool of men – the number of Welshmen aged between 20 and 35 was only 315,000.

On 10 October 1914, the War Office, under pressure from Lloyd George, sanctioned the formation of a Welsh Army Corps of two divisions. A National Executive Committee was formed and, in just over a year, it was able to recruit enough men for one division and one brigade. The table below provides a list of the units raised by the committee:

**Units raised by the National Executive Committee**

*38th (Welsh) Division*
  113th Infantry Brigade
    13th Royal Welch Fusiliers (1st North Wales)
    14th Royal Welch Fusiliers
    15th Royal Welch Fusiliers (1st London Welsh)
    16th Royal Welch Fusiliers
  114th Infantry Brigade
    10th Welch Regiment (1st Rhondda)
    13th Welch Regiment (2nd Rhondda)
    14th Welch Regiment (Swansea)
    15th Welch Regiment (Carmarthen)
  115th Infantry Brigade
    10th South Wales Borderers (1st Gwent)
    11th South Wales Borderers (2nd Gwent)
    16th Welch Regiment (Cardiff City)
    17th Royal Welch Fusiliers (2nd North Wales)
  Pioneer Battalion
    19th Welch Regiment (Glamorgan Pioneers)
  Artillery
    119th, 120th, 121st and 122nd (Howitzer) Field Artillery Brigades
  Engineers
    123rd, 124th, 151st Field Companies
  Army Service Corps
    38th Divisional Train (Nos.330-3 Companies ASC)
  Medical
    129th Field Ambulance
    130th (St John) Field Ambulance
    38th Divisional Ambulance Workshop
    Welsh Bacteriological Laboratory
  Veterinary
    49th Mobile Veterinary Section
  Lines of Communication
    38th Ammunition Sub-Park
    38th Divisional Supply Column
    43rd Field Bakery
    4th Field Butchery
    Five Depot Units of Supply
    49th Railway Supply Detachment
    41st Casualty Clearing Station

77th Sanitary Section
One Infantry Base Depot
*40th Division*
  119th Infantry Brigade
    19th Royal Welch Fusiliers
    12th South Wales Borderers
    17th Welch Regiment (1st Glamorgan)
    18th Welch Regiment (2nd Glamorgan)
    39th Divisional Cyclist Company

*Reserve Battalions*
    18th, 20th, 21st, 22nd Royal Welch Fusiliers
    13th, 14th South Wales Borderers
    20th, 21st, 22nd Welch Regiment

*Source: Report of the Welsh National Executive Committee* (1921)

# APPENDIX C: WELSH INFANTRY BATTALIONS ON THE WESTERN FRONT

## 1914

| Date of Arrival | Battalion | Type[1] | Division[2] |
|---|---|---|---|
| 11 August | 2nd Royal Welch Fusiliers | Regular | L. of C. |
| 13 August | { 1st South Wales Borderers<br>2nd Welch Regiment | } Regular | 1st |
| 7 October | 1st Royal Welch Fusiliers | Regular | 7th |
| 29 October | 6th (Glamorgan) Welch Regiment | Territorial | Army Troops |
| 6 November | 4th (Denbighshire) Royal Welch Fusiliers | Territorial | 1st |
| 7 November | 2nd Monmouthshire (Pontypool) | Territorial | 4th |

## 1915

| | | | |
|---|---|---|---|
| 18 January | 1st Welch Regiment | Regular | } |
| 13 February | 1st Monmouthshire (Newport) | Territorial | } 28th |
| 14 February | 3rd Monmouthshire (Abergavenny) | Territorial | } |
| July | { 9th Royal Welch Fusiliers<br>5th South Wales Borderers<br>9th Welch Regiment | K2 | } 19th (Western) |

---

[1](a) Although battalions started life as 'Regular', 'Territorial' or 'Service', casualty rates soon meant that officers and men were posted to any kind of battalion.

(b) 'K2', 'K3', 'K5' indicate units of Kitchener's 2nd, 3rd and 5th New Armies.

[2] This column shows which infantry division a battalion belonged to initially. Usually it stayed in the same division, although moves from one to another did occur. L.of C. means that the unit was engaged in guarding the army's lines of communication. *Army Troops* were at the direct disposal of the Army Commander, and defended his headquarters.

| 18 August | Welsh Guards | Regular (raised February 1915) | Guards |
|---|---|---|---|
| 6 September | 7th South Wales Borderers<br>8th South Wales Borderers | K3 | 22nd |
| September | 6th South Wales Borderers<br>10th Royal Welch Fusiliers<br>11th Royal Welch Fusiliers<br>13th, 14th, 15th, 16th, 17th Royal Welch Fusiliers | K3 | 25th |
| December | 10th, 11th South Wales Borderers<br>10th, 13th, 14th, 15th, 16th, 19th Welch Regiment | K5 | 38th (Welsh) |

### 1916

| 15 March | 2nd South Wales Borderers | Regular | 29th |
|---|---|---|---|
| June | 9th Royal Welch Fusiliers<br>12th South Wales Borderers<br>17th Welch Regiment<br>18th Welch Regiment | K5 | 40th |

### 1918

| May | 24th (Denbighshire Yeomanry) Royal Welch Fusiliers<br>25th (Montgomery & Welsh Horse Yeomanry) Royal Welch Fusiliers<br>24th (Pembroke & Glamorgan Yeomanry) Welch Regiment | Territorial | 74th (Yeomanry) |
|---|---|---|---|
| July | 26th Royal Welch Fusiliers | Service [3] | 59th |

---

[3] Formed on 16 July 1918 from the 4th Garrison Guard Battalion. This had arrived in France in June 1916 as the '4th Garrison Battalion'. The 59th (2nd North Midland) was a Second Line Territorial Division formed in 1915.

# APPENDIX D: A CHRONOLOGY OF THE MAIN BATTLES ON THE WESTERN FRONT

## 1914

| | |
|---|---|
| 23 August – 5 September | The British Expeditionary Force in retreat from Mons |
| 7 – 10 September | The Marne |
| 12 – 15 September | The Aisne |
| 10 October – 22 November | Ypres |

## 1915

| | |
|---|---|
| 10 – 13 March | Neuve Chapelle |
| 22 April – 25 May | Ypres |
| 25 September – 8 October | British offensive at Loos |

## 1916

| | |
|---|---|
| 1 July – 18 November | Allied offensive on the Somme |
| 14 March – 5 April | German retirement to the Hindenburg Line |

*1917*

| | |
|---|---|
| 9 April – 15 May | The Allied offensive at Arras |
| 7 – 14 June | Messines |
| 31 July – 10 November | Ypres |
| 20 November – 3 December | Cambrai |

*1918*

| | |
|---|---|
| 21 March – 5 April | German offensive in Picardy |
| 9 – 29 April | German offensive in Flanders |
| 27 May – 6 June | German offensive in Champagne |
| 20 July – 2 August | Allied counter-attacks in Champagne |
| 8 August – 6 September | Allied advances in Picardy and Flanders |
| 26 August – 12 October | The breaking of the Hindenburg Line |
| 28 September – 11 November | Final advances in Flanders and Picardy. |